JOBS THAT COULD KILL YOU

Also by Tom Jones:

Working at the Ballpark

Beyond the Blowout

The Making of Superior Energy Services

JOBS THAT COULD KILL YOU

TRUE STORIES OF PEOPLE RISKING THEIR LIVES TO MAKE A BUCK

TOM JONES

Skyhorse Publishing

Skyhorse Publishing books may be purchased in bulk at special discounts for sales promotion, corporate gifts, fund-raising, or educational purposes. Special editions can also be created to specifications. For details, contact the Special Sales Department, Skyhorse Publishing, 307 West 36th Street, 11th Floor, New York, NY 10018 or info@skyhorsepublishing.com.

Skyhorse® and Skyhorse Publishing® are registered trademarks of Skyhorse Publishing, Inc.®, a Delaware corporation.

Visit our website at www.skyhorsepublishing.com.

10 9 8 7 6 5 4 3 2 1

Library of Congress Cataloging-in-Publication Data is available on file.

ISBN: 978-1-61608-319-9

Printed in the United States of America

For Sarah and Megan

CONTENTS

The fishermen know that the sea is dangerous and the storm terrible, but they have never found these dangers sufficient reason for remaining ashore.

—Vincent van Gogh

JOBS THAT COULD KILL YOU

INTRODUCTION

I played on a softball team on Thursday nights for two years before learning what my teammate, Rich King, did for a living. Sometimes he would miss a game or two, later mentioning only that he had been away for work.

When I heard he was a U.S. federal marshal who once guarded Unabomber Ted Kaczynski, September 11 conspirator Zacarias Moussaoui, and former Iraqi dictator Saddam Hussein, I was taken aback that this modest man could be in that line of work. Months later, over coffee, Rich talked about the Hussein assignment, simply saying, "I looked at it as another job," as if he were merely tying his shoes.

Except for a Marine and a firefighter who live down the street, few of my friends, relatives, and neighbors (e.g., plumber, librarian, attorney, Realtor, teacher, dentist, small business owner) are likely to experience any serious physical harm while at work unless they get injured by accident. They don't go too far above or below the ground nor do they, thankfully, endure hazardous or miserable working conditions. As for me—before writing books—I wore suits, ties, starched shirts, and polished shoes for thirty years doing government work, and never felt at risk.

How is it, then, that some people end up in occupations that take them to that thin edge where they confront true danger and where the consequence of error could cause severe injury or death to them and others? And, what is it about the public's fascination with reality television programs like *Deadliest Catch*, *America's Toughest Jobs*, *Ax Men*, *Ice Road Truckers*, *Dirty Jobs*, and *Lockup* in which daring people, from crab fishermen and storm chasers to loggers and cops, show what separates them from those who dwell a little too long in the likes of Walter Mitty's vivid fantasy life? Sure, there are weekend warriors among us who seek thrills through rock climbing, skydiving, bungee jumping, deepwater scuba diving, and extreme sports, but these pursuits are more often hobbies or personal quests than paid work.

I wrote this book because I was curious to know why people like Rich King choose jobs where the odds of getting hurt are considerably greater than at a desk job and if there is anything that distinguishes them from those who squirm at the slightest discomfort. So, I set out on a search for men and women who would talk candidly about why they take on dangerous work, how they deal with it, what type of jams they get into, and what the job means to them.

I began by typing the words "dangerous jobs" in Google's search engine and up popped a list published annually by the federal Bureau of Labor Statistics that identifies the top ten occupations by the number of fatal injuries in the United States. Year after year, the following jobs rank high in bad things happening:

- fishermen (from extreme weather, shipwrecks, being swept overboard, slippery decks)

Introduction

- loggers (from log handling, tree-felling, poisonous plants, animals)
- aircraft pilots (from crashes, exposure to hazardous chemicals—namely, crop dusters)
- structural ironworkers (from falling, being hit by equipment or steel)
- powerline workers (from falling, electrocution)

Typically rounding out the bureau's annual top ten are police officers, garbage collectors, farm workers, roofers, and truck drivers.

I collected additional suggestions from friends and strangers, clipped newspaper articles about gutsy people (like a story about crop duster Gene Hamner's frightening crash in a vineyard), and picked up some ideas from television programs. I also got a lead on an interview during a flight from Houston to Belize City from a fellow passenger who said his wife's cousin is an alligator trapper. And, when I was looking for a cheap place to stay in Kodiak Island, Alaska, I met a woman on the Internet who said that her son-in-law, Matt Corriere, was the sole survivor of a tragic accident aboard a crab fishing boat.

My list of candidates to interview was almost complete when I went looking for a tree trimmer, crane operator, and foundry worker, but I decided to swap those job categories for a pizza delivery guy, cab driver, and psychiatrist, because the latter are vulnerable to becoming targets of an assailant. I wanted to hear if they had anything to say about being at risk. As psychiatrist Peter Yellowlees cautions, "You never know who is gonna walk through the door."

Time to hit the road. I started with bullfighter Joe Baumgartner, who, the day after the interview, got a concussion after being hooked under his chin by a bull's horns and flung into the air and landed on his head. Then to Florida to talk with storm chaser Jeff Gammons, on the road with the Ringling Brothers Circus to talk at center ring with tiger trainer Vicenta Pages, and to Jerusalem to listen to *Washington Post* journalist Griff Witte describe a story about Palestinian smugglers. Then off to Pennsylvania to drink beer and eat barbequed pork chops with coal miner Jeff Shiner, to New York City to meet with Ula the Pain-Proof

Rubber Girl, a knife thrower's assistant, and later to Chicago to talk with high-rise window washer Walter Diaz.

It became clear in the early interviews that sitting in an office cubicle is not for these people; rather, it is often the pull of an adrenaline rush that sucks them in, such as for search-and-rescue ranger Keith Lober, who hikes the rugged terrain at Yosemite National Park. "I'm an adrenaline junkie, like a lot of people in this business," Lober said. "We go from one adrenaline rush to the next. You get addicted to it. . . . What we do is critical, and it's important. We make decisions every single day whether people are gonna live or die, literally whether they will live or die. I love being involved in that."

Similarly, Bobby Burrell gets his adrenaline fix by jumping over the pit road wall during NASCAR races to change tires, despite being severely injured one time when a car crashed into him. "It's not a job for the weak-minded," Burrell said. "You have things hitting you so fast you got to think in a split second what to do. . . . You got to have a little bit of adrenaline junkie in you to go do what we do. Fear is not an option. If you're scared or have just a hint of fear, you could get yourself hurt or somebody else hurt."

Speaking of fear, wildlife filmmaker Andy Casagrande, who shoots video for the Discovery Channel and National Geographic, has the clarity and guts that characterize almost everyone featured in *Risky Living*. "I was scared the first time I ever got outside of the cage with a great white shark," he said. "But at the same time, I realized if I allowed my fear to invoke panic then things could get bad quickly, so it was best to keep my head and keep my courage such that I didn't invoke a chase reaction."

Some people just know how to make the difficult seem simple and don't flinch. Lieutenant Frank Weisser, who flew thirty-four combat missions in Iraq and now flies high-speed aerial maneuvers with the Navy's Blue Angels, says, "When you're in formation, streaking through the skies eighteen inches from another airplane, doing flips and rolls, and you're doing five hundred miles an hour and under heavy Gs, one-hundredth of an inch of movement in the stick would lead you to hit that airplane. That could potentially cause a four-airplane fireball."

Soldier Cameron Begbie, who fought in Fallujah, Iraq, during one of the fiercest military battles since the darkest days of the Vietnam War, is willing to dare because of his commitment to duty and allegiance to his buddies. "Kicked the door of this one house and got into a firefight," Begbie said. "There was four of them. They were coming out of closets, shooting. We shot back. We got into a little hand-to-hand. We're hooking, jabbing, stabbing. . . . It's kind of a barroom brawl without the alcohol. It wasn't a schoolyard fight where you sit there and you say, okay, we're both going home. One of us isn't going home. I guarantee you I'm gonna go home at the end of the day. Then, one of the bad guys pulls a grenade . . ."

For some, recognition attracted them to risk, as it is for veteran hockey player Jeremy Roenick. "That's all I want to be known as: a warrior that came to play every night," Roenick said. "I want people to say they didn't know whether he was gonna hurt us on the scoreboard or hurt us in the corner or hurt us in open ice. I want to make sure that people knew when I was on the ice, that something was gonna happen. . . . I've had over six hundred stitches in my face. I've broken my jaw twice—once in four places, the second time in nineteen places. Broke every finger at least twice. I broke every toe. I've broken my ankle, broken my wrist, broke my ribs, separated shoulders, dislocated fingers, ten or eleven concussions, nine broken noses, pulled groins, two coccyx breaks, hernia surgery on both sides."

It is the pride in doing a job few seek that drives coal miner Shiner: "When you go to work, you get into the elevator, the doors close, you go nine hundred feet underground, the doors open: Welcome to hell. We walk where the devil dances, that's what people say, because you're so far underground and you travel two or three miles in. . . . You've never seen anything that dark in your life. . . . To work underground, it takes balls."

For others, the decision to work where danger lurks is basically a family matter, as it is for commercial fisherman Joel Helgevold, who does what he does because "I'm a son of a son of a sailor. My dad's dad owned a boat, my dad owns a boat. I'm gonna own a boat, and that's how it is."

The forty-two men and women in the book might, at times, doubt themselves and pause briefly to seek safer ground, but rarely do they turn away. They know they could die, but they also know what search-and-rescue ranger Lober means when he says, "We seek and hire the guy who marches toward the sound of the guns when everyone else runs the other way."

Ralph Waldo Emerson wrote, "A hero is no braver than an ordinary man, but he is brave five minutes more." Although nobody in *Jobs That Could Kill You* claims to have done anything heroic, they would be ready to act if needed. They, in their own style, would be there for those "five minutes more."

In the oral history tradition of Studs Terkel, I tried to preserve the tone, rhythm, and speaking styles of the interviewees. Their words are edited primarily for clarity and brevity. At times, fragmented comments are rearranged for a clearer sequence of events. Some people asked to read their transcript before publication, such as Hollywood stunt-woman Katie Rowe: "Do I get a chance to read what you write before it is published? Since we fall down for a living, I don't want to sound dumb."

I hope you get a kick out of meeting these fascinating people who make their living working around beasts, fire, extreme weather, guns, high altitude, deep water, speed, explosives, big things, bad guys, and a lot of other scary stuff. I sure did.

KEITH LOBER

SEARCH-AND-RESCUE RANGER

"*I'm an adrenaline junkie, like a lot of people in this business. We go from one adrenaline rush to the next. You get addicted to it. Whether you're a city paramedic or a firefighter or a race car driver, I think there's an addiction to adrenaline. This job also has the plus of it being a mix of mountain climbing and drama. What we do is critical, and it's important. We make decisions every single day whether people are gonna live or die. I love being involved in that.*"

Keith Lober manages the emergency services operation at Yosemite National Park. On this winter morning, he leans back in his chair in his search-and-rescue office and talks about his work. "*Because Yosemite has such a high incidence of wilderness rescue, we spend a great percentage of our time rescuing people out of the backcountry, which is both emergency medical and rescue work. It's a law enforcement job, because law enforcement is designated the responsible party for search and rescue."*

★ ★ ★

"A protest against rules banning the sport of parachuting from cliffs in national parks went horribly awry yesterday when a veteran jumper plunged to her death from the top of El Capitan in Yosemite."—*San Francisco Chronicle*

BASE jumping is not allowed here in the park. They were doing a civil disobedience jump, where they're lining up and jumping. The last person to jump was a lady named Jan Davis. My instructions were to meet and greet everyone at the top, to advise them that it is illegal to jump from the top of El Capitan. I was not to interfere. I was talking to her: "You will be arrested at the bottom, you know that, of course." She said, "Yes, thank you." I said, "Have a nice jump."

She was in love with life and happy. This kind of sport is one of these things that people love doing; they're addicted to it. I appreciate it for what it is, but it is illegal, and so I enforce it, and I'll arrest you if I catch you BASE jumping, because they pay me to do that, but it doesn't mean I don't totally support it. I do, and I think it's wonderful. My personal opinion is that it's a sport and it should be authorized here in the park, but it's not. So, I was the greeter at the top, like the Kmart greeter: "How are you doing, Jan? All right, Jan, when you jump here, expect to be arrested. You know the rangers are gonna put handcuffs on you, they will book you, and then they will release you. Okay?" It's all very cordial.

It was a good management decision not to try to interfere, to allow them their civil disobedience, because if you try to stop it they're gonna jump someplace else, and do it in a hurried fashion. We thought that was more risky, so it was a risk decision to allow it. It backfired. She got killed. She impacted the ground as we're counting—by nine seconds from the top, the chute should open. So we're counting, "One, two, three," and between three and nine you should hear the chute pop open, and then "ten, eleven, twelve." You knew "thirteen" was the deck. Her chute didn't open. She hit so hard it set off car alarms a thousand feet away.

I'm an army brat, so I have grown up everywhere. When I was in my early teens, we lived in Alaska and my dad commanded the 172nd Brigade, which is a mountaineering brigade for the army. I would get dragged around on the glaciers and the mountains by sergeants. I think it started me down this path. Climbing is in your blood, or it's not. I mean, I was exposed to it, read about it, and knew that that was the direction I was headed. And a part of it was also the romance of rescue work, you know, the old stuff that was done in the Alps, which was as intriguing to me as the actual climbing.

I started out as a professional mountain guide in Rocky Mountain National Park, in Colorado. I did that for the first six years of my employment. I was young and had good knees and a strong back. I got out of it at around twenty-six years old, because I realized there was very little money in it and a huge amount of work; the glamour wore off.

Then I realized that I really liked emergency services work, so I became a ski patrolman, and then eventually a firefighter paramedic in Washington, D.C., which is a whole other story. You see so much so quickly in a big city system that it polishes your skill sets, because you get inundated with so much; it's like going to the University of Carnage and Trauma. When you come out here in a rural setting such as in Yosemite, there's very little that one hasn't seen.

In Yosemite, 96 percent of this park is wilderness. It's 1,200 square miles; it's bigger than some states and bigger than many countries. This is "climbing central." The thing that brought me here is that the incidence of rescue is so frequent, so constant, you do it all the time. Sometimes a case goes wrong or goes sideways and you wish you had done something different, but I don't dread or shy away from making those decisions, and no one here does. We seek and hire the guy who marches toward the sound of the guns when everyone else runs the other way.

We average 250 backcountry missions a year, but the meat and potatoes of this job is on the Mist Trail, which is the heavily used corridor of the Yosemite Valley up to Half Dome. There's a waterfall there that mists across the trail. Our job is to clean up people with damaged ankles who fall down on the trail. It's not glamorous, we hate it, it's boring, but it's got to get done. So we just go up there and we wheel them down. We have a litter that has a big wheel on it. We will do that in the summer, sometimes once or twice a day.

There's everything in between that and up to the big El Capitan climber rescues where they are three thousand feet above the ground. We have to go down under the face of El Cap and pull climbers off. We're very good at that. Back in the seventies, it was just an unbelievable operation. Those days are gone, because we understand the animal, and we can pull off an El Cap rescue in a matter of hours without blinking an eye. That's not bragging; we're trained for it. All the guys that we use have climbed the face of the Cap multiple times. They've done it at night, they've done it in the day. We've mastered that skill, and our technical expertise is the one thing that we're known for. But what we're not recognized for is the volume of calls that we have. We're the masters of disaster. We manage chaos—that's what we do whether it's an earthquake or a rockfall event.

Our operation gears up from the staff like you see around here, which is pretty much nonexistent right now, to a huge team the busiest five or six months of the season. We form emergency teams on the fly, but everyone knows their roles. We're very good at managing emergencies because we do it with such frequency. We cover so many different hazards from fire to rockfalls, from law enforcement to emergency medical traffic accidents to search and rescue; you name it and we will manage it. We operate comfortably in high-angle terrain, and we aren't necessarily always roped. We try to minimize our risks, but there are certain inherent risks of just being able to move in terrain that preclude you from being roped up. Most of my team is very comfortable in technical terrain, so the level of which they personally feel they need to rope at is much higher than what we force them to use the rope.

Less than probably 2 percent of our caseload is actually a real search; probably 40 percent is an overdue report that you got to follow up on. That's where people haven't turned up when they're supposed to, for whatever reasons: unrealistic expectations on the person who's reporting it, delays because of weather, or they just didn't get their itineraries right. But that 2 percent tends to be a big part of our workload, because a search for a person in a 1,200-square-mile park can be huge.

I'll give you three events that have happened here recently that were each slightly different but uniquely interesting. In the first one, I was the IC, the incident commander. I ran the operation and directed the troops. The next one is an avalanche where I was simply a rescuer, one of the team members that went out. And on the last one, I was the operations chief directing actions on scene. So the first one is a missing person, the second one is an avalanche, and the third one is a suicide where a man threatened that he had a gun and was going to jump off the upper Yosemite Falls, which he eventually ended up doing after a five-hour standoff with our tactical team.

The first event is the Steve Frasier search. Steve came to the park by himself, hitchhiked into the park from I think someplace like Atlanta. Why that is significant is that there's no trail for us to follow to find him, so when eventually we were told that he might be overdue, there was no way to track him through the system. A lot of people leave a car, they use a credit card or a cell phone; he had none of that. So we didn't know anything. We get a call on the ninth of November saying, "I have a friend who might have gone to Yosemite, but I'm not sure. He hasn't returned, and he had a plane ticket to return on the ninth, and it didn't get used. Is he in the park?"

One of the patrol officers takes the initial call—we get this kind of crap all the time, and *that* falls in the category of crap, because there's not enough information to deal with—and the officer goes, "There's no way to track that down." The next day it gets dumped onto my office. We discussed some strategies, which included running all the backcountry permits that were taken out and, bingo, fourteen days earlier his name shows up on a permit. All it says is that Frasier is going to Sunrise, which can be a trail, Sunrise can be a High Sierra camp, Sunrise can be a specific campground, but they are all in the geographic north middle section of the park. Then we developed a large investigative search team who are looking at permits and campgrounds, and some are running credit cards, looking for cell phone records. We're aware that we're not gonna have much to go on, but there's enough to indicate that he might have been here in the park. We don't want to end up in a bastard search situation, you know. "Bastard search" is just what it sounds like: It's a search for someone who's not in your jurisdiction and you're wasting your time.

We start searching in the north middle section of the park, a two-hundred-square-mile area, but it turned out it was the wrong place. What really solved this case was criminal investigators who persisted in calling back and trying to find friends who might know him, and they found someone who he had discussed his plans with. So we now changed the direction of the search 180 degrees and now had a four-hundred-square-mile area, because now we had the possibility of him being in the north—because that's where his permit said he's going—and in the south, because this person said, "He pointed out that he wanted to go to the south end."

So I jumped into the helicopter with the search manager and took a joyride with him, because I wanted to actually see the terrain that I was gonna assign people to. And as we were flying over, we find Steve Frasier. He had written "SOS" in the snow in ten-foot letters outlined in pine boughs. It stood out so dramatically that as we're going by, bingo, there he is. We flew the itinerary that he had given his friend, and he was on it. He just got snowed in. He's out there forty miles out in the backcountry and had four feet of snow drop on him. It was like the Donner Party, except he didn't have anybody to eat. He had been out there for thirteen days on two days of food, so he had gotten very skinny. I mean, here is a guy who had scratched his last will and testament into what we call a "bear canister," which is a canister that is bear proof so bears can't tear into it and eat your food (it's not to protect your food, it's actually to protect the bears from being habituated by constantly getting your food). And then the helicopter flies over. He was elated. We landed, and it's like, "All right, problem over. We did a good job; a life saved." Steve knew he was gonna die, until we arrived. He told us that.

In mid-February, a group of Korean climbers were siege-climbing the northwest face of Half Dome, where it's colder than can be in the middle of winter. What they're doing is they're climbing a technically difficult low-altitude climb, but it would mimic almost Himalayan in its proportion because of the cold and the snow and access problem. It has many of the overtones of a huge wilderness mountain in the far-out distant regions of the world because of the circumstances. It's a challenge.

So they're climbing it in winter, which is a very legitimate although difficult proposition. It's cold and miserable and nasty. To facilitate access to the face where the actual real climbing begins, North Face is like a 2,500-foot dead vertical rock wall. Just the access to that is a three-thousand-foot chute that comes up from Mirror Lake, and part of that chute is subject to avalanche in the right conditions. Now, the Sierra snowpack is a fairly stable snowpack, and avalanches don't happen with the frequency that they happen in the Continental snowpack, which is a real dry snowpack. But when they do happen, they can be catastrophic events and equally hard to predict. In this case, there was a real warm spell and rain was falling on the snowpack, percolating through it, lubricating it from below, and loosening the adhesion to the surface below.

There were about eight climbers, male and female. And, because the weather had been so atrocious, they were going up and down on fixed lines, meaning that they had fixed ropes from the base of the actual start of the climb to the valley floor, so they could access it safely.

I'm gonna guess that they were like a week into the climb. This one guy was going down the fixed lines, by himself, when an avalanche struck and swept him down three hundred to four hundred feet. He stopped before the pour-over, or he would have gone off like a five-hundred-foot cliff. But he's in the debris field of the avalanche, which, because it's a Sierra snowpack avalanche, the rubble is computer-terminal-sized blocks of ice—it's like being put into a dryer with bowling balls—and he has been ground up in that.

The report came in to us from members of his party around 4:00 PM—they had those little family-band radios, the kind you buy from Kmart, they're very common in climbing, inexpensive, and they work reasonably well. This guy was supposed to go to their base camp and he never arrived, and so the two teams—the one on the wall and the one at base camp—started talking and they realized he was missing. They sent another couple of people down the wall to go look for him. When these two guys go down, they find their friend ground up in the rubble, with a broken femur, a broken arm, he has altered mental status because he has got some kind of closed head injury, and he can't breathe right because he has some kind of compression injury on his chest. He's very critically injured.

Well, in February we're at our lowest staffing levels that you can imagine in the park, because we're seasonal, and at this time of the year, we're on an adrenaline deficit. So we're eager, we got something to do. We're like hound dogs, we want to run, every one of these guys wants to run. We release our units as they become available. We try to pair them up into groups of twos and threes and send them out so they can watch out for each other. Ideally, we would like to send them all at once, but that resource isn't there, yet we want to get it started, because even a rescuer who's ill-equipped on the wall—or not equipped to complete the mission—can actually get started fixing lines and carrying supplies up to the high points on the trail for the next team to come up.

We launched the rescue, but there's a certain hesitancy, because there's three things going on. One is we initially weren't aware that this was an avalanche. Two, it gets back to us that the Korean climber has actually been ground up in an avalanche, so that's two red flags of operational risk that we know as we walk into this thing. The third was ongoing avalanche activity. Since there's avalanches going on, what's the potential of more avalanches above us? Are our approaches, for the most part, protected and safe?

So we now have the three red flags, which is to say, Hold on, we can't put people into a known avalanche chute when they're already climbing through debris where the avalanche has run, or will run, or can run. Then, the incident commander pulls the plug. He says, "I'm not gonna send people in there. It's too unknown and too operationally hazardous. Pull the people back." That's a hard decision for a guy to make, because he's potentially signing the climber's death warrant. But it was good operational risk management. I have to give him credit for that. I probably would have made that same decision, but I wanted to run up there, get as high as I could, and get a scene size-up. I wanted a boots-on-the-ground feel for what was going on in there. I would have come to the same decision had I been in I think reversed roles. You really want to go get this guy, but we put our life safety at a very high premium, meaning that if we injure one of our people, we've made the situation worse. We say, "Our life is not worth their life." We're not gonna kill ourselves to get you. There's a point where we're gonna pull the pin and say a person is on his own for a little bit. We can't get everybody.

So we pulled out. I think the units all got back by about ten or eleven o'clock that night. You're dead tired, you crawl back in here, you're hammered, and you go, "Thank God I got out of there." It would have been an all-nighter if we had actually made it up to the guy and got him. You just hope that he's less critically injured and he's going to survive the night, but you don't know.

Well, the next morning, he was still alive. The two Koreans stayed with him in the middle of the face. These were intelligent, skilled

Alpinists, and they took good care of this guy. They had him packaged up right. We sent people back up the fixed lines and we brought in our helicopter with myself and Jack Hoeflich. He and I got dropped out the door on the hoist line as the two members of the ground team arrived. Jack and I are completely self-sufficient. We carry all the medical gear, all our rescue gear, all our own climbing gear.

We get the Korean climber on the litter, the helicopter snags him and takes off. We can request the helicopter to come back and get us, but we can actually get out of the avalanche zone a lot quicker if we just run. So we run the lines and climb out of there. The Korean ends up in the hospital and survives, and he's banged up, but he gets off the mountain. The other Koreans eventually abandoned their ascent, not so much because their friend got injured, although I'm sure that factored into it, but I think they just ran out of time, and the weather was never cooperative.

The third incident is something we dealt with just last week, which was we got a 911 call saying that there's a gentleman who had called his sister saying he's gonna kill himself from the top of the Yosemite Falls, and he's got a gun. He says his life is in turmoil, he's got legal problems, he's got personal problems, he's got life problems, all of the above. Which one stood out the most? Who knows?

One of the patrol officers and I get dispatched to be the initial crew to hump up to the top of Yosemite Falls. It's a 3,600-foot vertical elevation gain. You're doing that with cold-weather gear, military tactical gear, an M16 rifle, magazines, handcuffs, Taser, a vest. So it's a hump up there, and we beat the helicopter. This has the tones of a law enforcement event, but it also has a certain component of rescue to it, because the guy can change his mind anytime. He's self-medicated—he's drugged—he was staggering. It took us a while to find him because we didn't have a clear idea of exactly where he was.

I left here like at one thirty; it took me about an hour and a half, two hours, to get to the top. Well, it is *the top* of Yosemite Falls, it's full-on winter, there's eight feet of snow on the ground, and he's standing on a rock out in the middle of the river. There's snow, and a rock bridge that goes out to his rock, but he's pretty well-isolated out there. The only way that we can go out there is if we walked to the rock, but of course you don't want to do that, because if you fall in you're in the laminar flow of the Yosemite Falls and you're going over. He has tactically placed himself in a position where we can't go reasonably try to get him. You can't Taser him, because then you own him when he falls in the water. You can't shoot him because there's no reason to shoot him; you're trying to save him. And, he says he has a gun. So this becomes a police standoff with rescue overtones. And we have a rescue swimmer there who's in a dry suit; he's ready to go in, plus we have a hostage negotiating team that deals with people in stressful situations. It was kind of a no-win situation.

The standoff goes on for like four hours. Just before dark, he decides that's it, game over. He lowers himself down into the water and gets swept over the falls. We haven't recovered him yet because he got swept over and he's now in the ice cone at the base. We will recover him in two or three months. But I got to tell you, in twenty-five years in the business, that's the first time I've ever seen anyone purposely kill themselves.

If you're way too sensitive, this is not your job. I mean there's been cases that I probably still have huge misgivings about how they were handled, and I have lain awake at night. You know, the worst trauma doesn't affect me. You just move on to the next case. You become somewhat like a lot of emergency workers and disaster workers: hardened to human trauma and the tragedy of that we deal with. It's natural survival. You disown other people's human tragedy so you can move on to the next case. When you start owning it, that's where you start getting into trouble, but everyone does to a certain extent. There's always something that bothers them.

I'm fifty-five. I'm going to retire in about a year. I'm going to do something else. I just have a need to move on to the next chapter in life. I'll miss the adrenaline and drama of this job, and I'm trying to wean myself a little bit. I might go into commercial emergency services with a company that does international work. I worked for one company last year as a nongovernmental operation, so I had to take time off from my job here. They flew us down to South America to do recovery operations for a helicopter accident on a Peruvian peak. The helicopter was carrying ten people and it impacted a mountain coming back from a mining site. The mining corporation wanted the bodies of their execs returned to the families. The site was on a jungle cliff face; it was like an adventure expedition, with indigenous local people hacking their way through the jungle with machetes, and porters carrying loads on their heads, and different versions of venomous snakes. It was quite exotic. We got to the accident site on a big cliff face and recovered the bodies.

That's one of those things that I wouldn't go into full-time, but I'd stay on the Rolodex as someone who can be picked up on a catch-as-catch-can basis. I want to be deployed in the field and manage an accident scene, just to maintain the adrenaline flow, because I don't think I will ever get over it.

JAMES IRVIN

MIXED MARTIAL ARTS FIGHTER

*J*ames Irvin holds the record for the fastest knockout in Ultimate Fighting Championship history by beating Houston Alexander eight seconds into the first round of their fight. James is thirty years old, stands six feet two inches tall, and fights at 205 pounds. He runs a mixed martial arts training center. "This sport is still so new that it's all misconceptions, people don't understand. When I opened this gym about a year ago, the city would drive by our parking lot with a camera like five times a day until we had our permits and our licenses because parents were complaining that we were gonna be teaching kids how to barroom brawl. People think we're teaching eye gouging and fighting in a cage with bottles and bats. They don't understand. That's *partly because of the way the UFC was branded when it came out in the nineties. It was blood and guts, no gloves, no rules. Now, it's the biggest sport in the world."*

★ ★ ★

I am a professional mixed martial artist. I fight for the UFC, the Ultimate Fighting Championship. It's no-holds-barred fighting. There are actually rules to it, like there is no eye gouging, there is no groin strikes, there are certain submissions that you can't do, there are certain elbows you can't do, you can't bite, and stuff like that. I'd say it's the most fierce fighting: You bring the attributes from different martial arts and you blend them.

I didn't grow up in martial arts. I didn't wrestle, I didn't know karate, I have no parent that was into that. I watched the infant stages of UFC fighting in the early nineties like everyone did. Just watching these guys, I knew I could compete with them athletically.

I trained for many years to be an athlete. My dream always was to be a football player. I never doubted that. So when that washed out, I just don't think I was ready to give up being an athlete, but I never thought mixed martial arts fighting was it. I always felt like a tough guy, and I was always big and a mean-looking guy, but I couldn't back it up. I think I had been in two fights my whole life, in high school. I knocked both people out.

I went to my first fight and I thought I could compete with them. Little did I know what was really going on in the cage. At that first fight, I'm seeing these guys who are out of shape, they look like barroom brawlers. I'm like, I'm gonna whip these guys' asses. I went home and got a phone book, picked up the nearest jujitsu place that I could go to. If you don't know about Brazilian jujitsu, it's ground fighting; you start on the ground, most people fight off their backs; it's all submissions, no punching, no hitting; it's chokes and arm bars, joint manipulations, twisting your arms certain ways; it's hard to explain. So I went to this place, and I'm 240 pounds, and I start rolling around with guys there that are 170 pounds. I left there with like almost black eyes—not from getting punched—from being choked, with marks around my eyes. I think I got choked unconscious at least once my very first night. I remember going there thinking that these are the guys that I would have picked on if I ever had to. These are guys in a bar who would be the first ones that I went after if they ran their mouths to me. I instantly gained respect for them. I had piercings in my ears and nipples, and I took them out that night. They were all bleeding anyways.

After about six months of doing that, I got to where I could hang with everyone in there, not beat anyone, but none of them could make me submit no more. I was very comfortable on the ground, and I wanted to try my first cage fight. My coach at the time said, "Okay, we need to try and see how your stand-up is," so the next day in practice, I put boxing gloves on. I left there with a bloody nose, a bloody mouth, a fat lip. Coaches don't beat you up—they are the only ones who care about you; they are showing you your mistakes; they are playing pitter-patter with you. He could have knocked me out numerous times, but I left there with a smashed face. I left there thinking I need to keep on doing this. Then I went and joined a boxing place to learn kickboxing. Then I had my first fight. It's just evolved from there. This last June, I've been pro fighting for five years. I had seven or eight knockouts to get to the UFC. Usually it takes much longer. I've been fortunate enough that I had a lot of wins to get there. You start fighting at small area shows, like at Indian casinos where they are not regulated—they are a pretty scary deal. You kind of work your way up, and you kind of have something to prove. I remember a lot of fighting on a Friday, and then on Saturday all of us went to bars and were getting into fights. But that was before I realized this was gonna be my career.

I don't care how experienced you are, that fight-or-flight syndrome kicks in. I thought for about half an hour after my first fights, I was gonna have a heart attack. I don't even remember walking out to the cage. I remember bits and pieces of fighting. I don't remember leaving. I remember being backstage lying on the ground asking for an ambulance to come. I never had an adrenaline rush like that before. At that time it was scary. I didn't know what was going on. I don't do drugs. I mean, can I be having a heart attack? It was the adrenaline.

The last twenty to thirty minutes before a fight, I'd pee like thirteen times. That's your fight or flight kicking in. It's making your body lighter; a natural animal kind of instinct. It's your body getting ready. Brandon Vera, one of the top-level guys who fights in the UFC, pukes before every fight, right backstage as he is walking out, usually ducking off puking as they are announcing his name.

I've been pretty lucky. Most of my fights have been on the winning end. I really haven't been beat up. I've lost fights. I've been knocked on my ass and I got twenty stitches across my face two months ago when I got knocked out by Anderson Silva. That was the first fight I've ever really been blown out of the water, but I haven't been in too many spots where I was dominated and beat up to where I even got to consider giving up and just go, fuck this, I'm out of here. I've had people on my back trying to choke me out for long periods of times, but there are certain things you don't give up to. Chokes are one of them. As far as I'm concerned, if someone gets you in a choke, you keep fighting until you fall asleep, because they are not something that really hurts that much; a blood choke, especially. In a fight, there is so much energy you're giving, you should be fighting as long as you can. Usually, when people give up on chokes, it's at the same time that if I had held a little bit longer, I probably would have finished the guy. It's funny how that line is right there. But choking is one of the things that I don't feel someone should give up on.

There are different kinds of chokes. The carotid artery choke—or blood choke—don't hurt at all really. It's just pressure from both sides, and you just fall asleep. There's triangle chokes, they don't really hurt, but a lot of people give up because you get scared because you are pinned. There's also like old-school chokes, like a guillotine choke, when you get someone from underneath and you just squash them. That one sucks, but there's lots of ways out of there.

There also are certain submissions that will snap your arm, so you need to give up on them, and when someone is on top of you just punching you and punching you, a lot of times you know the refs will step in. The refs really make sure no one will get hurt. We have never had anyone die in a no-holds-barred fight yet, so they take real good care of us.

A lot of guys don't understand about mixed martial arts. Some guys think it's their way or the highway, like kickboxing is all you need to learn. It's not. You need to learn boxing, kickboxing, Muay Thai, wrestling, grappling, and then you got to take all those and practice and mix them all together. The sport is still so new that I could go to a kickboxing coach who is a world champion in kickboxing, but he doesn't know nothing about wrestling. I've had a boxing coach, a Muay Thai coach, and I wrestled with a bunch of guys where I really had to check my ego at the door.

I get inspiration from my coaches. I go in there "yes sir, no sir," doing what they say. What they say has a lot of impact on me, and I have faith in them. I pay them a lot of money to whip my ass in practice, to push me much harder than I can push myself. I have one coach, he has made me cry a couple of times in practice, not because he was hurting me but because he made me go to that point where I thought I was gonna pass out. He has gotten me so many times to that point on hard runs or running up mountains or something like that, that I'm really thinking, I'm gonna pass out if I take another step. But I've done that so many times, it's almost like I get a kick out of it now, seeing how hard he can push me. And there will be practices where I will start laughing, like there is nothing you can do to me. I push and push and push. It's about how much you can overcome, like be in a cage and be getting dominated and still not give up, and then come back and win.

You know, a good day at work for me is getting a bloody mouth and a black eye. My best practice is when I get beat up, because that's the only time you get better. It sucks. If I stay here in my hometown and just beat up all my training partners, you never get better. You can see a lot of these world champions—I'm not gonna say names—but for some reason or another, five years ago they were unbeatable. Now, they are getting beat left and right because those are the ones that stay at home and they have all their own training partners that they all beat on. They do the same thing for five years. But if you are looking at someone like Urijah Faber, or other guys that stay at the top, they are constantly traveling, constantly bringing in new partners, and most times the guys are better than you at least in one thing. A lot of guys don't want to do that, because it sucks.

I can go to a boxing place and they have all guys that have been boxing for five to ten years, and they will whip my ass. But, let me start kicking those guys, and things will change. Then when we go to a kickboxing place, they will kick the hell out of me. College wrestlers are the worst. Most have been wrestling their whole lives. I haven't been doing martial arts my whole life, so take someone who has been wrestling their whole life, and now wrestle him, it's like a joke. How can I possibly compete with these guys? They will get a hold on you and just pretzel you up, smash you on the ground, and throw you around. Deep down inside, I know that I'm not a wrestler. I'm just taking part of that and I'm gonna meld it with punching and kicking. I can see it in a lot of their faces, they are like, I can take this guy. It's a look I get all the time. Every time I go to a different gym, it's a look I get from these people, and they put in the back of my head that I got to stay positive, and I'm thinking, let me put cage gloves on, let me and you have no rules, and let's see what happens. For some reason I seem to be lucky when I get in the cage. I'm able to put things together. But in practice with a lot of these guys, it's a tough job.

What I do is, I practice to finish fights by hurting people. I happen to be a striker; it's something I gravitated toward. My first three or four fights, I don't think I threw a punch while standing and kicking. Like I said, I put people on the ground because I was so nervous, and that's what I was comfortable at doing. Then it evolved for me. I have the fastest UFC first-round knockout and the fastest UFC second-round knockout in the world: an eight-second first-round knockout, and a nine-second second-round knockout.

The eight-second first round was when I fought Houston Alexander. This guy was the scariest-looking guy in the UFC. They call him "The Assassin." He looks like a pro body builder, which is rare in our sport, because most guys don't carry a lot of muscle. This guy has a six-pack, a bald head, a big goatee. Like I said, I just have a knack for fighting the scariest-looking guys in the sport.

In his fights, he had come off a couple of big knockouts against guys that were much better than him, and he was known as a tough guy. I haven't had no one bullying me around yet, and I wasn't about to. Right off the bat, I threw a Superman punch at him. It's not something you ever throw at someone—it's where you throw a kick and you punch at the same time. You don't land the kick, but it's too late for them to cover the punch, because when you go to kick, people's first reactions usually are to block it. So, I walked out, throw my right kick at him—only about four or five inches off the ground, just enough for him to look down at it—and at the same time I threw my right hand. He actually didn't go for it because you usually you have to set it up by peppering him and hurt him with a leg kick. We both came right at each other, so he did half the job for me—a right hand across the chin, right hand, right hand, and his chin kind of kicked back. It's funny about getting hit in the jaw: Any tough guy can be hit right in the jaw, and you just go to sleep. He dropped like a bag of rocks. I remember seeing him fall. It's so fast I'm just thinking, finish, finish, finish, so I'm jumping down and I'm going to punch him, and the ref's already jumping on top of me. I had no idea it would be it was the fastest UFC knockout ever until they announced it afterward.

That's why I have these big knockouts in the fights, because I'm coming right at them and not giving them a second to breathe or letting them decide how the fight is going to dictate. That's the kind of fighter I am. For me, it's all about imposing my will. If I go in there and just get all barroom crazy and start throwing punches, that does me no good.

My fastest second-round knockout was against Terry Martin, which was my second UFC fight. I had been beat up the whole first round. He held me down and sat on top of me, barely punched me once or twice. It was very frustrating. So, in the second round, I walked across the ring and threw a flying knee at him. It's just what it sounds like: I jumped in the air and shot my left knee right across his face. It's pretty Hollywood-looking. He's out cold. Nine seconds. It's something I would have never expected to land and knock someone out with. That was the first time anyone has ever left in a stretcher in UFC history.

One time, I come off a couple of losses and I had to fight my way back. I fought Hector Ramirez, a training partner of mine that was a national champion wrestler. In training, he always whipped my ass. I didn't want nothing to do with him, but when the UFC gives you a fight, you have to take the fight. For three months, I was battling with how am I gonna beat this guy. I went into this fight, and sure as hell, he beat me up. I had a concussion, I had black eyes, I had a bloody nose, he mauled me the whole first round. I go back to my corner, I can't breathe, and I'm looking for a way out. I'm almost thinking of throwing in the towel, giving up. My cornerman, Scott Smith, calmed me down a little bit, and I kind of got my second wind. I went out there and—for some reason I'm pretty lucky when it comes to knockouts—I caught him on the way in with a big right hand and knocked him out.

Even though I won, I looked horrible. I didn't do the stuff we worked on, and it wasn't till I relaxed and finally landed my huge shot that you can see my body just kind of go, okay, here we go. But up to that point, I was rigid and tense for whatever reason. You are fighting high-level competition, and I will be scared to death, but if I go in there and do what I worked on and compete at my best, then I'm happy as hell.

I've always been a pretty humble person, so I'm not the kind of guy to flex and jump around and cuss. I always kind of keep my head down and just let my work show what I did. Most fighters are that way. There are a few that are very brash, but we all know your own ass kicking is only one fight away. I shake my opponent's hand, leave, inside feeling tremendous, then you hear the crowd, trying to take it all in, because that's three months of work for that twenty seconds where you finally get to "this is what I did this for."

Yeah, I get nervous, but it evolved from those beginning fights. At first, fighting was an ego thing, then it turned into a money thing. I started making big money because I was very good at what I did; then it turned into actually being able to make a living from this, and now it's about wanting to be a top-level fighter; it's about wanting to be recognized as a top ten guy year-round. It's about getting a chance to fight for a belt. Now, it's all a sport for me. I have money in the bank, I have the notoriety; now it's all about what I do in there on my own, getting in the cage and performing as hard as I trained. I push myself as hard as I can.

Anyone who has been in the sport understands that the first fight you fight is getting out of bed in the morning, every day. Everything hurts to hell. I wake up hurting, and I won't feel good till I finally start walking around. I have days when I will just stay in bed. I will lay there and keep hurting, but once I finally talk myself into getting up and get moving, it's like, okay, here we go. Then, I'm crawling out of bed.

In this job, it doesn't matter how good you are or how hard you train, every so often you are going to catch that punch that you didn't see, or you are gonna get hurt, or you are gonna get cut. Sometimes it's a something as simple as that. You never go in there feeling like a million bucks. There is always injuries and stuff. I've broken both my hands. I've broken my nose. I have a deviated septum. I've broken both my feet, and I've had knee surgery, let alone numerous bruised ribs, hyperextended joints, and I think I've had about thirty or forty stitches. But, going in there knowing that I trained as hard as I can is where I get all my confidence from. Knowing that I had the best coaches, knowing that I trained my ass off, knowing that I'm in good enough shape—those are the things that keep me from being nervous and not be able to perform.

I got at least five more years left in this sport, but I want to be remembered for a long time. I want to get a chance to fight for a belt and get a belt. I'm thirty now. When I'm thirty-five, I will probably look and see where I'm at, how my body is holding up.

RICH KING

Federal Marshal

A few days after returning from conducting a federal marshal's operation in Seattle, Rich King sits outside with me at a coffeehouse, talking about his career, including his assignments in the Ted Kaczynski "Unabomber" case, at September 11 conspirator Zacarias Moussaoui's trial, and at former Iraqi dictator Saddam Hussein's trial and execution. He is fifty years old.

★ ★ ★

I'm a deputy U.S. marshal.

Early in my career, the Marshals Service sent me to New York for an assignment on the first World Trade Center bombing, when we were doing the trial of those guys and the blind sheikh. Back then, I was just a regular deputy. Most of the time, I got put on night shifts and was doing security of the building. A couple of times, I worked on the court team where we're transporting jurors. We had different types of teams doing different things during that trial, like protection on the judge.

I would say, back then, I was an average guy with tactics and pistols. Then this guy in our district wrote a proposal that gives us an eleven-man response team here in Northern California, so that like if you're working a warrant and all of a sudden you locate a guy and you think he might be a problem, you can have all our guys on the same sheet of music with an operations plan. You then can just put out a call, and we'll go and take this guy down as safely as possibly. Or if you have to do any high-threat moves, you got guys operating on the same piece of paper and they're a little bit better shots, a little bit more tactically oriented; it's just better and safer. We put in over 350 hours of training just on the handgun alone, to where your arms are so sore you can't even hold an empty gun. But it's served me well, even to this day. Now I'm older, I'm not in the shape I was back then. That training I got has still kept me head and shoulders above the rest of the guys, and even though I don't practice as much as I used to, I'm better than most of the people that are shooting.

[The Unabomber,] Ted Kaczynski, was my first big thing when they moved him to Sacramento. He was caught in his cabin in Montana. Anytime you're arrested on a federal warrant, you go before the nearest available magistrate, so he went before a magistrate in Montana, but he had mailed a letter here that blew up in an office and killed somebody. So they decided the jurisdiction and trial is going to be in Sacramento. I remember we flew him out to Mather Air Force Base, and we went and picked him up and put him in his own little cell, all to himself. I was in the motorcade for that movement, in the follow car right behind him. I was armed with a 9mm MP5 [submachine gun].

Yeah, we talked, but it was real small talk. He'd get by himself and would hum classical tunes. He always asked for books. Once he was in custody, he was no threat at all. In fact, he was kind of a klutz, because like the first day he tripped and fell going up the stairs to our courtroom. We always sent people in waist chains and handcuffs. Well, since he fell, they didn't want him to hurt himself, so I always had to hold on to his arm and walk him. I had to have hands on him from the time he left the cell till he got in the courtroom.

Everything went fine. I think they had half the jurors picked, and then he decided to take a deal. He pled life imprisonment instead of facing the death sentence. When we got him out of here, we flew him straight to Colorado.

When I first came on with the Marshals Service, we traveled quite a bit; they call it "special assignments"—like witness security, where we give someone new identities. Sometimes they have to go testify in court and then, depending on the nature of what he has been doing, we may have a detail on him. I was traveling a lot, and I enjoyed going out and seeing different parts of the country.

Well, we started getting shorthanded in the Sacramento office and weren't hiring anybody for a while. I thought about trying out for our special operations group but really didn't want to devote that much time to it, and my kids were in high school. But then they made selections for the special operations group, so I went and tried out. Since then, all my things have been with the special ops group, like my two tours of Iraq.

I was in Baghdad twice. The first time, I went over in September of 2004. Basically we'd had one rotation of six deputies that went over in April, and my team relieved them. Our team got split up, one half was assigned to the Ministry of Justice, and that's what I was assigned to; the other half of the guys were assigned to interview people for the upcoming trial on the war crimes for Saddam Hussein and all his cohorts, like Chemical Ali. I don't remember when Hussein was caught in Tikrit, in that hole. I can't remember when he was caught because I really don't pay attention to details; I'm more of a single-job-oriented guy: Give me a job to do, I go do it; then give me another job to do.

My job when we went over there was we were trying to set up a training academy to train the security officers who provide security in their different courthouses, for Iraq's Ministry of Justice. We also went to their courthouses, looked at them, and then would say, "Okay, you need to get this done, this done, and this done to upgrade your security." That's what I did for my first six months.

I went over for the experience. I really didn't know what to expect, wasn't ready for it. It took me a little bit to get used to the environment. When we got there, the first team had only three days to get us up to speed with projects they had set up that we're supposed to continue. My first three days in Baghdad I didn't sleep very much. We're staying in tents with cots, and it was 118 degrees.

We set up an academy with a contract company right in the middle of the desert in Al-Hillah, where the ArmorGroup—I think it was— would train the Iraqi security guys, teach them how to shoot, teach them proper searching techniques. And then we would go down and oversee the training to see how they're doing.

It's a fine balance: You're there as an advisor, you can't tell them to do it, but you're also overseeing it, so you're trying to say, hey, get young guys, don't hire a sixty-year-old guy to go through a three-week thing in the desert when it's 115 degrees. You don't know who they're bringing in. The guys you're dealing with during the day could be the same guys that are out at night shooting at you. So, you would kind of just watch them, and then if something didn't work out, you said, "You need to get rid of this guy, you need to get rid of that guy." After my first tour there, I was glad to come home. I was glad to get out of there.

I went back again in September of '06 for what they called the "Iraqi Higher Tribunal." It was my decision; I wasn't forced to go back. The [second] Saddam trial had already started. I was gonna go back to the Ministry of Justice to do what I did before, but I was assigned to take over the security at the trial.

You got to remember you got a little courthouse, and you got approximately 120 Iraqi police that are assigned to just do security at this courthouse. They have a lieutenant and a captain that's basically running it, and we're advising them: You put guys here, you rotate them at these different times. And then you're also dealing with security for Iraqi judges. Say, an Iraqi judge is Sunni and he's got an Iraqi police officer that's Shia. Maybe their tribes conflict: "I'm above him, he won't tell me what to do," and you're trying to explain security to them. So a lot of the security issues I had to do with were just trying to please people, and you can't please people when you're trying to maintain security standards. I mean, one time I had two Iraqi police who didn't see eye to eye and all of a sudden they're squaring off and they've got Glocks and AKs. Thank goodness they put the Glocks and AKs down before they went to strapping. I had to go running out there to separate those two guys. So, basically, I'm dealing with attitudes and security, not to mention now and then you got the mortars coming in that land near the compound.

When the Iraqi judges would go into session for the Hussein trial, the military and we would work together. The U.S. military had control of the detainees at different locations. I know what base they were at, but I can't say. They would bring them in helos at night and then move them out at night—it was only probably a six-hundred-yard drive from the landing pad to our courthouse.

The military basically controlled the basement of our courthouse where the cells were. When court came in session, the military would bring the defendants up in one old elevator that you could only put one detainee and one soldier in. I had three other deputies assigned to me to monitor things like badging—people had to get badges to get in, and all badges were scanned outside about two hundred yards before you even entered our compound. They had a magnetometer and one of these new body scanners—when you could get it to work—and we had another body scanner on the fourth floor, prior to entering the courtroom. Then we had cameras all throughout the courthouse that we could monitor. We had like 130 cameras.

The defendants basically were treated as prisoners of war and had to obey the guidelines. A few times a prisoner would refuse to go up to court, but we had procedures. Saddam was defiant and egotistical. I would actually have to read a damn document to him through an interpreter. It was basically to read the Iraqi law, like, "You have been ordered to appear in court according to section so and so; if you fail to do this, you will be removed." I had a six-man response team of all Iraqis that would actually go down into the basement—that's the only time they would really go down there—they would put hands on him and escort him up to the court. I was nervous because we videotaped everything we did like that, you know, just for our protection and everybody's protection. But I read him the thing. It was like he was playing a game. He goes, in English, with an accent, "Mr. Marshal, you want me to go to court, I'll go to court." Just like that. And he would say, "I'm not afraid of the dogs"—the dogs were the Iraqi police.

We got notice the execution is going to come down real quick, and we need to set up an operations plan to move him. The Iraqi judges wanted to do it as fast as possible. This was right around Christmas, in December of '06. He was hanged on December 30. There was me—I'll not say names—but it was four of us that went with the military who was gonna be transporting him. We knew where, we didn't know when, but we knew it was coming up. So we drove out to their place, had a big meeting, and then we actually did a walk-through at the site of what we're gonna do.

The U.S. military was gonna sign over custody of Saddam to the Iraqi government. Things about security had been talked about and we're still communicating with Main Justice because they want an American presence, someone to make sure he's not beaten while he's in Iraqi custody. After many phone calls, they finally said, "Okay, get the U.S. Marshals Service there," even though our headquarters was saying, "No, don't do it."

On the twenty-ninth, I went to work on my normal thing at the ISOC. I was there at probably six thirty in the morning, and my boss calls and said, "I'm sending you." So, four of us from the Marshals Service went to a meeting, and then we headed off to another location to start the process. We met up with the military and then motorcaded to the death house where they were going to perform the hanging. By the time we got out to the site, it was like thirty-three degrees. It was one of the coldest nights I have ever been in Baghdad, so I kept jumping in our Humvee. I wasn't prepared for the cold, and I was cold as hell.

I didn't really take anything with me. I took some rations and my backpack, but all I really had was my regular Royal Robbins 5.11 pants—light tactical pants with pockets—an Under Armour shirt, and an automatic M4. I had my vest on—a level-4 plate carrier—and my Rhodesian rig: It's the thing that carries all your magazines. I think I had put my long gun in a Humvee with a military guy that was posted right outside. I had a jacket, but I left the jacket in a container where we kept all our equipment in the palace inside the Green Zone.

All I wanted to do was go get sleep. I was tired, and I wanted to get back to my trailer and sleep. I was cold. I was hungry. I had started work the morning before, and now it's in the morning of the next day, the thirtieth. I'd worked a couple of long days before, and we all just wanted to get it over.

We did our stuff with getting the security set. I want to say it was something like fifteen high-ranking Iraqi officials that were gonna view the execution. They each had their own protection, and everyone's got guns. Now, you're talking high-ranking officials that we are gonna search. We say, "No phones, no nothing, no protection is going with you." It ended up turning into a nightmare. The Iraqi officials all wanted Iraqi protection details, their own guys, and we're saying, "No, you're not going. Yeah, this official is going"—like the head of the Ministry of Justice—"Yes you're going, but it's just you, no phone, no camera, no nothing." Not all the Iraqis want to get their faces shown, especially the ones that hanged Saddam. So they're all running around with AKs and balaclava masks on. You don't trust anybody. You don't know who is who, so it was kind of an uneasy feeling.

The military got Saddam in a helo at probably about two o'clock in the morning. At about two thirty, they put him in a holding cell while they were doing everything else in the death house and getting the VIPs. Myself and another marshal were right outside the holding cell.

We stayed with Saddam probably for about three hours.

Saddam's cell was a hole in the ground, just big enough to piss and shit in. That was it; just a square holding cell with a door, no bars, no windows. He was by himself. He was dressed in a suit without a tie, and he had a coat on. He was fine. He basically just sat over in the corner. He had a book, a Koran. I don't know if he was reading. He just sat there. Me and my partner were going in and out. We would kind of switch, until it was time.

There also was an American contractor that was like an advisor to a couple of Iraqi guys that were in charge of the Iraqi correctional officers on how to run things for a prison. So it was like us two, this American contractor, and the correctional officers, and then some of the Iraqi military and our military would come in and say, this is going on and that is going on. There also were other high-ranking Iraqi guys. We're all just kind of sitting there waiting, basically waiting for us to be told we're going to march him from the holding cell to the death house. It seemed like a long time.

Finally, once the VIPs got in the death house and the decision gets made that they got everything set up, basically the Iraqi correctional officers told him it's time to go. He just got up with his head held up and walked out of the holding cell. Didn't say anything. All businesslike.

Rich King

Now, you got a big presence of correctional officers. They walked out of the cell. Some of the guys that were running around the death house wore masks and some of these guys didn't wear masks. The guys that were gonna actually do the rope and pull the lever, they were already in the death house. That was all done by Iraqi corrections. We had nothing to do with it. The death house was all Iraqi. Once we got to the door of the death house there was no American presence inside.

From the holding cell to the death house, it was about a two-hundred-yard walk. You had to walk out the holding cell and through a big metal gate. On the side of the metal gate, they had a door open. They all walked through the door and then you had about a hundred yards of a straight, beat-up, asphalt-dirt road. I walked to the death house along on the left, to the rear. Basically all we were told was just to make sure Saddam's not violated and is not beaten.

It was a little noisy because we had protection up top. We had helos flying low. The sun hadn't come up yet.

I think they hanged him right around six o'clock in the morning. I remember it was still dark outside. The back wall of the death house was all lit up inside so you could see perfect shadows of the outlines of the gallows, the noose.

They walk him along and then there's another little gate, and they go through the gate. Then they get to the door of the death house. I'd been in there two days before when we did our walk-through. When we're talking about the death house, it's real primitive. It's these mud-type walls and a dirt floor. Just a set of gallows built up.

As soon as you walk through the door, there is a scale that they weigh him on. Whatever his weight is, that's what they measure the rope with. From there, there's a small room he goes into where he's read a court document in Iraqi that explains his sentence. Then they got his prayer rug. He gets to fold his prayer rug out and is given time to pray and do whatever he wants to do. From there, he just comes out and then goes right up the steps. I could see him—his outline—walk up the steps. You could see him turning. You could see the Iraqi correctional officer go to put the hood on and Hussein pull back and say, "I don't want the hood." Then you could see the shadow of them putting the noose over his neck. He stands there. Then, you saw him drop.

Once he dropped, it got real loud in there. I remember all those head Iraqis start chanting and praying real loud. It's like celebrating at a soccer game.

After it's all done, we got the VIPs out of there. Saddam was down on the dirt floor when I got there. He was on the ground with a Z in his neck. You could see his neck had snapped. The military put him in a transport bag and then got him on a chopper and they took him up to Tikrit.

I just remember it got done. I looked at it as another job.

STEVEN FRICK

ASTRONAUT

*C*aptain Steven Frick graduated from the U.S. Naval Academy in 1986. He flew twenty-six combat missions during Desert Storm, was aboard an Atlantis *Space Shuttle flight* in 2002 that docked with the International Space Station, and was the commander of the Shuttle on his second trip to space in 2008. The forty-three-year-old astronaut has logged more than four thousand flight hours.

★ ★ ★

Risk, that's one of the things we wrestle with, because it's not just the perception of the public, it's also our perception of us—I mean, the professional crews in the vehicle and also the mission control team that manages it from the ground and makes all the preflight decisions about how we are going to plan the mission, and how much redundant systems we are going to have. After the *Challenger* accident in 1986, we flew for many years with no serious accidents. You start thinking it's pretty safe, but you only fly four or five times a year, so when you actually do the math and look at the number of failures we've had—a total of two in the Shuttle—over the number of missions that we've flown and the number of people we have lost, our chance is only about one in sixty, or so, that you're not going to come home, which compares to crab fishermen, who are running about one in two hundred or three hundred, something like that. Though we can go years and years without an accident, your exposure every time you launch on a mission is actually much higher than anything else that is considered normal, noncombat kind of duty. It actually compares pretty closely to combat, like an infantryman that was hitting the beach on D-Day [where there was about] one in sixty losses on that first day. We have to convince ourselves that that's really the risk that we're taking, and we have to think about that when you are thinking about how you are going to plan a mission and how much additional risk you are willing to take to be aggressive, and get as much done on the mission as you can.

Most folks that end up as astronauts had a life before. My life before was flying with the navy. I'm still a captain in the navy. I started out flying F/A-18s off of aircraft carriers. Did a sea tour when I was young, including flying in Desert Storm; did some missions over there; came back; went into the test pilot track; did some aircraft testing for a couple of years; applied to NASA, and then got picked by NASA to be a Space Shuttle pilot in 1996, and ended up down here at the Johnson Space Center in Houston, Texas. We get folks from the navy, folks from the Air Force, and folks from the Marine Corps to be Shuttle pilots.

I had always imagined being a fighter pilot flying off of aircraft carriers, so that's the route I went first. I was always interested in space, probably like everybody my age that grew up watching the Apollo missions. It was intriguing, but it also seems like an unrealistically ridiculous goal.

We're used to flying tactical jets, which seem pretty complicated to most people that fly, but the Space Shuttle is a whole different level of complication, something that is going to be able to launch on a rocket and go all the way from zero sitting on the launchpad up to about sixty miles and 17,500 miles an hour up into a stable orbit above the atmosphere. You have to release an unbelievable amount of energy and keep it harnessed that whole time. Then once you get up there, this vehicle has to turn from a rocket into an orbiting space vehicle and handle all the bizarre aspects of space, which is you're up in a vacuum. You're not in a nice atmosphere like we have down here. You got to generate all your own electricity; you have to keep the air breathable; you have to get rid of heat that all your electronics and the humans and all the systems are putting into the vehicle; and you're going around the earth once every ninety minutes. Roughly forty-five minutes of that is in sunlight where you're just getting baked. It's a couple of hundred degrees out there with no atmosphere to kind of mitigate it a bit, and then you go into darkness when you go around to the dark side of the earth. The earth blocks you from the sun, and then it gets really cold. So you get this combination of having to keep the vehicle from getting too hot in the sun, too cold in the darkness, and then back and forth again while you're generating power, and while you're getting rid of the heat, keeping all the systems going, and doing all your work.

At the same time, you got to fly this thing in a controlled manner so you can rendezvous and dock with the space station. You got to carry big pieces of payload and move them around, and when that's all done, you got to wrap it up and fire your rockets one more time to drop down into the atmosphere and use the friction of the atmosphere to slow yourself down enough so you can land. It's an unbelievable amount of heat that you have to dissipate as you're coming into the atmosphere. So you're going 17,500 miles an hour and you got to get yourself slowed down to about the speed of an airplane to land it on a runway.

Things for the Shuttle are way different than what an airplane has to do just to fly from point A to point B. And there is no way to service it, so you have to make sure that your systems are incredibly reliable, because if, for instance, you lose all your electrical power, you die. If you lose your ability to get rid of all the heat you generate, your systems are going to overheat, and you die. You have to make sure that you have complete confidence in your systems, and your backup system, so you can get safely home. That's what makes it so much more complicated than a regular airplane, which means it takes a lot longer to learn. We spend a couple of years learning how to fly this thing and manage it on a spaceflight before we can even be assigned as a crew member to a mission.

It's a very different experience than when we flew combat missions from the USS *Saratoga*, an aircraft carrier that was in the Red Sea during Desert Storm back in 1991. We would launch off that carrier, fly all the way across Saudi Arabia—a flight which is a pretty low threat—to get to either Iraq or Kuwait, which is like an hour and a half flight. Then, you'd fly your mission in the risky area, which was pretty short where you were getting fired at or were under threat. And then you'd return.

Shuttle missions are different. There are obviously no things like taking surface-to-air missiles or ground fire when you are in orbit. It's more the ever-present concern about a systems failure that could put you at risk, or micrometeoroids that could hit you with no warning. The Air Force tracks all the bigger pieces up there, and they can tell us if we're getting close and we maneuver to avoid them. Then there are really small dust particles that hit us all the time. They're not big enough to really do any damage, but there's a certain percentage of debris up there that's too small for the Air Force to track but big enough that if it hits us, it is going to do serious damage. We are very much aware of it, but there's nothing you can do, and you won't know until it hits you. The main risk is to our thermal protection system. If it hits like the leading edge of the wing—which is a really fancy composite material that takes most of the heat on reentry—and breaks that, it basically will do what happened to *Columbia*, which is you would burn up on reentry.

Nothing big has happened on my flights, but during both of my missions we took a hit on a window, which was probably just from a speck of dust. But when you're up in orbit, that glancing blow from dust is maybe an impact velocity of twenty thousand miles an hour, so a piece of dust hitting you at twenty thousand miles an hour still can make an obvious mark. For us, it looked like a big stone came off a truck and hit the window; it left like a pockmark but, luckily, we didn't have anything hit in a critical area that caused us to have to do something about it.

You're assigned to a mission more than a year out, so you spend that year both training for the mission and also working with the operations team on the ground planning on how you're going to do it. Basically, you have that trade-off of do we want to risk being a little more aggressive on this one activity so we can get a little more done? Do we want to risk spending more hours awake?

Our normal day is, you work for sixteen hours and then you have to stop yourself and jump into the sleeping bag, turn the lights off, go to sleep. Eight hours later, the lights come on, and you get back to work. You might do that for twelve or thirteen days, so you try to figure out how we can get as much done as possible but still not be so tired that you can't handle the challenges of reentry. We have all those kinds of discussions ahead of time, and then you start grappling with the personal ramifications of the risks and how they affect your family.

One personal consideration is how many times do you want to expose yourself to this if every time you do it, it's one in sixty, you know? You start doing it five or six times, you're running an awful lot of risk. Some guys fly a couple of times and say, "That's about as much as I am willing to put my family through. I think it's time to stop," and think about doing something else. Others just take it one mission at a time. Every time you go through it, it's really difficult for you and your family. It's much worse for the family, because we are real busy during the really dangerous times like launch and reentry, whereas they're having to just watch it from the ground and they got nothing to do but worry.

The strange thing about the way we train versus the reality of spaceflight is we spend an awful lot of time practicing for all the little things that could fail and how we could work around them so we can either continue with the mission or get safely on the ground. We get very proficient at it, but the reality of spaceflight is, historically, all of the really bad failures we've had are things that there's really nothing the crew can do about. For example, in the *Challenger* accident, the rocket burned through and broke the vehicle apart. There was nothing the crew could do. On *Columbia*, it burned through the thermal protection system and basically burned the vehicle up from the inside. There's nothing the crew could do.

Back with *Apollo 13*, they basically had a tank that blew open and they were able to get back home safely, but you know if it had gone on just a little bit more, there was really nothing the crew could do. That's kind of the reality of spaceflight. There's not much we can do about that, so we don't spend a lot of time worrying about that during the mission. You understand that there are risks, but you don't spend every second worrying if the rocket is going to blow up or not. You stay busy all the time.

You're the most apprehensive before launch. We go out to the launchpad and strap into the Space Shuttle three hours before launch. The pressure suits are pretty uncomfortable. You're lying on your back and are strapped in really tight. After about two hours, your back starts hurting.

During those three hours, you don't have a lot to do. So that's the time where you're kind of nervous; maybe a little concerned about what could be happening beneath you that you're not seeing or hearing. You listen to the ground team chatter on the radio about how the vehicle is doing and how they are progressing toward the launch count. We have a few little things to do in the vehicle, but we're mostly just waiting. Then the last nine minutes, after they give you a go for launch, go by pretty darn fast up to the point of launch, and then launch goes fast.

On launch, initially, we don't have much time to look outside. The visuals and the feelings are very disconnected from each other. On my side, I look outside right after the engines have fired and we're leaving the launchpad. I have to make sure we're heading in the right direction and the engines are working. I glance out and watch the launchpad drop away as we do a roll maneuver so you kind of watch the world spin, until the shuttle stabilizes.

We recently were reviewing the in-cabin video that we shoot during launch. We've done this hundreds of times in the simulator. You go through the same sequence over and over and over and over again, and normally we just have our operational communications where one guy is confirming the computers are correct and the engines are good and the maneuver is correct—you hear this sort of standard communication. For the real launch, you're hearing guys hooting and hollering, "Woooa, that's incredible!" The thing is shaking hard and it's pushing you hard from the thrust of the engines. We don't have any simulator that can simulate it. You're getting pushed off the launchpad with about 2 Gs. You glance outside your window and you're watching the earth kind of drop away. It only takes about twenty or thirty seconds for the sky to go from blue to black as you get up through most of the atmosphere. The physical feeling is an amazing experience, because we just can't simulate that.

Once you get to orbit, it's completely different because your body goes through a lot of physiological changes when you get up into zero-G. Your fluids shift up in your body because they're not being held down by gravity. Your body thinks that you are way overhydrated because all this fluid has kind of come up into your torso and head, so you spend the next day basically peeing it all off and getting back to sort of a new equilibrium.

The periods of very high risk are relatively short. It only takes us eight and a half minutes to get from the launchpad up to where we shut the engines down and we're safely in orbit. That's a pretty narrow window of severe vulnerability where a lot of things could blow the rocket up. The Space Shuttle just keeps pushing and pushing and pushing as you accelerate toward space. It's a great ride. For about the first seven and a half minutes, you have burned off so much fuel that the engine thrust is really pushing you hard. When we get up to 3 Gs, we start throttling the engines back to keep it at 3 Gs so that we don't overstress the vehicle or break anything. Being at 3 Gs for about a minute is pretty hard. You have to force yourself to breathe because all this equipment on your chest is pushing you back into the seat, and you really have to struggle to make sure you're paying attention to everything you need to do.

Two weeks later, before you come home, you're in this kind of a dehydrated state, which works for zero-G but is terrible for when you get back down here on earth. We could black out on reentry, so the last thing you do before firing the rockets to come back is drink about forty ounces of salty water. You feel like you're just going to burst. Then you drop back into the atmosphere and get back into some Gs. Suddenly you are really thirsty. It wreaks havoc on your body.

Reentry is very different. It seems to go by quickly. It takes about an hour from when you fire your engines to slow down and drop into the atmosphere, and it takes about an hour from that point to landing. You fire the engines over the Indian Ocean and coast from there all the way across the Pacific Ocean. For both my missions, it just happened the sun rose right about as we came past Australia. We were coasting over the Pacific and after being up at two hundred miles—which is kind of our orbital altitude when we are with the space station—you're now down about maybe fifty miles, just touching the top of the atmosphere. It feels like you are incredibly low and going just ridiculously fast. You have this phenomenal view—I don't want to get too into the details about the way the orbital works—and you come in rolled way over on one side so that one of us—the commander who is sitting on the left or the pilot who is sitting on the right—is looking right down toward the ground and the other guy is looking up toward space. The guy who is looking at the ground looks down and can see this incredible view of the Pacific and the storm clouds and the islands as you pass over them. But if you look out any of the windows that are pointed up at the blackness of space, you see that orange glow of the super-heated plasma that's caused by our reentry, and you're like, wow, that's amazing. Before you know it, you're crossing Mexico and the Yucatán Peninsula and over the Gulf of Mexico, and then suddenly you're over the west coast of Florida heading toward the Kennedy Space Center, and you are just a few minutes from landing. It goes by pretty quickly.

On reentry you're only in the really high heating part for maybe twenty minutes. After you've gotten through the high heating part and the vehicle seems to be working pretty well, you're almost certainly home free. We reenter at maybe a G and a half or 2 Gs at most. You've been floating up in orbit for essentially two weeks and you've gotten used to that. So when you start coming back into the G-field, you start feeling these accelerations on your body and on your inner ear. It plays tricks with you, and you have to work hard to make sure you don't get vertigo. Just think of like if you went on one of those whirly rides in the carnival and then stepped right off it—think about how your head kind of spins. We'll get that just if you turn your head wrong on reentry. We have to be really careful about how we turn our head, because I'm going to hand-fly the orbiter all the way to touchdown. I can't be consumed by vertigo.

It doesn't end when you land. You come to a stop on the runway, the mission is over, you get home safe. Then we crawl out. You feel tremendously heavy, because you haven't been using your muscles for two weeks and you have been in zero-G, so you feel like you weigh three hundred pounds. You quickly take your pressure suit off, because it's heavy and it's hot. You sit down in a chair in kind of like a big RV that they pull up to the orbiter. I swear they were driving that thing in circles around the runway and I couldn't figure why they were moving already, so I looked out the window and no, they're sitting still. Then I looked back to the middle of the room and sure enough we're back turning. It takes about half an hour, at least, for that feeling to go away. The carnival ride doesn't end with the touchdown.

Without a doubt, I think almost every astronaut will tell you the most dramatic and memorable thing about a spaceflight is the view of the earth. You orbit once every ninety minutes. You're only two hundred miles up, which sounds like a lot, but with the diameter of the earth you seem like you are in a high airplane. You can see every direction as you go around the earth, and that view is just astounding. I think most astronauts could just sit there and stare out the window for their whole mission if there wasn't anything else to do. As it turns out, we're paid to do this stuff. We have to accomplish so much in a short time, but you're always trying to grab a few seconds here and a minute there to look out at the earth, especially if you are flying over someplace that's real important to you, like your hometown or where your family lives or interesting places you have visited in your life. You really want to see those things from space and kind of store that image in your memory.

You also look forward to being up in microgravity in zero-G. Floating around is just the most amazing experience. To do that for a sustained period of time like on a two-week Shuttle mission, it's like being a little kid again on the best carnival ride you can possibly imagine. You can sit there and do tumbles, you can float around, move your body around in ways you can't possibly do it even in water. It's like being the most weightless you could be when you're down diving but without any water resistance. Now, the price you have to pay to get that experience, for a lot of guys myself included, is the adjustment from living your whole life in 1 G to having your body get used to zero-G. For me, the first six hours are not too pleasant. It's like getting a flu that comes on fast, but then, thankfully, it goes away fast. There are some folks that I have flown with on both my missions that are just awesome spacemen. They get up there and are instantly comfortable and happy in the space environment, and when they come back home they are instantly comfortable and happy on earth again. But it doesn't work that way for me. That first day for me is pretty unpleasant.

The Shuttle is still scheduled to fly for a couple more years before they retire it and move on to the Constellation program. The way the astronaut life works is you keep doing what you're doing, and you hope something good is going to come down the line. You come back from a flight and you're back at the end of the line, waiting to see what happens. I may, or may not, be lucky enough to fly again.

Photo Courtesy of: **ANDY CASAGRANDE**

ANDY CASAGRANDE

WILDLIFE FILMMAKER

*T*his thirty-one-year-old is a busy man. We quickly got in the interview before Andy Casagrande flew from Hawaii the following day to New York City to pick up a $300,000 high-speed camera that he would be using in Costa Rica on assignment to film army ants for National Geographic. Months later I sent him an e-mail requesting his photo for the book. His reply: "Good to hear from you. I'm in Mozambique with the crocodiles. Sorry for the delay. I have been busy, busy. Just spent the past month in Tanzania shooting cheetahs with a high-speed camera. Off next to Patagonia to film the Orcas eating the seals!"

★ ★ ★

Andy Casagrande

I'm a wildlife filmmaker. I like to make films about animals that are struggling to survive so I can inspire other people to sort of give a damn about these animals that are just doing what they've been doing for thousands and thousands of years. I mean, humans have evolved at such a fast rate from when we used to scratch stones together and build fire and go hunt with spears, and now we jump out of helicopters and snort cocaine for fun and do random frivolous stuff, whereas a lion still hunts a zebra on the plains in Africa like it did thousands of years ago. And, elephants in Africa have been poached almost to extinction throughout the years. It's bizarre because for some people their favorite thing in the world is to see elephants and what they do in the wild, and other people only see them as ivory and some way to make money.

How I got in this line of work? I think I was just born this way. I guess the true link to this career was great white sharks. Ever since I could remember, I've been fascinated with great white sharks. I think the first time I ever saw them was on a National Geographic documentary. When I saw this shark swim across the television, I thought it was fake. I thought it was something from Hollywood— at that age I didn't even know what Hollywood was—but I knew what cartoons were and what movies were about, and I thought this was a fake animal. I'm not talking *Jaws*. From that point on, I was just fascinated with them.

When I learned that great white sharks were actually real and tangible and something that was actually living in our oceans, I couldn't stop thinking about them. That particular animal took up more of my time and thoughts and fascination than any other thing in the world. Part of it also was an interest in the ocean. I have always been fearful of sharks and the *deep, dark ocean*. They're pretty scary, but I think that's what drew me toward them. I had to learn more about them, because it was a fear of mine, and as I grew older the fear increased, but so did my fascination to the point where I'm like I just got to get to know these things in order do the whole counter-your-fear thing. So I went to school, studied a little bit of biology and psychology, and I graduated with a degree in sort of biopsychology, and then I went into software. It's a long story, but after working at a software company for two years, it just dawned on me that I'm way too young to be sitting at a desk for nine hours a day, 365 days a year. I got to get out of here!

I thank Google a lot. I basically Googled "great white shark researcher," because that's what I wanted to be. I found a few different research teams in California, Australia, and South Africa. And, I'm a musician, so I ended up writing a song about great white sharks. It's kind of a funny little educational song about conservation. I sent it to these research teams around the world and the one research team in South Africa called the White Shark Trust wrote back to me and said, "Your song is excellent. It's hilarious. We love it. I know you don't have a lot of experience with sharks in general . . ."—because at that point I had never dived with sharks—but they invited me to come down there. Long story short, I moved to South Africa in 2003 and lived there for two years.

When I moved to South Africa, I was working as a research photographer. I bought some cameras, went down there, and was photographing great white shark dorsal fins (every great white shark dorsal fin is like a fingerprint; they actually call it a fin print and you can identify unique individual sharks through their dorsal fins). I started in still photography and then quickly realized I'd rather capture these animals and their amazing grace at sixty frames per second instead of a couple of frames every minute that you use with a still camera. So I became a video cameraman, and over the two years there I developed my skills as an underwater cameraman.

Basically, one day National Geographic Television showed up in Cape Town to make a documentary about great white sharks and about the research team I was working for, and at the end of the two-week film shoot they offered me a job as a National Geographic wildlife cameraman. The only stipulation was that I had to move to Washington, D.C.—that's where their headquarters were—and from that point on I've been working for them and I've been able to film lions, jellyfish, crocodiles, cheetahs, bears, army ants, king cobras, manta rays, baboons.

Some of the most valuable things I have learned working for National Geographic were from other cameramen. A lot of the older veterans that I have worked with have really helped me to understand the behavior of animals. What it really boils down to is that you really need to think like the animal. If you're filming hyenas, you need to think like a hyena. You need to think about how hyenas hunt, how fast they can run, where they can hide, what they like to do, everything.

With regard to sharks, you have to think like a shark, you need to be as fast as a shark or as calm as a shark, or if a shark is getting aggressive with you, it's often better to get just as aggressive back, because everything in the ocean swims away from a great white shark. If you swim away from it, it's just like triggering an instinct in that animal, in that the shark will chase you just as it chases a tuna or a seal. But if you swim straight at a great white shark, it throws its thinking off, because nothing really does that. We don't really know what it's thinking when you're swimming at it with a high-definition camera, but under most circumstances it swims away. The bottom line is this: It's best to think like the animal thinks.

With wildlife filming, you often go there trying to capture something natural, and you really hope to capture some amazing behavior that's never been captured before. I guess I just really want to capture interesting things that haven't been seen before to help reinspire people to care about this endangered wildlife that we have. It's funny, because anthropomorphism is sort of a dirty word in the natural history documentary film world because it's apparently just not proper to anthropomorphize animal's behavior into human behavior and emotions. But often, when I'm watching lions play with each other, it's amazing; you can't help but feel that they're having a lot of fun playing. When the cubs are playing with their mother, and they're biting at her tail, and she is maybe not in the mood, but she puts up with it, because they're her little cubs. It's funny, because I see other little babies pulling on their mom's pigtails here on the beaches and wondering, you know, it's kind of the same thing.

The magic formula is to get as close as you possibly can without interfering with the animal's natural behavior. That is sometimes not always possible, because we do our best to try to blend in the environments that we're working in. If we're filming crocodiles, you need to have full camouflage, almost as if you're hunting. If you're filming crocodiles hunting, then you need to be hunting the crocodiles. They can't realize that you're near them and trying to capture their behavior otherwise they're gonna be too focused on you crawling up next to them as opposed to crawling up on a wildebeest and pulling it into the water and removing its head.

Great white sharks are easier to film. You just jump in the water, and if you're brave enough to get outside of the cage, they will swim right up to you. They'll get as close as they can before either they bite your camera or you bump them with the camera to let them know that they're a little too close for comfort. We utilize a cage for a last-resort safety box, but you really get limited amount of footage from within a cage, because the sharks can only swim so close to the cage without hitting it, and also when you get outside of the cage, the sharks react totally differently. If they're swimming around the cage, they just swim around the cage and check it out. But if you get outside of the cage, it's as if they're thinking something different now and they come a lot closer. Depending on the shark and your safety and comfort levels, we do some risky things, but they're always calculated. For instance, every great white shark is unique. They all have unique personalities, and you can actually tell a lot about a great white shark by its physical appearance. The sharks that look scarred up, beat up, missing teeth, little tears at their eyes, and their noses are bloody, that's most likely an aggressive and dangerous shark. If you see a shark that's clean, smooth, with very few scars, and is really placid and relaxed, it's probably a safe shark to dive with. It's as if you go to a bar, you see some guy with a bunch of tattoos and bloody knuckles and scars all over him, you're not gonna walk right up to his face and take his picture. But if you see another guy that seems to be pretty polite and relaxed, you might walk up to him and say, "Hey, mind if I take your picture?"

The cages usually are aluminum cages, sort of the material like aluminum baseball bats, because it's strong and light, but to be honest, the sharks can thrash that cage and shred it if they really wanted to. There is documented video footage of great whites dismantling cages when they get frustrated enough. The cage is about the size of, I don't know, maybe your bathroom depending on what size your bathroom is, but it can fit usually two to four people. We utilize it as a last resort, sort of a bunker as if when you're doing battle at some point if things get really rough, you head back into the bunker and hunker down.

I was scared the first time I ever got outside of the cage with a great white shark, but at the same time, I realized if I allowed my fear to invoke panic then things could get bad quickly, so it was best to keep my head and keep my courage such that I didn't invoke a chase reaction. Great whites aren't stupid. For an animal that has outlived dinosaurs, they must have some intelligence to survive this long.

The main protection while filming sharks underwater without cages is the camera. Often these cameras weigh seventy pounds and sometimes they are the size of your television, but underwater they become neutrally buoyant. Often, if sharks get a little bitey, you can bounce them with the camera. The interesting thing is that the camera obviously has a lot of electronics, and sharks have these unique senses that detect electronic and magnetic impulses throughout the water column and they're actually drawn to the camera, which makes for great shots, but at the same time, it makes for very close encounters with them. As soon as they bite onto something that's very hard and metallic, they quickly realize, hey, this isn't something that I normally eat.

Sharks aren't malicious and demonic as a lot of Hollywood films like to depict. Yeah, I've had my fins bitten by sharks, and it's a bit unnerving, but it was because I wasn't paying attention. The one thing while filming sharks is it's not the one that you're filming that you have to worry about, it's the two that are underneath you or the one that is coming behind you. That's why we often have safety divers with us while we're filming dangerous species like tigers, great whites, and bull sharks. While you're filming, you're so focused on filming the shark in front of you, you don't realize that there's three behind you or one coming up straight from the bottom, and unless you have someone watching your back, you might get bit.

Yes, I have been caught off guard: by lions. It was in Tanzania, in the Serengeti. I was filming lions throughout the morning and then I put my camera down, because I had to go to the bathroom (I had to go number one) and I jumped out of my Land Rover. Next to the bush where I was peeing I noticed a lioness was there crouched and looking right at me. She was about five feet away. I hadn't seen her because she was concealed by a bush, but luckily just as I saw her the driver of my vehicle also saw her and quickly reversed the car toward the lion to spook it off. That was pretty scary. Because you're filming these animals all day long, you can become complacent and you're like, oh, this lion is only hunting the wildebeest or the zebra. You get so close to them to the point where you could almost touch them, and you start to become a little desensitized to the fact that these are wild animals and serious predators. So you have these mental checks every so often to realize that you never can lose respect for the fact that *this is a wild animal with razor-sharp teeth.*

When I got my job with National Geographic, I worked for two years on staff with them and they would send me on assignment. But I kind of grew tired of Washington, D.C. I don't really like cities that much. I really prefer living along the coast or even in the forest or in the jungle, anywhere I can be around wildlife. So, after two years of working on staff there, I decided to become a freelance cameraman such that I could work for National Geographic just as much as I did in the past, but also I didn't have to live in Washington and I could live anywhere I wanted. They would call me for assignments and fly me to wherever I was going. That also allowed me to work for other production companies like Discovery Channel and Animal Planet. It's kind of the route that most wildlife filmmakers eventually go, because if you tie yourself to one production company, you do have job security, but it's nice to be able to pick and choose assignments.

The start of every assignment begins with extreme focus. They say, "Andy, we need you to go back to Africa and film lions." I know then I got to get up to speed again on the latest lion research and what's happening. So I focus on the particular animal and then secondly, I focus on technology and all the best cameras that I need: night cameras, high-speed cameras, infrared cameras. You focus on every aspect of the film that you need to accomplish, having all the right equipment, the right crew, the right vehicles, the right food, the right everything. And then once you get there and all your batteries are charged up and your cameras are all ready and you start rolling on your first tape, that's when the adrenaline kicks in, because you know that you can't miss any shots when you're in the field. You realize you're capturing wildlife as it happens, and you got to be at the top of your game. If you're not, then you might miss the kill, or you might miss the amazing light. Photography itself means "light writing." With photography, and cinematography, the better the light, the better the pictures you're gonna get. So you have to be up before the sun. And it's all about being physically fit, mentally healthy, and you just got to enjoy what you're doing because if you're not, then you might as well be working at the bank.

One of the main objectives is to get as close as possible without interfering with an animal's natural behavior, but there comes times when you do get too close and at that point the animal realizes that you've crossed over its comfort zone, and you both realize it simultaneously. It's basically up to you to decide what to do. Sometimes it's a tough call. Often it's just a matter, for example, of you slowly backing away with a shark standing ground. I've filmed grizzly bears up in Alaska, and one of the experts we were working with said among the bear attack studies that he did, a high percentage of people that ran from grizzly bears were actually chased and attacked, as opposed to basically sort of standing your ground. It's almost like you're talking the bear down; you talk softly to it to show that you're not being aggressive. If you charge the bear, then you're probably gonna lose. Every animal has a different personality and a different behavior; they will react with fight or flight.

With lions, it's a lot more black-and-white. When you see a pride of lions hunting, they're in a stalking mode in which they crouch low and stalk from cover to cover in order to keep hidden from their prey. As they get closer and closer, they get to a point where their muscles tense up and you can tell that they're about to engage in chase. Right before the lion is about to initiate its pounce, it's pretty easy to tell that it's pretty tense. That's when the adrenaline really starts going for me. When you're filming a lion as it is stalking a zebra and you realize that the zebra has no idea that the lion is there, but you're watching this all unfold on a high-definition camera and you're realizing, wow, if this lion kills the zebra right in front of me people are gonna be able to see this.

Lions have a lot of respect for how they kill their prey. Lions will pull a zebra to the ground and immediately go for its trachea to suffocate that animal to silence it in order to decrease the likelihood of hyenas and other predators coming to steal that kill from them. I have, on the other hand, watched four or five hyenas grab a wildebeest, pull it down, and start eating it from its private parts up into its body cavity. It's alive for ten to fifteen minutes as its intestines and kidneys are being ripped out; basically everything is ripped out from its lungs to its liver to everything, and it finally dies when they rip its heart out, which is one of the most gut-wrenching things to film, let alone to witness.

The sounds of hyenas killing anything is like a horror movie, because they're cackling, they're laughing, and you hear the sound of flesh tearing, and the dying animal usually is crying out in pain. It's pretty horrendous. It's very similar with crocodiles: They will grab a zebra or a wildebeest, and they will usually pull it into the water and immediately three or four other crocodiles will latch onto that animal and they will each grab a leg and then they all start their little death rolls. Crocodiles don't really have serrated teeth, so they basically just grab a hold and try to use blunt force to tear an animal apart. It would be like someone grabbing you with pliers and pulling in different directions. I'd rather just have someone strangle me and then eat me later, as opposed to being eaten alive or ripped and drowned and quartered. Sometimes it's tough to watch, and you really hope that that animal escapes and it doesn't succumb to a very unpleasant death, but sometimes it is just inevitable that that animal is not gonna make it and that these predators have to feed. That's when I just have to realize this is just a job and this is the animal kingdom and I'm glad I'm not a zebra right now.

The job can be incredibly taxing, from all the thirty-six-hour plane rides to the waking up before the sun rises, going to bed well after the sun sets, and sometimes spending eighteen hours out in a vehicle following a pride of lions. All you may have is a couple of bottles of water, some PowerBars, and hopefully a good driver that tells good jokes. It can be mentally challenging, because we will often spend three months in one place. A few days will go by or sometimes even weeks, and you may feel that you haven't really filmed anything that worthwhile. It's not because of any dysfunction, it's more that the animals just aren't in the mood. Or, it's that global warming seems to have affected a lot of animal behavior around the world. I can't tell you how many times I have gone to a place where the experts say, "I just don't understand, the manta rays are always here at this time. It doesn't make any sense, they're always mating right here on this reef, but we haven't seen them at all this year." You know, things are changing in the world.

Author's note: *In 2011, Casagrande won an Emmy award for "Outstanding Individual in a Craft: Cinematography-Nature" for his camera work on National Geographic's* Great Migrations.

ROB DICK

BOUNTY HUNTER

*R*ob *Dick sits behind his office desk talking about hunting people for a living. His file of unsolved cases will keep him busy for some time. He's forty-two years old, stands five feet eight inches tall, and weighs 170 pounds. "It's a lifestyle. I don't have Christmas Day, because it is the easiest time to get people. They're always at Mom's home. I'm always somewhere on Christmas. Thanksgiving is the same thing. It's kind of a rough lifestyle if you have a family, because the job is always taking you away."*

★ ★ ★

My job is a bounty hunter. I track down people.

I fell into this work when a roommate of mine got a DUI, and his dad and I went down and bailed him out. We were talking to the bondsman and I said I got law enforcement experience as a deputy sheriff at the jail and that I have my private investigator license and was doing investigations on the side. So we started talking. I didn't like working the jail; I wanted to be on the street and be more active. The one thing you find out is you can't be a part-time bounty hunter. There's just no way to do it. You can't really have another full-time job because as you start working cases, all of a sudden, you get a call and you have to just got to go. You got to be free to do that.

I get hired by bail bond companies to find people and get them back either into court or into jail, depending upon what the circumstances are. I'm paid by the bondsman whenever I get the guy in custody, whether I do it or law enforcement does because whatever I was doing solved the problem. I'm probably chasing about twenty-five to thirty people at any one time. I have four companies that I do full-time work for, which allows me to have enough to sustain myself.

Normally how it works is, it's a 10 percent bond. If the bond is $10,000, a loved one puts up a thousand bucks and bails the client out of jail. The bonding company then puts a piece of paper up with the court saying that that person will appear in court. It's basically insurance. Now, as long as they go to all their court appearances, everything is fine. The 10 percent that the loved one paid is how the bondsman makes his money: That's his fee for putting up the liability. If the guy went to court and did everything like he was supposed to, no one will have to pay anything else.

If a defendant misses court—let's see this case. [Dick opens a file on his desk.] The bond was placed April 13, and the defendant missed court December 11. In this case, the court issues a forfeiture for the bond to the bail bondsman—that basically starts the clock. We have six months plus five days for the mailing to resolve this by getting him a new court date and getting him back into court—sometimes people oversleep and miss it—or, if he's actually not wanting to go, then it's a matter of getting him into custody either by law enforcement or by us picking him up. Like on this one, the guy missed court, and a $25,000 felony warrant has been issued for him. So, we'll contact the jail and get a booking photo to make sure that it's actually the right person. I mean, just because a guy comes in and signs the paperwork the next day doesn't mean it's not his brother or somebody else, so we get the booking photo from the jail where he was booked. There are a lot of things that we go off of, like a description, tattoos, whatever information the bail agent takes when they bail, which hopefully is as truthful as can be. Hopefully there's a bail agent looking at you and saying, "You have a tattoo? Show it to me," and then writes it down.

I look at the people that bail as different kinds of people. There are the guys and girls that basically have never been trouble, then they get in trouble, bail once, and it's a done deal. It's a learning experience, and it's over with. And then you've got these guys that are continually in trouble but are just kind of plugging along. It's not like they are really career criminals, but something is always happening to them. They get into trouble, go to jail, and then they just don't go to court. They think it's like a hair appointment and blow it off. They're not really running. They just don't pay attention to it, and it catches up to them. I tell them it's never a good day to go to jail.

And there's the ones that are the career criminals. That's all they do: just get into trouble, go to jail, spend time in jail, get out, get caught up in the same stuff, do it again. They know the system. They know what's going on. They know they are going to go to jail, do some time, get back out, probably mess up again, whatever. From our standpoint, they are not such a bad person to deal with. We're not law enforcement, so we're not arresting someone. They understand it's part of the deal. They didn't go to court, and now it's "catch me when you catch me," but now you're caught and you don't want to piss anybody off, because you're going to need to bail again.

Surprisingly, the more meaningless the case, the worse or more dangerous they can be. When I say that the people who have the lesser crimes are more dangerous, I mean, say you get a guy who's driving on a suspended license. That's a bailable crime; it's not just a ticket. Okay, you get bail. When these guys miss their court date, they don't know what to do, because they don't understand how the system works. They'll fight. They'll be crazy because they're scared. They have no concept of the fact that, dude, all you got to do is go get cited and get a new court date; I'm going to take you over there and they are going to give you basically a ticket, issue you a court date—which is an arrest and which clears this bond—and that's it. They believe they are going to go to prison for the rest of their lives.

One of the things that you have to be good at in this business is trying to read people from the first contact, whether it be on the phone or in person. You need to kind of find out where they're going. One time, we chased a child molester guy all the way to Guam. The mom was the cosigner. The bond was $30,000. In finding out about her financial standing, we found she actually had $2 million, just in her checking account. I mean this lady was pretty well off. She doesn't want to pay the thirty thou, yet she would spend three grand a month to put in an account to keep this guy living in Guam, just to not deal with his situation. The whole time, of course, she's lying to us, saying, "Oh, I don't know where he's at. He took off. I don't have to pay this," but at the same time, she's paying for his lifestyle to stay on the run. It surprises me the stakes one family member will go. I don't understand how they think that way.

Well, in that case, it was another family member that didn't want to see the mom having to keep paying him. For whatever reason, that family member didn't think it was right that the mom was going to continue to pay and the kid is just living over there off of her. He's wanted by the law, and there's a bail bond over his head. So the family member gave us the tip that took us to where he was at. We ended up going over there and getting him put in custody. They extradited him and now he's in prison.

I look at my job like a game of hide-and-seek. It can be pretty draining depending upon what it is. A lot of the problems with some of the people, like the drug cases, for example, they may be running high for four to five days with no sleep; just running, bouncing here and there and everywhere, and you're trying to stay up with them. We've had some exhausting trips. Usually we're never by ourselves. We're usually with a partner, so you can try to feed off each other as far as one sleeps and one is awake in order to try to keep up.

I've found people everywhere: attics, under the kitchen sink, behind the water heater. There was one place—a condolike setting—where there was a dresser with a hole cut out in the wall going into the next condo where they could run to get away. And one time, I went into this attic and found a note where apparently the guy had hid from the cops. The note said, "Stay up there. I will let you know when they are gone."

The risk of my job is a little bit lower than say for law enforcement. Law enforcement is the unknown to you. An officer comes up, he's going to arrest you if that's what the situation dictates, meaning you're going to catch a fresh case. There's a little bit more of wanting to get away. But we're only here for this existing case. I mean, obviously, if I come after you and you are in a meth lab, then probably there's going to be consequences, because law enforcement is gonna have to get involved. Unfortunately, the risk to me can sometimes be quite great, because I don't know what's going on. So we have to be as safe as possible when we take somebody into custody. What I mean by that is you don't give a person an out. Make sure about all the doors and windows so they can't get out the back door and run away. You come in with a partner and you make it known that this is why I'm here, and you're going into custody. If I have to tase you with a Taser, I will, and you're not going to like it. That's my job, and you're going to have to do your part and go along with it. Then we'll take them.

Yeah, I can give you an example. The case was just a burglary; no big deal. It was a Nevada case. We ended up meeting with the wife and having to take her car for the bond. Hoping she could get her car back, she reluctantly told us where he was staying and pointed to where the apartment was at. We get there, stayed late into the night, and he never showed up. We were just doing surveillance from our car, then went and got some sleep. In the meantime, her conscience got the best of her and she told him that we were there.

We came back early in the morning and as we pull up, we see him. He's got the pickup backed up to his door, just throwing everything out of the apartment into the back of the truck. He's trying to leave. So we fly up there and I say, "I have a warrant for your arrest," and we take him into custody. I can't identify myself as law enforcement; however, I usually call them by their name to make sure that it's them. Usually it's hard for a person, even if they are using a fake name, not to respond to the name they've had for twenty years or whatever. They'll turn, or try not to, but it's too late at that point. Then I'll explain to them why I'm there. If it's a felony case, I may be taking him at gunpoint, drawing him out, and cuffing him up. It just depends on the circumstances.

In this case, we had him kneel down, took him into custody, and put him in our van. Now we're faced with all his stuff, and we don't want to just leave it unsecured. While I was looking at it, it appears to be a lot of stolen merchandise; you know, six TVs and all these radios. We're going to have to call law enforcement. We don't really care so much—it's not that we don't care—but it's not our job to create a new case for him or cause more problems. We're not there to deal with this; however, we have to have law enforcement there to secure the scene, and it's something that's on them.

If he had complied with everything and we got him into custody, the officers might not have to go there. Now, though, we got this mess, because the officers are going to have to figure out to whom this stuff belongs. The officers arrive and are looking around and they say, "By the way, who is this guy?" We show them the guy in the back of the van, and the officer says, "We got to talk, go ahead and leave him there for a minute." The officer comes over and says they've been looking for this guy for a week because he shot somebody while this guy was breaking into a car. The homeowner had come out with a shotgun and confronted him, then the guy shot the homeowner. We had no idea. The dangerous part in this case is that this guy might think that's why we are there. I mean, you never know. That's why everything has to be done the safest way possible to take them into custody, no matter what. The homeowner lived, but they had been looking for this guy for the shooting and we had no idea. We were just looking for him on our burglary case.

We usually try to overpower the situation by numbers. There's been times we've wrestled around with people trying to get them into cuffs. They're trying to fight just to get away, for the most part. I think the Taser has changed the whole game. I mean, it's a completely different deal now. You just don't fight much anymore. Before, you may have to fight with pepper spray. Pepper spray might make a person mad or it may not work at all, and you're gonna get effects of it during the fight on you as well. It gets into your eyes, you can't see, it's uncomfortable, it hurts. But the Taser is a wonderful tool. It fully incapacitates someone if you have to use it. I mean, people nowadays, you pull a gun on somebody, they know you're not going to shoot them, and they'll laugh at you and run away. On the other hand, they don't want to get tased, so they're going to comply for the most part. I have a Taser, pepper spray, guns, handcuffs, baton; everything that normal law enforcement would have as far as tools.

It's always an adrenaline rush when it comes to an end. It's finally over, and you've got another one. We get them all, every single one. I've never missed. *Never.* I don't count anymore. I'm sure it's over five thousand catches. You can locate anybody in this day and age. Now, there have been close calls as far as bail time is concerned, or maybe you found them and you can't do anything about it.

I do quite a bit of work in Nevada, where [under the law] I can go to the cosigner and say,

"Hey, where is this guy?"

"I don't know. I haven't seen him."

"Is that your Lexus in the driveway?"

"Yeah."

"Give me the keys. It's mine, now!"

Then they start going, "Wait a minute, maybe I do know where he's at." I can hit them hard and quick in Nevada. Anything that they own actually becomes recoverable to the dollar amount of the bail. If they own the house, you can basically say, "I'll give you five minutes to grab what is most important, get out of my house." That really gets a lot more cooperation.

Once, we actually took a bar. Yeah, a bar. The cosigner owned a bar and he was kind of not being cooperative—it was his brother that had taken off, but he signed for him. So I walked in and told everybody to get out: "The bar is closed. We're seizing the bar and locking it up." You're protecting the assets of the bail bond company by taking *their* assets until either the bond has been paid or we find that guy. That case is still ongoing. The bar's been closed for three months. That's the breaks of the brother cosigning that bond. He may lose the bar to pay that bond if we can't find the guy.

I like my job because it's like a puzzle. Everybody you talk to tells you half-truths. You got to figure out in each sentence which part is fake and which part is true, and then you got to talk to this guy and you get this half, and then you got to get this other half and you got to kind of put it all together until you actually find the person. I think that's the most intriguing part about it: It's hunting down and being smarter than the person you're chasing. People go to great lengths at trying not to be found.

I've never been shot at, but I've had guns pulled on me where we kind of pulled guns at the same time. It's not an everyday occurrence, but it happens. There's a lot of firearms involved in going into people's houses. Hopefully, when I'm telling you that I will kill you, you'll believe me more than you want to die. I've had to do a lot of talking as fast as I can.

I was in one shooting incident [where I fired a shot]. That day, I wasn't really dressed as I normally would be. If I'm going to approach a house to take someone into custody, normally you're going to have your vest on, and gun belt on with all your tools. In some instances, these things unfold too fast and you can be caught unprepared a little bit. In this case, I had a fanny pack with my short-barreled firearm—a more compact version of the .40 Beretta that I usually carry. I come across this guy in the truck I was looking for. The truck just happened to be going down the road. Boom, there he is! This guy had been in prison before for manslaughter; a real career criminal. The bond was substantial because of his felony warrants. Anyway, I'm behind him in a car and he ends up going into a dead-end court. I was by myself so it was kind of a bad situation. I tried my best to block him in, which didn't work. He backed up his truck, and as I exited the vehicle, I presented my firearm and told him to turn the truck off. We ended up in kind of a standoff to where he was facing me in the truck and I've got him at gunpoint, and I'm now ordering him to turn off the truck and comply. I also make sure he knows there's a warrant on him. This guy was a really bad guy. He decided he would rather run me over and kill me than go to jail. I was instructing him that if he chose to try to kill me with his vehicle, I would kill him: "You need to shut the truck off."

I'll never forget: He just smiled and then floored it. As the truck was coming at me (I knew there was nothing I could do; the truck was going to hit me) and as the hood of the truck hit my hand, I leaned forward and pulled the trigger. In my mind, it looked like the bullet went through the windshield and hit him right in the forehead. As I flew over the hood and landed at the side of the truck, he slapped his hand to his head and slumped over. I started to approach the truck, and as I look, he starts to come to and realizes he's okay, and then starts to take off. My first thought is to jump in the back of the truck, but then I'm thinking he's probably going to die from the bullet so I don't want to be in the back of that vehicle going down the road when he decides to die. He takes off like crazy and I get back in my car. By now, it's kind of a bad situation because I can't really pursue him. Law enforcement units are coming, because it was a shooting.

Turned out it was like a '64 to '66 truck, the kind with the windshield that has a slant to it. The police found the truck and said the bullet would actually have hit the guy right in the forehead, but it hit and made a dent in the windshield and went straight up. There was some glass that hit the guy in the forehead, and him seeing it in his mind that he was shot, he had the same effects of like he was shot. Then he realized he wasn't shot, and boom, he takes off. The funny part is that it was the first actual shooting I had been in, so your stress can make you perceive things differently. In my mind, I saw a hole in his head. I had perceived the bullet had gone through the windshield and shot him. I guess I didn't follow up with a second shot because I thought that the first one had done it. I went to a .45 caliber after that for a little bit more power. Hopefully, that never happens again.

I think that I'm safe enough that I would like to say that I'm always going to win any situation. I mean, being on the run, that's not a life. They can't sleep. They can't rest. They're running, looking over their shoulder, jumping at every little noise. It's a horrible life. We're on the other end of it trying to keep up with them, but we don't have to look over our shoulder.

Photo Courtesy of: **SAN JOSE SHARKS**

JEREMY ROENICK

HOCKEY PLAYER

*D*rafted by the Chicago Blackhawks in the first round in 1988, Jeremy *Roenick is a nine-time All-Star. He is thirty-nine years old, stands six feet one inch tall, and weighs two hundred pounds. We talk in the locker room after a practice session of the San Jose Sharks.*

★ ★ ★

I didn't hang out on the corners or cause trouble growing up as a kid. I was always doing the sports thing: I played soccer, hockey, baseball, football. I got better and better and came to love sports. I was an average student. I got good grades because my parents demanded them, but I was never much of a bookworm. I just excelled at sports and I think if it wasn't for sports, I'd probably be that nerdy kid with acne all over my face that hung out. And, if it wasn't for sports, I probably wouldn't have the personality that I have today.

I actually got put into hockey by the mom of one of the little toddler kids that I used to play with in the apartment building that I lived in. Thanks to his mom for asking my mom if I can keep him company with skating lessons; it carved out a career for myself.

I excelled at hockey, and that seemed to be my niche, so I went with that. I was a better soccer player than hockey player, but there really wasn't much of a future in soccer unless you played in Europe, and that really wasn't in the cards for me. Hockey really wasn't a goal of mine until I was maybe ten or eleven years old, and I saw the Olympics in 1980. I thought I wanted to do it, but I didn't really have the opportunity until maybe I was sixteen or seventeen.

You know, I really thought that I would end up at this level, but I never thought that I would excel like I have. When you think pro sports or pro hockey, you think "the best of the world." I never looked at myself as one of the best in the world, for whatever reason. I think that's probably helped my growth.

I never try to let anybody beat me. I always wanted to prove myself to the best players in the world, and I think that's maybe how I became one of the best players in the world and was able to compete at a very high level and accomplish the things that I have accomplished. To play over 1,300 games, score over 1,200 points and over 500 goals, never in my wildest dreams had I ever thought that I would be able to push myself to that level. The love of the game and the fierceness that I have in terms of not failing is the kind of emphasis that I went by my whole career. I hate losing more than I love winning.

I really think hockey players are the most humble, most respectful, and appreciative bunch of guys that you will find in pro sports, bar none. There is no other place that you can emulate the feeling of the camaraderie of the game and the competitive nature of team sports like a professional hockey locker room. I really feel that it's stronger than baseball. I think it's stronger than basketball. I think it's stronger than football. The egos are in check here, and I think the respect factor is immense. You go to a basketball player and ask him who the best player in the game is, and you probably get nine out of ten saying that it's themselves.

It's your teammates—the people that you are with; the people that you're going to battle with every day—that are gonna give you the strength and the confidence to succeed in what you do. You are marching in with twenty other guys next to you that are gritting their teeth and that got your back. You are gonna go in with your chest high and your guns a-flaring. That's pretty much the basis we go by in the National Hockey League.

I think everybody in this locker room will say that I'm a battler, that I'm gonna give 100 percent effort, and that I'm gonna come in and have my heart into it. I'll do whatever it takes to win a hockey game, whether it's knock somebody in the head, put a puck in, or take a hit to make a play. I think my players know that I'm a warrior, that I'll go through whatever to succeed. That's all I want to be known as: a warrior that came to play every night. I want people to say we didn't know whether he was gonna hurt us on the scoreboard or hurt us in the corner or hurt us in open ice. When somebody else on the ice knows that there is a possibility of pain being inflicted, they're gonna be more aware. They might be a little bit more skittish and a little bit more reluctant to make a play.

I don't think you teach that. I think you either have it or you don't, and that's what separates the elite players from the good players. I didn't think I had it in me, but [Coach] Mike Keenan dug it out of the depths of my body and taught me that I do have it. He grabbed me by the throat and threatened my life, saying, "If you don't finish your hits and you don't play physical and you don't bang bodies, then you'll never play a game in the National Hockey League." That was in 1988. I weighed about 155 pounds. He scared me to death.

I didn't have it until I knocked the first guy out, and the whole crowd went crazy. I was just finishing a check and making sure that they knew I was out there—that then kind of became my persona. When you check somebody by hitting them so perfect in the chest with a shoulder—like somebody taking a pillow and hitting you in the shoulder—it just mushes right into your body and you don't feel a thing. It still doesn't matter how many times you do it, it's a never-ending feeling of pleasure to know that you've done something good, you've made the crowd excited, and your coach is looking at you and saying that's a good job.

Intimidation is just letting somebody know you're coming after them, letting somebody know that you're gonna knock their head off, knock their teeth out. It's more to rile up your own teammates. You do a lot to get your own teammates going. Like I said, what am I gonna do to help my team win tonight? Some of it could be physical, some of it could be mental, some of it could be on the score sheet. If you think you're gonna get the best of me, you're gonna have to go through a lot of pain. Some people aren't willing to go that route, and they're weeded out quickly. They're very easy to spot and aren't around very long.

What we do best is we play injured. It's the warrior mentality. You're not gonna be considered a warrior until you show warrior traits, and warrior traits are playing when people don't think you can. People think that you're not gonna succeed, but you push through it, and the pain doesn't stop you from trying to succeed. I'm never afraid. Never intimidated.

When I came into the league, guys looked ten years older. They had no teeth, long hair, beards, no abs, and they weren't in shape. Nowadays, kids look ten years younger than they really are, they're ripped to the gills, work out twelve months a year, are bigger, stronger, faster, more talented, and they can skate like the wind. It's night-and-day difference, and I've had to adapt to that shit. I didn't do the gym work and the bike work and all that stuff during summertimes until I was twenty-seven years old. I took the summers to unwind, let the aches and pains go away, and get my body ready for another year. Nowadays, you got to do it all year.

It's big business now. I made 95,000 my first year as a professional athlete. I got up to making nine million for a bunch a years, then eight million, then seven million. Rookies nowadays make a minimum of 500,000.

At this point in my career, I'm a lot smarter. I know the ins, I know the outs. I know the dos, I know the don'ts. I'm not as fast as a lot of the guys, but I make up for it in the way that I think the game, and I get in the right positions to make it easier for myself. Being smart is just as important as being strong and fast.

I've had over six hundred stitches in my face. I've broken my jaw twice, once in four places, the second time in nineteen places. Broke every finger at least twice. I broke every toe. I've broken my ankle, broken my wrist, broke my ribs, separated shoulders, dislocated fingers, ten or eleven concussions, nine broken noses, pulled groins, two coccyx breaks, hernia surgery on both sides. Man, it's pretty crazy.

What's a good day? A good day is when I wake up and I can get out of bed without having to stretch myself out and not feeling the aches and pains. Or, when I come to the rink and everybody is in a good mood and we go out and have a good practice like we did today. I can go home, pick up my kids, and have a nice dinner with my family. That's a perfect day.

A bad day? A bad day is when I wake up and my back hurts, my knees hurt. There's days when it takes thirty seconds to get out of bed. Some days it takes two and a half minutes. Then I come to practice after we've lost, and it's glum in the locker room, and guys are like feeling sorry for themselves and not being appreciative that we have one of the best jobs in the world. I kick those guys in the asses and say, "Wake the fuck up and let's go to work."

★**Author's note:** *Two months before the start of the 2009–10 National Hockey League season, Jeremy announced his retirement. He played in 1,363 regular-season games and scored 513 goals, which places him third on the all-time scoring list of American-born players. At his press conference, he said, "My body can't do it anymore even though my head and my passion are still in the game."*

TREDALE BOUDREAUX

ALLIGATOR TRAPPER

T *redale Boudreaux was born and raised in southern Louisiana. We sat at the kitchen counter in her house as she talked about trapping alligators.*

★ ★ ★

Trappin' or huntin', it's pretty much the same thing. It don't matter to me, we say it both ways. I mean, you can call it trappin', because we actually are trappin' 'em.

There's over a hundred trappers around here. I'd say ten women, maybe, but that's pushing it. It's what the guys do. I've always been a different kind of woman. Since I was probably like six years old,

I had my own horse and I was always with the guys—always the one girl. I didn't care, it never bothered me.

My dad has a business, so in my high school days that's when I took over. He didn't have time for it no more, so he gave it up. I accumulated all his land, and then I was a full-time alligator trapper.

This year, the season starts the day after Labor Day. You have to buy you a license to shoot alligators. If you get caught without a license, you'll get fined or they'll bring you to jail. It depends on how bad it is. Your license expires when alligator season ends.

The Rockefeller Wildlife Refuge, that's where we get the tags. It's twenty-five dollars. After you get your application, you have to go to the people whose land that you are gonna be huntin' on and get 'em to sign a paper saying that you can hunt on their land. Like say, if I asked my next-door neighbors if I can have their land to hunt on, then I would go to the tax assessor's office to get my neighbor's land information.

You put that all together with information about what kind of water is in it: like freshwater, brackish water, or saltwater. There are more alligators in freshwater. You get less tags for saltwater, because alligators don't stay in there very much. So, that's how the refuge determines how many tags you get.

My dad and his dad, they all used to trap; they hunted everything. I know his dad did it back in the days, but it was just mostly me and my dad. As a kid, I loved being outside and taking chances and learning new stuff. Always been that way. My dad was like that, too; he's not scared of anything. I'm more cautious now because I'm a single mom, so if something happened to me, my parents would have to help.

My biggest memory with my dad was he wrestled a gator one time. I thought it was dead, but he noticed the gator come off the line, so when he grabbed it, it shot up in the air and body slammed on the water. My dad ended up getting it. I don't know how he did it. I guess he had his knife and he stabbed the gator in the leg. That right there scared me. I was, I'd say, ten.

Sometimes when the gators would get off the line, my dad would actually take his wallet and all that out of his pants, and he would take his shoes off and get out of the boat. He'd hold on to the boat and then he would drag his feet on the bottom of the river—or whatever we were in—and he would kick where he knew the gator was at and then wait for it to pop up so he could tell if it was dead or not. He was crazy.

About a month before alligator season, we will go looking on our land to see if we spot any gators, and then we will come back and put lines where we see 'em at. They like deep water, so you'll find 'em more in deep ponds. That's your best bet of finding 'em. They sunbathe on the side of the levees right next to the water, that's what they do. If you look around, you'll see they're going back and forth to another deep pond, and they have a trail, so you can pretty much tell what they're doing. They're scared of you just like you are scared of 'em. Most of the time a gator won't mess with people unless you're messing with him, but if they have babies nearby, that's when they would probably mess with you.

Every once in a while we hunt in the Sabine Refuge. Every three years, you put your name in and they have a lottery-type drawing. I had been helping other people out there for years, so I kind of knew my way around, but the first year I ever put my name in my name got pulled. That first year, we had 145 tags—one alligator a tag.

We usually have a little drive ahead of us when we hunt on the refuge, so we wake up about four o'clock in the morning and be gone about five. You have your shells; you have all your boat requirements like your flares, whistle, life jacket. You have extra hooks—we use from a size seven to twelve. We got our lines—thirty-foot; that's how far we make our lines. Then we make leaders for 'em, so when we do catch an alligator, we don't have to cut on our main rope. We just cut the leaders off and put on a new one.

We set like a hundred lines out there. On the refuge, we catch gators with the cheaper pieces of chicken, like thighs and stuff like that. It'll take us over half a day to put out the lines. We get there

I guess about six or something like that, whenever sunlight would happen. There's me and another guy in my boat, and then my other helpers, too.

You get you a stob, or you find you a mesquite bush or something to tie off your line to. Then you get your cane pole—bamboo cane; we go cut 'em before the season and cut all the leaves and stuff off 'em, and we'll let 'em dry out so they'll get hard where they don't bend—I'd say about a six-foot cane. And then we put on a clothespin with a little string coming off of your cane. We hook our line to that where it drops down to about three inches above the water. If you know there are no small gators in there, you can put it low [otherwise] the small ones are gonna get to it first. Most of the time we put it higher, and the big ones will jump out of the water and grab it and swallow it. We'll also put some flagging on 'em so that we could see 'em.

After we do that once, then we bait everything that we have, and then you leave that alone for the rest of the day. After a couple of days, it gets to stinking. Each day, we'll go to our last line and then we'll work back toward our truck, which is a lot easier, because your load of gators gets heavy. We go to each line, and if the line is still up we'll just pass it by and go to the next one. Usually, the first day you get like thirty gators, forty at the most. And then the next day, you probably get twenty-something. It goes down. It usually takes us at least five days to catch a hundred of 'em because as your days go by, you get less and less.

The first day of alligator season on Sabine, which is always a good day, we had, I think, thirty-something alligators in my boat—it's a sixteen-foot, aluminum hull. Oh yes, that is a lot of gators. They would be piled up. You kill a big ten-foot, which weighs from eight hundred pounds to no telling how much, and you and your helper is trying to get this gator up into the boat and that boat is coming up where the water is almost coming in it. We were maxed out. We had less than an inch left that the water came over. Stuff like that is scary. Being I'm a girl, I'm not as strong as a guy is. It takes a lot out of you.

There's been a couple of times that we have shot alligators and we thought they were dead, but they're really just stunned and come back to life in the boat with us. I remember one time going with my dad when he was still huntin' with me. I was on the front of the boat and he was in the back, driving. He pulled out a gun and shot that gator not far from me and killed it.

Once we catch the gators and kill 'em and get our stuff done, I'll throw 'em behind my truck and bring 'em to the seller over on the next ridge. I make sure the gators don't fall out of the truck. I don't have no tailgate on the back of my truck, so I got to watch so they don't slide out. I keep my eye on my back window. We pretty much strap 'em down, they ain't going nowhere. We have to cover 'em, though because the sun will wilt the hides. We used to put plastic over them, but now we use mowed grass sacks. We'll dip 'em in water and then cover 'em; makes 'em stay cool.

When I'm huntin' on my land, I put the gators on the four-wheeler with me. I put my leg on top of a gator to hold it in place, and I'll drive standing up with my knee over it. Then take it back to my truck or wherever I'm at. I'll just grab 'em by its two front arms and throw it. Sometimes they're slimy and slippery, but you grab their arms and you can throw 'em pretty well. I'm a girl, but I'm pretty strong.

Last year, we got paid I think it was thirty-seven dollars a foot. We sell the gators whole. He buys 'em from us and then he sells 'em to somebody else. When we get to his ice truck, they have a platform out there. We go one by one: We pull an alligator out, we measure the length and read the tag number—we have to tag every alligator. Then we throw it in the truck on ice. We have to hurry it up and go sell 'em so that the hides and the meat will stay good. After we sell the gators, we have to pay 40 percent back to the refuge.

Gators are heavy. My biggest one I caught was an eleven-footer. I was by myself down on the levee. When I pulled it up and seen how big he was, I was like, oh my God, this is gonna be bad. It wasn't dead yet. I was standing on the side of the levee, and I pulled its head up out of the water where I seen he swallowed my line that's hooked to a wooden stob—when they jump out of the water and get the bait on your line they swallow so it's hooked in their gut or in their neck, and it hurts 'em when you pull on it. They can't do too much. So I pulled him up just out of the water and I seen how big his head is—from their nose to their eyes you can tell how long they are. I've been doing this so long you can tell how big an alligator is. So I started making some phone calls on my cell phone; told the guys they got to come help me. They ended up getting there and we killed it. We had to end up shooting that gator like ten times. It took like five of us to load that thing in the back of the truck.

Most of the time, a big gator like that I shoot with a .22 Long Magnum. And, most of the time the first time you shoot something like that, that gator is gonna cut up and he's gonna go crazy and he's gonna start flipping and throwing himself around. Sometimes it makes 'em so mad they'll come out and get you, so you got to kind of be careful. The bigger the gator is, the harder their head is, so you hit 'em in the soft spot in the middle, right above their eyes. The bullet can hit them, but sometimes it won't penetrate 'em in their skull. I've had times where you're shooting a gator and you're hitting it in the bone, and the bullet ricochets. And, there's been times I've had little chips of bone in my face and in my arms.

After I shoot my gators, I hit 'em in the head with a hammer to make sure they're dead, but first you got to poke on 'em with a stick or a cane or anything; you don't just go and touch it, that's one bad mistake. Then, I just grab on top of their mouth and put their head down so they can't bite you, and I just beat 'em with a hammer. How many times? Depends on how mad I'm at 'em. Sometimes it only takes me two times. You bust that little spot behind their eyes, because you pretty much know that they bleed pretty good. I like doing that to save bullets.

Oh, there's a lot of things that can go wrong, especially with the rope you use to catch 'em, and how when you shoot 'em, they twist. It's just their natural thing when you shoot 'em. I guess their nerves just automatically start 'em rolling. They roll to drown their prey, but the rope it can easily get caught up in your arm or your boot. You don't notice that when you're pulling the rope and then it gets caught around you. It can pull you under and drown you.

I heard one time some people went to shoot a gator and this gator got mad. They hit it, but it didn't kill it. The gator jumped straight out of the water onto the land with the whole length of the rope, and then it ran back in and it clipped people that were standing right there. It flipped 'em. Ever since then it kind of scared me. You got to be careful. You just got to look at what's all around you.

A hurricane come through this past year. A guy in a big rig said he had caught an eighty-five-mile-an-hour wind. The hurricane hit while we were alligatoring in Holly Beach. That's about fifty miles away. It got bad. We were huntin' alligators while we were out there in the boat, down in the marsh, and lightning was hitting all around us. I was scared to death.

We knew the hurricane was coming. We launched our boat and we went out in the rain anyway. We were determined. We caught some alligators, but it wasn't much because when lightning hits, they go back in their holes. We had ran our traps the day before when the sun was hot. It started raining later that night, so the alligators we caught that's probably when we caught 'em. Then we spent the night on a beach in a camper, and that thing was rocking. I thought it was gonna flip, and I worried about how high the seas were gonna get. It was horrible. Maybe you're gonna wake up the next morning and you're gonna be in the Gulf!

My dad called me all night long. He was like, "Tredale, you need to get out right now while you got a chance." He had me a nervous wreck, and I was like, "No, Dad, I'm gonna stay. It's gonna be all right." I've got my three helpers with me, plus there also was another guy in a camper trailer that was alligatoring. At three o'clock in the morning, they got up and went and checked how high the water was, and it wasn't bad. The storm chasers were out there, but the water hadn't gotten that high. I mean, it was high, but it wasn't dangerously high where it would harm us. I slept maybe an hour. I was glad that day was over. I probably had maybe fifteen gators that we brought back to sell. I wish everybody had a chance to experience that. That's living.

I like it. I guess it was just the way I was raised. Most of the guys around here are like, "I can't believe you do that." But it's fun to me. When you see what you got on that line, you start jumping around and get all excited. That's the best feeling in the world right there. Some people think it's nothing, but to me that's why I do it. I love it.

I couldn't see myself living in any other place. I love it down here. We've always got something to do. We hunt during duck huntin' season. We also go fishing in the Gulf and out here in the canals, the lakes, the rivers, wherever we can go. You don't get bored. We do it all.

I got some pictures of gators if you want to look at 'em. . . .

Photo Courtesy of: **KEN THOMAS**

JIM DICKERSON

Prison Guard

*J*im Dickerson works at Pelican Bay State Prison, which houses many of California's most dangerous inmates. The prison is located in a remote, forested area in the farthest north region of the state. When we met in an area a few feet away from the warden's office, he suggested I put on a jacket over the long-sleeved blue shirt I was wearing. The inmates' clothing is the same shade of blue. He wanted to minimize any possible misidentification between an inmate and me.

"This is a job that not too many people would do. We've had people come in here for employment and walk out the first day, saying there's no way they can do this job. I don't know if you really get used to the violence, but you see it all the time, so you do get immune to it a little bit. You got to realize most *of the guys in here are lifers. There are days it can be scary. I don't know if 'afraid' is the right word; I don't know really if 'scared' is the right word, but you just get apprehensive. You could be standing out in the yard and it just goes sideways. It happens."*

★ ★ ★

I'm a correctional officer here at Pelican Bay State Prison. I've been doing it for twenty years.

Basically, what we do is manage incarcerated felons, managing their day-to-day activities from when they get up in the morning till they go to bed at night. We're like an adult day care for men who have been removed from society because they're unable to conform to society. We have to provide for them all the basic human services that me and you have to pay for on the street, from feeding them, getting them clothes to wear, linens for their beds, taking them for dental, the optometrist, psychiatrist, any medical-type needs. And we have to provide for their security to make sure that they're safe all the time, plus make sure that they stay within the prison walls. A prison is basically a world within a world.

The other correctional officers are my brothers. I've seen my fellow staff punched and stabbed. I've seen one shot. You have to be able to depend on your partner. We rely on one another for our lives and are in life-and-death situations daily. Your life may depend on them at any split second whether that officer is a gunman or he is standing next to you or he is just a set of eyes. I'll do whatever it takes to protect my partners out there, and if that means jeopardizing my own safety, so be it. That's who I am, and that's what the job has pretty much made me. But as for dying, as far as getting stabbed or anything like that, I don't really worry about it. You can't keep coming through those gates every day worrying about "am I gonna live or die today?" I know that some people, unfortunately, are scared every day they come in here for work and are scared when they go home. I don't worry about myself. Maybe I've been doing it too long.

I work on the security squad, which is we're basically in charge of the security within the prison, more so than the regular line staff are. There are only about eight handpicked fellas on the squad. It's not a job that you can just apply for or get from seniority. It's something that you're asked to do.

We respond to all alarms anywhere in the prison. We're up in the general population area. There's nine cameras on each yard. We record everything that goes on in those yards. It's not a job that a rookie could really step into because they don't really have an understanding on what goes on inside here to be able to effectively do your job. You need to be educated in the ways of the prison and how things take place.

Because I'm on the security squad, when the inmates see me coming or my partners coming, they usually run the other way. They don't want anything to do with us because they know it's not gonna be good. That means somebody is in pretty deep trouble. We're coming to get you, and when we get done with you, you're gonna lose a lot of privileges.

Their behavior is gonna dictate what I do. Everything falls back on them. It's their behavior that they're responsible for, and then I'm calling them on it. It's not really *me* making those decisions; *they* made that decision to do whatever it is they're doing. I'm just there to enforce the law to the fullest. The State empowers me with the authority to do so; it's not that I get power hungry or anything like that, but I know that I have the law behind me. I don't negotiate with these fellas, and you can't plead with them; you just tell them once: "Look, this is how it is. You're responsible for your actions and you need to take responsibility for it, or these are the consequences."

Back at that time I started, we would refer to inmates more as "convicts." They were very well-institutionalized and were more manageable, but Pelican Bay has a different mission. They usually send us the inmates that are pretty incorrigible, guys who were pretty much out of control. We're dealing with the worst that the State has to offer, guys who the State had a difficult time housing at other facilities. It's not uncommon to see eighteen- and nineteen-year-olds here. They haven't done enough time yet to settle down. They're still rambunctious and pretty active in violence. If they don't get their way, if they don't agree with orders, whatever, they're gonna run their mouths at you.

The older convicts have a different value system than the young guys do. When you tell convicts "no," they accept no and they go on. I'm still *the man* to them. Some of the fellas who have been housed here for years, they know me, they've been around me, they know that I'm fair and honest with them. I'm not out to do anything dishonest, but I'm still the man. I'm the law enforcement to them. There's that separation, and there always will be. I'm gonna treat them respectfully, and I expect them to treat me respectfully.

I think the inmates see you for what you are just after talking to you for a minute or two. These guys are masters at manipulation. They can see pretty much right through anybody because they spent their whole life manipulating people. They know if they can get something over on you or beat you out of something or manipulate you into doing whatever it is they want done.

You can't take a lot of things here too personal. If it upsets me, I get mad, but I keep it on a professional level. I'm not gonna seek out that inmate and try to retaliate or anything like that. The walls have eyes and ears. You can't get away with anything here. Somebody is always watching, somebody always finds out—staff and inmates alike—so this is a job where you must always maintain professionalism. You really want to show as little emotion as possible. We don't discuss anything that goes on outside the prison walls with them. We make sure that their needs are met, but we don't discuss our family, we don't discuss our activities, we don't discuss anything about our personal life with them. We never cross that line.

I walk out on the yard and see things, not just visibly but audibly, too. You can hear if the yard is normal, if things are going well, or you can hear if there's a problem from just the noise level of the yard itself. Unless you've experienced it, you wouldn't know. It's tough to describe. It's like listening to a motor; you can tell if a motor is running good or if it's got a mechanical problem. You can hear it as soon as you step on the yard that there's a problem. You step out there, and if it's normal, it sounds somewhat like a football stadium or a baseball stadium—a lot of chitchat; just normal people noise. And if there's problem, it's like you can hear a pin drop. You know something is about to happen.

For the most part, they segregate themselves on the yards, by ethnic group. They do intermingle a little bit but not too much. But if there's something going on, they'll be segregated well away from each other. The southern Mexicans population is probably the largest out there on the yard, but we have the Crips, we have Bloods, we have nonaffiliates, we have Asians and American Indians, we have different white factions.

Years ago we would run up to a thousand inmates out there at a time; now we run maybe two to three hundred at the most, because of the violence. We try to keep everybody contained in smaller groups of people out there, so they're more manageable when something does go bad. Years ago we didn't have fences up on the yards; now the yards are chopped up.

There's times I've been standing out in the middle of the yard when violence has erupted to the point where we have had to use deadly force. I've been involved in quite a few; they're all different but they're all the same. The safety of myself and fellow officers comes first; the inmates come second. Sometimes we go charging in and break up the fights, and sometimes we utilize chemical agents, which is something we're using more now than when I first started because we didn't have chemical agents back then. It's made the job probably a little bit safer, because now we have a variety of other force options that we can utilize that's safer for everybody involved, instead of just going from physical force straight to deadly force. With physical force, we get in there and actually pull the fellas apart and utilize our batons to stop the violence. With deadly force, we use the Mini-14 rifle. I've been in numerous situations where I've taken the slack out of the trigger.

We had a little stabbing at work today. This was about nine thirty this morning. We could hear radio transmissions that the yard was down, and we responded to that. I worked the cameras on it and then assisted with the call. A couple of white boys were cleaning house—cleaning house is when they perceive somebody is no good; perhaps that person didn't follow their orders to do whatever it is they wanted him to do. That's part of the prison culture. All the groups do that, all your gangs, all your races.

I don't think they got to utilize the razor weapon on the guy. He was just a little dinged up. The guy lived in a housing unit that the whites felt was undesirable, because the fellas down there didn't participate in a riot against the black inmates, so they're gonna assault all those white inmates that live in those two housing units at the first opportunity they get. Today was an opportunity that presented itself, and they capitalized on it. They physically assaulted him with their fists.

But we did find a razor blade out there on the yard, which is one of their weapons of choice. There's not a whole lot of metal left inside a prison to make weapons out of, so they utilize razors. There's a razors program where we exchange razors at night with them when they shower. We hand them razors and they're supposed to hand us the razor back, but if you're not paying attention, they can beat us on those disposable razors. They'll take that blade out of there and put a piece of foil in it—it's about an eighth inch wide. Sometimes they'll put a handle on it and melt it into a piece of plastic. Then, they'll try to slash somebody with it—usually slash the face or their neck to send a message.

Respect is probably one of the most important commodities here in prison. That's their value system. It's not a commodity that I can go and take away from them. Your word is very important, and only you can tarnish that image. If you are disrespectful, if you lie to other inmates, be dishonest to them, not keep your word, well, it's a life-or-death thing. There's been thousands of killings over disrespect. The inmates know they're incarcerated, they don't need to be reminded of that. These guys don't forget. If they're in their cell and if something were to take place—perhaps you were less than respectful to them—they know someday they're gonna be out of that cell. They may physically assault you the next day, next week, next year. You could be feeding them and you'll get that food tray back in your face.

Communication is probably your strongest tool. Sure, we can go in there and beat on people when the time is necessary for us to have to do so, but communication is pretty much the key; with that, you can effectively manage the population, to a point. You know, a lot of these guys have been incarcerated for their entire life, since they were twelve, fifteen years old. If you can effectively communicate to them, a lot of your management problems are dealt with and you don't have them getting out of control.

Back in '93, '94, we fed them in chow halls, which were small dining rooms attached to the housing units. One particular day, we had multiple stabbings where the inmates were eating. They coordinated an effort where they jumped up and stabbed numerous people at the same time. Fortunately, no staff were injured. But there was an officer standing near, and when an inmate jumped up and stabbed another inmate and slit his throat, he then turned at the officer. By that time, I had already drawn on him and pulled the slack out of the trigger. The inmate tossed the weapon down and got down on the floor.

We don't utilize the dining rooms anymore because of violence issues. Now, they eat in their cells. When I work extra shifts I'll be involved in the feeding of the inmates. We're armed with batons and chemical agents, but basically all we're doing at that time is taking the food to them, opening the small food port, passing the food through. They're standing right at their cell doors. That doesn't prevent them from reaching out and grabbing hold of you or your equipment or reaching through and stabbing you.

I've been spit on, I've been kicked, I've been gassed with numerous substances more times than I care to think about. No, it's not water out of the sink. It's called "gassing." They make a mixture of stuff like feces, urine, blood, saliva—just about anything they can put in it— and then they'll throw that in your face, hoping it will get in your eyes, in your mouth, in your nose. They'll do that at any given time. The smell is just nauseating, because they'll let that stuff ferment for a couple of days. It's nasty. They cover your jumpsuit and your boots in it. You got to take all your stuff off before you go home, because you don't want to take that stuff in your house or on your family, perhaps give them a communicable disease, HIV, hepatitis, and who knows what other diseases are out there that they don't even have names for yet.

You learn to keep your mouth shut and you wear safety glasses when you're walking on the tier or standing next to an inmate. You look to see if his hand is clear. You're always watching the guys. You try to protect yourself as best as possible, but there's no getting around it. They might do it for just a personal reason. Perhaps they don't like you or maybe they just want to change their housing. They know if they assault you, they'll get a change of housing. And if they don't like somebody, they'll throw it on each other. It's low life-forms that do that.

With experience, the job becomes easier, but we have a lot of state and federal restrictions, and some of those things make it tougher. I don't think the general population of society really has a clue about what we actually go through. When they incarcerate somebody, they just lock them up and throw away the key and forget about them. People are incarcerated, not to punish but to isolate them from society; basically like taking the trash out of society and get rid of it so we don't have to deal with it.

We're not the knuckle-dragging guards that they used to show in movies. We're out here managing people, communicating with people, trying to make the best of a pretty lousy situation. We deal with a lot of violence, and we deal with it the best that we can with the tools that we're given. We're not just beating down inmates all day long like sometimes it portrayed. Sure, we have a lot of very evil individuals here and sometimes they're violent. Some of these guys are very intelligent, but they chose the life that they chose; they made those decisions. Sometimes we have third-, fourth-generation guys here who basically never had a chance at all in life. Their fathers are locked up, their father figures are locked up, their uncles, grandfathers. Basically, it's not so much a choice of "if I'm gonna go to prison," but "when." They fall into crime because crime is easy. Pretty much anybody can do that; it doesn't take a whole lot.

The inmates may dislike you and they may put violence upon you, but for the most part, most of it is not personally against you. Most of it is just against the man, against society, against law enforcement, against holding them back or keeping them down. They see us as a symbol of that. The police on the street lock them up and throw them here, and now we have to live with them for the next twenty, thirty, forty years. Basically, we're in here doing time just as well as they are. We're incarcerated just as well as they are in a sense, and part of that mentality weighs on you.

When I was younger I could get out there with the inmates and toss it up with them, but when you get older you don't want to get involved in physical stuff anymore, because you don't bounce out of bed the next morning like you used to. I stand back and analyze myself now, because I'm almost fifty. We get hurt and we stay hurt longer. This job has a way of ending a lot of people's careers. If you're on top of your game, you sense something is not right as soon as you walk on to a yard or into a housing dorm. Am I still able to do my job effectively, or is there someone else that perhaps I should step aside and make room for?

I always try to look my best, always do my best, always try to give 100 percent. I still find it stimulating. You always got to be thinking; you always try to stay one step ahead of the inmates. It's a difficult job at times, but it's a rewarding job. You find a way within yourself to come in here, do a good job, and go home safely.

I'm at peace within myself. You have a little bit of control over a few things, but it's pretty much up to the guy upstairs. I'm not really a religious person, but I believe that some things are within our control, some things are not. My life, my destiny, my death are probably not within my control. God will make that decision, when it's time.

ANTRON BROWN

TOP FUEL DRAG RACER

*A*ntron Brown *drives Top Fuel drag racers in the National Hot Rod Association and is the only driver in history to win races in both Top Fuel drag racing and in Pro Stock Motorcycle racing.*

"It's like we're doing things that are mentally and physically not right. We're trying to keep this car on the ground when even an airplane takes off into the air at over two hundred miles an hour. We have front and rear wings for down force, where our front wing puts close to over five to seven thousand pounds of force at three hundred miles an hour to keep the front end down. Our rear wing puts eight to ten thousand pounds of down force on the rear tires to keep the rear down. When the car is on the racetrack, the back tires are

literally fighting the vehicle, because what happens is that the front tires try to stay on the ground as the back is driving the front end up, so the car actually starts bowing up. Where I had a four-inch gap underneath the car at the start, by the time we're halfway down the racetrack, the race car bows up so much that you actually could take a basketball and roll it underneath."

★ ★ ★

I'm a NHRA Top Fuel dragster driver. I drive cars that have over eight thousand horsepower, and we accelerate over three hundred miles an hour in a little bit over four seconds. It's a very intense sport because of the rate of acceleration. We strap into this vehicle that's only about four inches off the ground and we accelerate in eight-tenths of a second to over one hundred miles an hour, so basically when you mash on the throttle, you're over a hundred miles an hour and we're pulling 3.8 to 4 Gs right off the start line. Then, when we get to about a hundred feet out, our clutch is applied and we accelerate to where our car takes off even harder, to almost 180 to 200 miles an hour, like in one and a half seconds. The crazy part is we're over 4.5 Gs right there.

We get to the 330-foot mark—the length of a football field—in two seconds, and then we pull over 5 Gs at that point, and we hold those 5 Gs all the way, which is incredible for a land-moving vehicle. Usually, you don't have any Gs by the time you get to top speed, but sometimes we're still pulling a G and a half, because the car is still trying to accelerate.

When we get to the finish line, we're still pulling a G and half, then we hit the parachute, which pulls 4 negative Gs until we stop, so it's a 5.5 G swing. The car just jerks. Your whole body is going from a G and half positive to a 4 G stop, you know what I mean? It feels like I'm trying to hold five of me from going forward. The seat belts are strapped tight in this harness restraint system trying to hold me in this race car so my head doesn't slingshot forward. Before we had all the restraints to tie ourselves into cars, we had people like Don Garlits and Joe Amato, who had to retire because they were actually separating their retinas from their eyes from the G-forces of slowing down that fast.

I'm a kid from Trenton, New Jersey. The deal is that my dad, my uncle, my grandpop got into drag racing at an early age, from street racing to drag racing. When I was born, my dad and uncle were at the Sportsman level of drag racing and ran our family excavating business. On the weekends, we were racing. I would be out there at the age of twelve helping take transmissions in and out of their race cars.

I always liked the big drag races and seeing the greats like Don Garlits, Joe Amato, Eddie Hill, and Gary Ormsby. I grew up seeing all these superstars at the Nationals and I'm like, I want to do that one day. I want to be like John Force. I want to be like Gary Ormsby. I was just a fan of the sport since a little kid, so I had that dream and desire.

I was always an adventure junkie. When I raced motocross, I used to jump those big hundred-foot triples and big tabletops, and I was always the first one to jump something. It's like a natural high where you can take a deep breath and you feel these tingles going through your body, like you're on the edge. That's just something that drove me.

Today is Friday, and we won't start qualifying till about three o'clock. I usually show up with the team at around noon to get my fuel set up. We work with a very dangerous fuel called nitromethane. It's volatile; it doesn't light off of a flame, it lights under combustion. Nitromethane is the "N" in TNT, the dynamite they use to blow up mountains and bridges. That's the reason our cars can make so much horsepower. Also, we have to be really safe where we lock up the fuel because with all the terrorist stuff.

We have a regular 500-cubic-inch engine and we use 90 percent nitromethane, which makes these motors have close to seven to eight thousand horsepower. In our eight-cylinder motor, each cylinder can produce close to a thousand horsepower. In fact, it produces as much horsepower out of one cylinder as a NASCAR does out of their whole engine. It gets pretty intense.

That's one thing that makes our sport so dangerous. If we have a misfire or something when we're on the racetrack, the engines can blow up and they blow up hard and heavy. We blew my motor up a couple times this year, but the lucky part about Top Fuel dragsters is that the engines are behind us. So it doesn't blow up in your face; it blows behind the race car.

It also happened to us one time in Bristol, Tennessee, when it actually blew up while I'm in the car. We're on the racetrack where I'm doing about three hundred miles an hour. Prior to that, the car is running hard. We dropped the whole hydraulics and it blew the motor, kicked the rods out of it, and when that happened the car rolls all over the place and kind of makes it intense to get this vehicle stopped. The parachute is deployed, but it's getting oil in it and there's oil on my brakes, so now I'm trying to slow the car down with oil on the brakes and in the parachute. Luckily it was deployed.

I'll take you through a whole run. First of all, it starts in the staging lanes, where I put on my suit. I have a layer of Nomex-like under-wear—it's like long johns, top and bottom—you put that on for flame protection. Then I put on fire-retardant socks over top of it. Then I put on my driving suit, which is a five-layer SFI 20 Nomex suit with layers of Carbonex to keep flames off of me. Our suits can protect us for three minutes in a fire before you even feel a flame, just in case they have to take that long to put a fire out. Then I put on my five-layer retardant boots, and I got gloves and knits I put on underneath the gloves. There's also a head sock that I put on before I put my helmet on, and my helmet has got a big ol' blouse-like thing that comes from the bottom of my helmet and tucks inside my suit. That keeps the fire from touching my neck and face.

Once I get myself dressed up and all dialed in, then I go sit in the race car. That's when all the real stuff starts. I climb over the roll cage and slide in. It's a real tight cockpit, almost like a jet fighter plane cockpit. I got seatbelts that harness my legs and it's got a double strap that goes around my legs to keep my thighs down, and then you have a strap that comes over your lap that locks your pelvic area tight. And then I have an arm-restraint deal that locks my arms so that my arms can only come up about a foot above my thighs so my arms can't come out of the cockpit and take a limb if there was an accident, if you know what I mean. And then I have a HANS device that slides above my neck; it kind of comes over the top of your shoulders and rests on your chest muscles. The HANS has got clips to the back of the helmet so your head only can turn about a quarter inch each way. It will only let your head go so far down and then it stops. And there's another strap that comes over my regular strap and clicks into my belt. Then I have a chin restraint system for when I take off.

It probably takes my guys a good five to seven minutes to strap me in. That doesn't sound like it's long, but it's a long time just sitting there to strap me all in. Then you got to wait in the staging lanes where I'm getting myself acclimated.

Right before we're about to go do our run, my guys will make sure to evacuate any fumes in the cylinders so you don't blow up the engine once it's started. Then they will add fuel, like regular 87 octane, to the injector to start it up. Once the car starts firing up, I'll switch to nitromethane. We have fuel pumps in our car that will pump 110 gallons in one minute through a quarter-inch hole. The pressure has over 500 psi that can shoot probably from here all the way up on the top of a mountain. I mean, we've got a lot of stuff going on.

Now, we're idling. Once I get the signal from my crew chief—he will place his hand inside the cockpit and wave me forward—I will start rolling the car forward through water that's in the burnout box. Once we roll through the water, I'll hit the throttle, ignite the tires, and start doing a burnout with the tires spinning for about sixty to seventy feet. I'm doing that to heat and seat the tires, which will actually take a coat of the rubber off and make them hot and sticky so they will stick to the racetrack. You feel all the vibration of the motor, and you can feel all the raw horsepower. The vibration of the chassis twists up the car. When I do a burnout, I'm not whacking it wide open. We have a throttle stop that only pulls the [carburetor] butterflies up maybe three-sixteenths of an inch. It just lights you up. I mean, that's the part of the run where it wakes you up. It gets you ready and gets you all pumped up and tense. You got to get ready for this because you're trying to drive an untamed beast down the racetrack. You don't know what it's gonna do, and you got to stay on top of it to control this thing.

Then you will stop on the racetrack, push the clutch in, put the car in reverse, and back it up to the start line. So now, I'm backing up, backing up, keeping everything in the groove of the track—that's the dark part where the cars run all the time, and it's the stickiest part of the racetrack. You want to be in the groove, so when I say "in the groove" I mean you're in the middle of the racetrack where all the cars run at. Okay? So I'm backing up in the groove, just keeping her straight, and I'm looking at my pit man in front of me, who will tell me if I need an inch over to the right or an inch over to the left. Then he tells me to stop. I stop, put the car in forward, let the clutch out, ease the car up the start line, and my pit man stops me right before the two staging beams on the racetrack. You got to check both beams of the "Christmas Tree" for them to activate, so you can take off the start line.

When we're all about ready, we do the final adjustment for the fuel flow and then I'll put my helmet shield down, take my last deep breath, and get myself ready for the motion—because you're about to pull 4 Gs right off the hit. I'm just relaxing myself and I'll say, "yellow go, yellow go." I'll put the fuel pumps all the way on, pump the brakes to make sure that I got a good brake pressure to hold the car back, take my foot off the clutch, put it on the dead man's pedal in the middle, and brace myself for the explosion that's about to happen off the start line.

I'll take my hand off the brake a little bit, hold it, then all of a sudden you see all three yellows on the tree come on at the same time, then my body will do what it does, and you let the brake go, you drop the throttle, then BAM! You feel the acceleration, you feel your stomach touch your backbone, because you're pulling 4 Gs. I weigh 150 pounds, so right there I got six hundred pounds of force trying to push me into my seat. It's like I'm holding a heavyweight sumo wrestler against me while trying to take off and drive the car.

You don't realize it, but you can't breathe, and you actually black out for a split half second because when you take off, your eyes blink real quick and then you're already eighty to a hundred feet out there at 150 miles an hour in less than a second. From there, you're trying to maintain and stay in the groove in the racetrack. You're seeing the car trying to dart a little bit to the right or dart to your left, and you're trying to finesse it because once you make one move to move it right, the car moves right real quick and you got to make a countermove to bring it left to hold it straight. You're never just moving it right and holding it straight. You got to move it right and bring it left to bring the car straight because the back end of the car always kicks out a little bit. Once you get out there, the car is sashaying back and forth.

By half track, you're doing 280 miles an hour in three seconds and you're trying to keep the car in that tiny groove, which feels like it gets narrower and narrower, because you're going so much faster. And then, the coolest part about the whole run is what it feels like. What happens is, when you're going that fast in a Top Fuel dragster, your peripheral vision narrows to where you can't even see the sides of you no more. It's like you're looking out of a telescope right at the groove. All you see is the groove. It looks real big in your eyes and everything else around you is black because your peripheral view is taken away as you accelerate. It makes you feel like you're in *Star Wars* where this vehicle takes you to warp drive because of the rate of acceleration that you feel. What happens is, the more and more we do this, the more and more we can slow this down in our mind. It feels like slow motion even though we're going that fast. The more runs you do, your mind slows it down where I could come back and talk to you for half an hour about what happened all the way down the track on a four-second run.

Once you pass the thousand-foot cones on the racetrack, you take one hand off the wheel to hit the chutes. When you take your hand off the wheel, you're traveling over three hundred miles an hour, and by the time you get your hand over to hit the chutes, you're through the finish line. We cover the last three hundred feet in eight-tenths of a second.

If you've missed your chute button at the finish line, by the time the chutes deploy you will be halfway in to the shutdown area. That's too late. It happened to me one time and I just barely got the car stopped. The car was hopping and skipping and then you got to let off the brake and let the car wobble and settle back down. I was trying to think of everything I could do to get the longest amount of runoff to make the racetrack longer. All I is see are holes where I want to go, but if you pick the wrong choice, it can be deadly. Some people panic and lock up. When people get afraid, their mind stops thinking and they lock up and they brake more and crash. It's like they don't let their mind think. I've been racing for so long that I got to the point where my mind just does it. It's like I feel the car hopping and then my mind says to let off the brake and let the car settle back down.

I'm aware about who I race against, but I don't worry about it. I used to look at the other person and get up a little bit more, because maybe this guy is a world champion, but honestly I put the same effort forth every round. We win or lose drag races by thousandths of a second—not hundreds, not tens—thousandths. I mean, I won the final round of a drag race this year by three-thousandths of a second. If I had just jerked on the steering wheel one little eensy bit wrong on that run, I would have lost that race. In our sport, we don't get a second lap. You get only one shot to shine. If you go out there and go through four rounds, you win and you go home a national champion at the end of the day.

Antron Brown

To me, there is no ego here. My deal is, I just want to win, to win as a team, not as a person. I'm only as good as my team is, and if we're not successful together, it doesn't make a difference how well I drive the car because if my team don't do their job, we're not gonna win that drag race. This is my passion, this is what I always wanted to do. I live, eat, and sleep it. It's like when I'm in that seat, it's me and that machine, like we've got to become one.

CAMERON BEGBIE

Soldier

"*There's a lot of stuff I haven't talked about in so long. I apologize if I bounce back and forth. If somebody asks what happened to me, I say I got injured over in Iraq clearing up houses. They tossed grenades at us.*" *Cameron Begbie served as a navy corpsman for six years before being wounded in Operation Phantom Fury, a major battle in Fallujah, Iraq. Approximately ninety-five U.S. Marines were killed in the fight, and more than one thousand were wounded. A reported 1,350 insurgents also were killed.*

Two days after the interview, Cameron started training to be a city police officer. He was one of eight applicants selected out of 550.

★ ★ ★

I miss the military. It wasn't the fighting, it wasn't the shooting guns, it wasn't fast-roping out of a helicopter—it was the people, it was the camaraderie. It was knowing that every day you went to work with people that are going to give their best because they know you're giving your best. I don't have to worry about the guy to my right or left smoking weed. I don't have to worry about them being hungover when they show up to work. It was that integrity level that I appreciate.

When I enlisted, I just wanted to get in the medical field. I wanted to become a corpsman. As a corpsman, you have two options: You're either a blueside corpsman and work on ships for the navy or, if you're lucky, a greenside corpsman and you work for the Marine Corps—the Marine Corps is part of the navy. I went into the Navy because I got the chance of going with the Marine Corps. It means the world to me. You see a Marine: They are proper, they stand up tall, they will do anything for you.

The Marines don't have their own medical department. We are their medical department. So I got to be linked to them. When they went on hikes, I went on hikes. When they slept in the woods, I slept in the woods. When they slid down ropes out of helicopters, I slid down ropes out of helicopters. When they go to combat, we go to combat with them—we shoot, we move, we kick doors. It's just that when somebody gets hurt, corpsmen take over at that point. We have to get you to the rear where a medical team can take a look at you. We're like police officers in a firefight or kicking in doors and all of a sudden, the paramedic runs in to get his wounded out. Your mind-set changes and you put on a different hat. If we're in a firefight and are in an open street, we're laying down fire at the same time as we go grab somebody hurt in the middle of the street and get them brought back to somewhere concealed to work on them.

In the beginning, I was with the third platoon and went wherever they went to take care of them. Say we're on a hike or we're on the shooting range and there are multiple casualties, who do you take care of first? Well, you take care of the worst injured person first, because that person might lose their life. But when you're in combat, you take care of the least injured person first, because that person has the best chance of surviving, not the person that has it worst.

As a corpsman, we're only supposed to carry a 9mm Beretta as our sidearm. The days of wearing a cross on your arm are done, and you're not going to read my name tag and see it says "U.S. Navy" on it or be able to see that I have a little medical caduceus on my collar. That's a target, so we don't wear them. The first people that are going to get shot are the radioman, the medic or the corpsman, and the platoon commander. Back in World War II and the Korean War, they used to wear the red cross on the sleeve, and according to the Geneva Convention, they're not supposed to shoot you and I'm not supposed to shoot them. But you see in the news, they are cutting heads off. I carried a sidearm, grenades, and my M16. If you're going to shoot me, we're fighting, too.

By the time the Iraq war was going, we wanted to get in the fight. When I joined the military, there was no war, but you train for it and you want to see if you can do it. Our average age was probably about twenty. I was twenty-three. None of us had any combat experience, and I wanted to be tested as a corpsmen. I'm not a warmonger nor am I one of those guys that needs to have the action. It's just something that's internal; you can't explain it. I don't think any one of us was like, hey, let's go kill people. It was just, let's go see what we can do. They need us.

In August 2004, half our battalion goes to Kuwait—that's what we're told—for two weeks of combat training. We heloed in. It was like a tent city. About a week and a half into it, we start seeing the rest of our guys from the battalion trickle in. We're like, this isn't right. My platoon commander pulled me aside and he said, "Doc, I got to talk to you." He was a young guy and brand-new to the Marine Corps. "I want to tell you, before I tell the rest of the guys, that we're crossing the border in to Iraq on Wednesday. I'm going to tell the guys tomorrow. I want you to know first."

If things are going down and are bad, corpsmen were the ones that had to stay calm and act like everything is going to be fine. Docs aren't supposed to sweat under pressure. They came to me if they had marital problems. They came to me if they met the wrong girl Friday night and now things aren't right Monday morning. They came to me if they were just having a rough day. I was "mom." Whatever they needed, I was there for them. I had to keep my head cool for them. But I was a little bit scared. This is the real deal. I had to sleep with all these guys at night knowing what I knew, and I couldn't say a word.

The next morning we had a platoon meeting, and the colonel gave us our orders: "We are going to war, gents. Prepare." There was kind of a relief, because this is what we've been training to do. We don't have to worry about *if* we're ever going to go. It's like, okay, we're there, we're part of the show.

We leave the next day for Iraq. Some of us were flying in. Some of us were driving. I flew in. Over the loudspeakers of the plane they're playing "Bombs Over Baghdad" by Outkast, the rap group. We're sitting on these little mesh seats in one of these huge planes, and when we are landing, they nosedive for a combat landing—turn, turn, turn, turn—and then land. You want to throw up.

We went to a little air base for a day or two, and then we heloed over to Camp Fallujah, a big base. As soon as the group that drove us to the camp pulled in to where we were going, mortars hit. Had a few guys get hurt, but they were fine. That was our first day. It was like, okay, this is game time.

Fallujah, at the time, was a stronghold for the insurgency. That's where people were getting their heads chopped off. That's where the insurgents burned and hung the four [Blackwater] contract workers from a bridge. It was the Wild West. We then started dropping leaflets from planes saying we're coming in at this time, on this date; if you want to stay and play, great; if not, leave.

I was nervous, but it's not like I had an option to be there. It's not like I could raise my hands and say, "Not happening." I was a mess. I was scared crapless. Like, what I am getting myself into? The Marines, they're human. I mean, they were scared, but they were ready. That's what they trained for.

It was nerve-racking leading up to the battle of Fallujah. The city is a quarter to about a half mile away as the crow flies. We're in an old Iraqi army training camp, windows blown out, sleeping on cots, we're in our little foxholes. We're sitting on roofs watching our planes come in and level the city, the best fireworks show ever, and it's like, wow, we're going in *there*. We're taking mortar attacks every day from the insurgents. As long as you hear the whistle of the mortar, then it wasn't coming directly at you. You knew you were fine. If I run, I could run into it, because you have no idea where it's going. After a while, you're like just, ah, another one.

So, like I said, we would sit up there and watch these planes drop bombs. Then we got the order that we're going in. It was known as Operation Phantom Fury. Our rules of engagement in Fallujah was that if it breathes, if it moves, you shoot it. Like I said, we had dropped leaflets and said we're coming in. But the way the insurgents had it set up is that the most dedicated of them were protecting the heart of the city and the weaker, lesser guys were near the outside of the city. When you think you're going to get Allah and your seventy-two virgins, you're all dedicated. They were using women and children, any means necessary to get to us. Did we shoot everybody? No. Could we have? Yeah. Would it have been justified? It was war.

This is November 7. Early morning. We left Camp Fallujah at about four thirty-five in the morning, if I recall correctly. It was kind of overcast, chilly. We got in the AAVs—big amphibious assault vehicles. It's like *Star Wars*: .50 caliber machine guns, grenade launchers. We all pile on the back, in a troop compartment. How many should it hold? Twelve. How many do we fit in? Twenty-five to thirty. We're crammed in this thing, and when they take us down the road to the outskirts of the city where we are going to stage for the assault, another platoon hits a roadside bomb and one of my Marines lost his right arm and right leg.

We're sitting outside Fallujah taking mortar attacks. We're in the sand. Basically, sitting and waiting. We're just target practice for their mortar rounds. We're far enough away for them to hit us with small-arms fire, but they could still reach us with their heavy weapons. Our F/A-18s come in and flip upside down, look at their targets, fly back around, come in, and then light up their targets. And, we're watching Apache helicopters come in lighting the things up, too.

Nervous? The pucker factor hasn't set in quite yet. It's kind of surreal, like I'm watching a movie. I remember when I was a kid, my grandfather would tell me stories about how he got drafted, and I was always scared out of my mind to go in the military. I remember sleeping at his house and being up all night scared to death. So it was always a fear for me. Now, I'm sitting there, living it. I can't even describe it, just that I was in awe watching these planes do what they did, and the fact that I was scared out of my mind about what we were going to encounter.

Everybody was just kind of in their own little state of mind. There was a lot of coordinating going on. I remember replaying scenarios in my head like, am I going to be able to do this? It's easy to take care of somebody when there's no fire going on around you, but when I'm getting rounds going around me, am I going to have the courage, the balls, if you will, to go out there under fire? I know they are gonna be there for me, but am I gonna be able to do enough for my Marines? That was a scary thought.

We sat there all day. Later that evening, we piled into the AAVs again, not knowing what's going on. We're uncomfortable, and now we want to get out and fight so we can get out of this thing. Then, on November 8, after midnight, we get the call. The ramp drops, we peel out and cross into the city by foot. We had an Abrams A1 tank with us. We cross over a berm, railroad tracks, and are lined up on a wall getting ready to enter the city. Our mission was we're going in, going to kick ass, clear every house, clear every road. We had Marines coming from all edges of the city, and we were going to take the city back.

We hang a right down this alley, but it was too narrow to where the tank couldn't move its turret. As soon as we all got into the alley, there was a firefight. We started getting lit up with rounds coming downrange.

You have heard of the flight-or-fight response where some stay and fight, and some flee? Well, my butt cheeks were so tight. It was terrible. My initial reaction was to run, to find cover, but there was no cover. Like, I'm out of here. I felt like I'm in this narrow little fatal funnel. I remember I took a couple of steps and thought: Wait. I got my 9mm. I got my grenades and my rifle. I got my medical gear. These were my Marines. It was my sense of duty. It's where I was supposed to be.

Then, I turned and engaged the insurgents by firing off rounds, shooting at muzzle fire. It was pitch black, but we had our night vision goggles.

Now, this is our first major firefight. All these guys are green. We have no idea what to expect. It lasted probably about twelve to fifteen minutes. It was kind of a flash because it was so new and we were just getting our bearings. I don't know if we hit anybody or killed anybody, but the firing just stopped and we're like, now what do we do? We ended up going to this abandoned house and kicking in a door.

I remember sitting on this little girl's bed. You could tell it was a little girl's room because of the bedding and pictures of soccer and families up on the wall. We're sitting on her bed trying to get a few minutes of sleep and the bed falls. I felt so bad about it.

Later, we left the house and started moving. It was constant fire and move, fire and move. We're shooting at moving curtains. We're shooting at muzzle flashes. We're shooting at the occasional dumb ass, excuse me, that runs out in the middle of the road. We're stepping over bodies as we go. There's a lot of abandoned dogs running around. They haven't eaten in weeks and they would go and start eating dead people. Bodies were hanging out of windows. People are stepping out of corners of buildings with rocket-propelled grenades firing at us. I've never seen that much carnage.

By now, we're on this major road with shops and stuff, in the middle of a firefight. We're out in the open, we have no cover. You hear the whistle of bullets going by your head, and we have the tank there. It's firing off its rounds. The concussion from those will put you on your butt if you're not careful. There wasn't really a time to sit there and think. The training started coming back, like muscle memory.

"Marine down!" I was like, where? Well, it's at the back of our platoon, and I'm sitting there going, crap, I got to go all the way back there? We're in this firefight, and it's probably two hundred feet back. So I run back, get to the Marine. He wasn't shot; he was dehydrated. See, we haven't eaten and we're probably about twelve to thirteen hours into the fight. The water supply is low. We got him underneath an awning of a shop, strip him down, and start pumping fluids in him, trying to at least get him to where he can kind of get back on his own feet.

We continued moving. We get to this group of houses and came across this guy and his son walking down the street; the son was an older teenager. We see him go into this house, so we go in after him. Now our rule, like I said, was we are authorized to shoot. Well, we go in, put them on the ground—don't shoot them. They are carrying bags of rotted vegetables. They said they just came back from the market. We are like, "Dude, the market has not been open in a while. We know you weren't out shopping." A translator quizzed them. They haven't eaten or drank anything. We have them in zip ties— these little plastic handcuffs—and we have them on their knees, in stress positions. I have to be in there during the interrogating because if something goes wrong with these people, I have to be there to take care of them. They are dehydrated. Were they probably shooting at me a few minutes ago? Yeah. But I can't discriminate against them. I mean, I have a duty to take care of them and that's the oath I took:

to take care of anybody that's injured or wounded. So I fed them real quick and got them some water.

You have to understand, the bodies that we had time to search, we're finding crisp one-hundred-dollar bills in their pockets. What was happening is that the main bad guys were sitting there saying, hey, here's a hundred-dollar bill, go fire a few rounds. They are poor. They've been oppressed for so long. They know nothing but torture and violence. So they are scared. We sent them back to the rear to be interrogated further.

We had a couple of INGs with us—Iraqi National Guard—but God help you if you are anywhere near them when they were shooting. If we were going into a mosque or something, we took them with us basically out of respect because it is their country. They're probably better now with a little more training, but they were shooting all over the place with their AK-47s.

We keep moving and come up to this little row of houses where we start taking fire from this mosque right across the street. For a country that is so about Allah and Mohammed, they're sitting there firing at us. We go in and clear the mosque. It was an open room with like an altar at the front and prayer mats in there. Now it has a bunch of shell casings from us firing in there.

There was a boneyard—we called it a boneyard—it was a huge junkyard next to this mosque. This is going to be our base of operations for the next day or so. Then I get the call, "Corpsman up"—the Marines have a saying if they are down: "Corpsman up"; it's their 911 call. So I run across the street. There was a guy underneath a tractor trailer that we shot; didn't kill him. We had to get to him out and I was like talking a little bit Iraqi that I knew. He had two bullet wounds to his leg, a bullet wound to his abdomen. I patch him up and start putting IV fluids in him, put him on a stretcher. Now, this guy just got done shooting at us, you know. His weapons are still underneath the tractor trailer, and we're sending him back to five-star medical care compared to what he knows. He was in shock, I think, because we're not the mean creatures he thought. We're not

Satan. I'm sitting there thinking, did we shoot you? Absolutely. But now I'm fixing you. To be honest, I took care of more Iraqis than I did my own guys.

A night or two later, we're sleeping outside on the dirt of a gorgeous house. The people have been gone about a month and a half. Everything is abandoned. We used that as our base of operations. From there, we send out squads of about fifteen guys. I would go with them every once in a while. I wanted to be them; those are my Marines. I mean, I've been with these guys for two years.

That night was one of the few nights that they actually fought us. They usually wouldn't fight us because they were afraid of our night superiority. But we're taking fire from this house. We're getting lit up and are firing back, sending rockets in. We leveled the second story.

The next morning, we go into it to do our body count. We blow the door, go inside, find a guy in there, probably in his mid-thirties. We put him on his face, go through our motions, searched the house. There is no trick room to this house—there is a first and second story. The top story is now gone and he's sitting there going, "Nothing happened here last night. What you are talking about?" There's rice in the house, weapons in the house, spent shell casings. "This is my uncle's house. Nothing happened here." We're like, "Dude, you have a sunroof, what do you mean nothing happened?"

Well, he was jaundiced, like orange color when your liver starts to fail. He had diabetes and was severely dehydrated, and he had kidney failure. Now, I have to take care of him. I would have been perfectly content pulling out my pistol and shooting him. But it's an ethics thing. My guys are going, "I don't know how you do it." I knew a lot of the insurgents didn't want to be there. A lot of them didn't understand why they were there, so I guess that's maybe how I justified it. We sent him back for medical care.

We go on about our day, kicking in doors and shooting and moving. When you're out on patrol it's pucker factor all the time. Fighting in a 3-D environment, such as a city, is tough. You don't know where they are. It's their neighborhood, they're dug in, they know where to go. We don't. We're going off an aerial map.

Every time we'd leave for combat patrol, we'd pass by this guy that we'd shot and killed who was buried, but he wasn't buried very well. His legs stuck out of this little dirt pile, and as the days go by, you'd see his face turn more blue and flies start coming. It was just a shithole.

November 13 comes along. That morning, we moved to a different base of operations. It was a one-story school, surrounded by two-story houses. It was a terrible location. Whose bright idea was this?

We go out clearing houses. Kicked the door of this one house and got into a firefight. There was four of them. They were coming out of closets, shooting. We shot back. We got in to a little hand-to-hand. We're hooking, jabbing, stabbing. We all were. It's kind of a barroom brawl without the alcohol. It wasn't a schoolyard fight where you sit there and you say okay, we're both going home. One of us isn't going home. I guarantee you I'm gonna go home at the end of the day. Then, one of the bad guys pulls a grenade, goes to grab one of our guys, who then throws him over this little like brick wall. The bad guy drops on the ground, grenade goes off; that guy is dead. My Marine lives. Just one of those things that you do what you have to do at the moment. We killed all of them. We secured that house. When you're done, you're done; then you move on to the next one.

Now, we're six days into it, and it's around four thirty, five o'clock in the afternoon. We kick this door, get inside. We squeezed them into the house. They are ready for us. This is their final stand. They had holes cut out in ceilings and holes cut out in walls. They started lighting us up pretty good. I had a couple of Marines shot inside the house, and we started calling "landslide," which means book it out of this house. We got our guys out, we scurry across the courtyard wall under fire. I'm carrying a Marine out. We get to the street side of this wall. We have Marines on the other side of the street covering our butts, and we're taking fire in the middle of this firefight.

There's fourteen insurgents in this house. They are the hard-core ones. They were trained with Chechen weapons and gear, with full-on body armor. They're shooting from the house, and we're shooting back at them. I have two Marines wounded right in front of me, and I'm working on them. One had a gunshot wound in his leg, the other guy took one to the shoulder. We're hunkered down. We're stuck. Neither wound was fatal, but you don't know that at the time. All of a sudden: *boom, boom, boom, boom, boom*! They started lobbing grenades over the wall at us, and I got hit. They lobbed five grenades, but I only remember one. It took out ten of us.

The back of my left leg was shredded up pretty good (I just took a piece of shrapnel out of there about a month ago). My left arm took shrapnel in and it came out the inner part of my forearm. My fanny was torn up. At that point, I was frozen. I remember thinking, I'm done, I'm gonna take a round to the head any minute. My ears are ringing from this grenade that went off a foot away from me. What saved me was, as I was sitting on the ground working on the Marines, the gate to the courtyard of the house is right in front of me. The grenade landed close and I think it bounced off the wall. I didn't find out till later, but my flak jacket was riddled with shrapnel. I remember this burning sensation from the hot metal.

I was prepared to die.

I hear, "Corpsman up, corpsman up," because I have nine other guys wounded. I couldn't move. I was sitting there going, what the hell just happened? We're all still stuck there. The fighting is still going on and I have no recollection of how much time passed, but all of a sudden the ground started rumbling a little bit and one of our big AAVs was pulling up the road and using its .50 caliber machine gun, just firing into this house.

I tried to get up but couldn't. So a buddy dragged me and carried me over to where all the other Marines were. There was blood everywhere. There were a few of us, like me, who took the worse hits. We get inside this AAV. I'm sitting there and bleeding. My ulnar artery was severed. I was trying to control that bleeding. Like I said, I train my Marines to take care of themselves, so there was this stud, he was able to open up my bag and he said, "Doc, this is what I have, what do I do?" I was trying to tell him what to do as he's passing me gear for myself. I was in no way, shape, or form able to take care of anybody else at the time. I had no function in my left arm. He is working on the other guys.

We get back to this triage place, and we are all lying on the dirt. I think there might have been Army medics there, working on us now. One of the guys came up and said, "Have you had morphine?" I said, "No, I gave it to everybody else." Then I got my morphine.

I got put into an ambulance with some of the other wounded, and we got sent back to Camp Fallujah, where the actual doctors and trauma surgeons were. Then, they flew me back to the states, to Bethesda, Maryland. I remember getting off the plane on a stretcher and getting loaded on to this bus. I remember driving down the road and having this feeling of abandonment, like I abandoned my buddies and had let them down in some way. I was relieved, though, that I'm driving down a road and I don't have to worry about cars shooting at me or blowing us up. You know, everybody at that hospital was great, and people from all over the country made blankets for us.

I've had seventeen surgeries, and I still can't feel the outer portion of my arm. I can't spread my fingers, I can't cross them. That's the way it is. But I would never take it back.

MELISSA STEELE

FIREFIGHTER

O*n a rare day off from work, Melissa Steele, the twenty-four-year-old firefighter, talks about the job she loves, and needs. "I remember I once jumped off the roof after seeing* Mary Poppins, *thinking that I could fly. Well, I hit a tree and then hit the ground, but at least I had my umbrella, which didn't work. It was like no hesitation. It was just fun. I wanted that adrenaline. I just crave the risk, and then overcoming it."*

★ ★ ★

I'm a firefighter. I've been in my current position with Cal Fire for three years. Before that, I was with the United States Forest Service for four years.

I never thought this job would become a reality, because I'm not that big. I'm five foot and weigh 125 pounds. When I was about five years old, I saw a big, red, pretty fire truck and knew that's what I wanted to do. It was one of those things where if I found a little fire truck figurine or action toy, I'd want it. It's funny when I talk to my parents about it because they remember me saying, "I want to be a fireman," and them always saying you can do whatever you want.

In high school, I saw a flyer that said, "Do you want to be a wildland firefighter?" and I thought, I'm gonna go to that seminar and just listen to what it was about. Then, I decided that this was something that I had to do.

My dad is a mechanic and my mom is a nurse. They've always impressed on me hard work. If you work hard, you can go far. I was good at school, but it wasn't that I wanted to be a professional student forever. I wanted to start fighting fire and to start working. I actually started with my first fire job the day after I graduated from high school. That was with the Forest Service. Basically, I graduated and then the next day I had to be at the station at eight in the morning.

Growing up, you would see these stereotypical, big, strong men jumping out of a fire truck. I don't ever remember seeing a female, but I remember always feeling like I could anything they could do. I don't know why, I've just always been that way: If they can do it, I can do it. So one day I just decided I'm gonna try it. I got to the station and was so nervous that I didn't think I would be able to pass the test, but I told myself you can do it, you can do it, and I passed.

My first season, I went on some crazy fires. About only two months into it, one of our sister fire engines rolled off a cliff in the Klamath National Forest and killed three coworkers. One was eighteen, one was twenty-seven, and then a captain getting ready to retire the next month, he was fifty-four. That was a big turning point for me. It definitely puts in perspective of how fast things can change and you can lose your life, but not once did I ever want to switch careers. I never thought that it wasn't right for me.

On a daily basis you have training. What you do is you wake up in the morning and you have breakfast as a group, as a family. I was living at the station five days a week. You train from probably eight thirty in the morning all the way up until lunch, provided you don't get any calls, because then you got to go. The training was physical as well as operational: how to run everything on the engine and how to pull the hose the correct way. When I started, I rode on the engine in the back as a newbie, and you get all the really unfortunate jobs like, oh, the toilet's backed up, go fix it. On the fires, they pretty much will try to break you in real quick because you're saving their life, too, if something was gonna happen, so they want you to know your stuff.

I probably have the most awkward way of fighting fire, because I'm half the size of these guys. They can pull the real heavy five-and-a-half-inch hose right off the fire engine. I have to climb up on the engine, wrap the hose around myself, and use my legs to push off, because I can't just pull it down. But it works, and I've gotten good at it.

My first fire was a wildland fire of about twelve acres, at one in the morning. I'm at the station sleeping, the call goes off, we get in the engine, and as you're in the engine you're putting everything on and you're fumbling to get dressed. You're putting on your Nomex pants and shirt, which is fire resistant but it's not fireproof; your gloves, your fire helmet, and then you have a shroud that goes around your face and right under your nose—it's connected to your fire helmet to protect your neck area.

It was black outside and I remember seeing this red glow and thinking, what do I do? I mean, I've trained for this for a while, but this is my first one. It's a fire, and you're thinking to remember all of your watch-outs. "Watch-outs" are situations to think about, like what's the wind doing, what kind of fire, what is the topography, or like watch out for what side of the mountain the fire is on because depending on what side, you will have less or more vegetation on that side (it's more shaded on the north side and more dense than on the south). So you're running through your watch-outs real quick as you're responding to a fire.

We got there and before we jump off the fire engine, the fire captain would say something like, "This is our plan of attack; you're gonna take the left flank, and you're gonna mobile attack it, which means just drive the fire engine as you're fighting fire." My assignment was I was the nozzle person. Of course they throw the new person on the nozzle every single time. You get out and you grab the hosing, and you just start fighting fire—up with the nozzle, down with the nozzle. I had two guys behind me telling me exactly how to do it: "There's flame behind you, there's flame behind you, turn around!" The hose is about 150 pounds psi and about a hundred gallons a minute, so it's going. I could hardly hold it. I have this thing called a "hose strap" that a lot of the firefighters *don't* use because they don't need to, but they're available. I kind of made my own where you wrap it around the fire nozzle and you wrap it around your body, and by using your body weight to keep it down, it keeps the hose steady so that you can manage it. So we're walking up and down a ravine that has probably a 50 percent slope. Hiking that thing was crazy.

Afterward, my feet were so bloody from blisters because you're breaking in new boots; you're never ready. I remember putting duct tape around my feet and calling my mom and saying at seven in the morning, "I just had my first fire. I don't know why the heck I chose this profession." She said, "You'll either love it or you'll hate it, but you'll finish the first season."

After about two years of struggling, I found my technique. I do things a little bit differently, but I've earned trust of the other fire-fighters and they know that it's doable. I love it, and now it's second nature; you don't even think about it.

After four years, I decided I wanted to switch from the Forest Service, because Cal Fire is all-risk, which means structural fires, vehicle fires, medical assistance—they respond to everything, no matter what it is. I wanted more. I'm an adrenaline junkie. The wildland fires and the vehicle fires are fine, but I wanted to go into structures, to climb high-rises, and, you know, to do stuff like that.

There are fifteen people altogether in my battalion: fourteen men and me. This has been so much closer of a brother-sisterhood, because they're more focused on being a traditional fire department, like it's the shining your boots every single morning even though you don't really know why you're doing it, but you're doing it because that's what our brothers did in the early 1900s. And, we have a fire station where everybody is in one room, with separate beds. Everybody respects everybody, and it's great. I do have my own bathroom, though. I had to lay that down.

In this job, you have two families. You have the family at home, and you have a family that you live and work with every day at the station. I see my coworkers more than I see my family, and that's rough. I love both families very much. The fire department is so traditional and so honorable. I love it.

I'm small, so one of my strengths is I'm the first one to go into confined spaces, like an attic. I'm not too fond of that, but I'll do it. If the attic was on fire and the house wasn't, you want to get to the attic space to put the fire out before it consumes the whole house. I've been put in a situation where no one else will fit up there, and, well, everybody looks at me. So you go up there as a spy, seeing where the fire is and what you can recommend to put it out. It's usually dark, dingy, and hot. It's incredibly uncomfortable being up there, and sometimes people have junk up there that you don't want to be around. It's quick, though; you're not up there very long.

When a call goes off at the station, there's a complete different package of thoughts than I had with the Forest Service. Like, we got a vehicle accident the other day. This is in the afternoon, two o'clock. The only thing that comes over the call from the dispatcher is the type of call it is and where it's at. That could be anything. We heard it was an accident five miles north of the station, so I'm thinking, oh my gosh, it is 106 degrees out here; I hope that person is not lying on the concrete, because they're gonna burn their skin. And I'm thinking it's going to be hot in our turnouts. And then when you get there and you see them lying on the ground, your training goes in. In that situation, the person came around the corner too fast, he hit a guardrail, the airbags deployed, which saved his life. He only had one small fracture in his rib, so everything worked out good.

You also have your mask that is called a "self-contained breathing apparatus." You put it on, and it's got a hose connected to it. That's what you're breathing through so you don't have to breathe toxic air. Wearing that was something I had to overcome if I want to fight a fire. I did not like anything over my face at all, but I trained on it day in and day out. My captain would wake me up at night and say, "Melissa, come on, we're going to train." We'd go out to the engine bay and he would put a mask on my face and turn off all the lights and make me search around with my air on. At some point, he would turn off the air valve, so basically all you're doing is sucking the mask up—it's that sensation of you can't breathe! The first couple of times you just want to grab the mask. You can't hear him even though he is yelling at you: "Turn on your valve, turn on your valve!" You don't hear it because you're just panicking. I had to overcome that. In a real fire situation, if you grabbed your mask you could be dead in seconds from breathing supercharged-heated air.

Fire clothing does not breathe and so it gets soaked with sweat. Say you have a fire at ten o'clock in the morning and afterward get back to the station, we hang out everything on the front of the engine or wherever. Then if at two o'clock you get another fire, you put it back on and go. When we put on those turnouts on a 106-degree day, if you're not hydrated, you're gonna get sick. Turnouts? When you think of your professional firefighter, you see them. Turnouts are the big yellow bulky clothing that you wear.

Those eighteen-pack bottles of water you can buy at Costco or anywhere, I'll drink probably nine bottles of those before ten o'clock to keep myself hydrated. We do have Gatorade on the engine, and we also have water. They're now starting to talk about banning energy drinks like Red Bull and things like that—which I'm completely addicted to—because they're having people become severely dehydrated.

I work better under pressure. If I have five or six things going on, I can prioritize them in my head, like when we pull out of the station, I'm looking right and we say "clear right" for the driver, so he doesn't have to look. I have one radio in this hand talking to dispatch, and I'm typing in the GPS for the location with the other hand. Then we pull up. If it's a fire, what side is the fire on, where am I gonna put the ladder, you're thinking all this. I get so focused, but once you're done you're kind of like oh, I didn't remember getting there. It's not like you black out; you're just so focused on it. I work better that way.

Normally, you work three days a week, straight seventy-two-hour shifts, and then you're off for four days. I've never had a four-day-off—ever—because I'm also a volunteer for the county fire department, so when I'm not fighting fire and getting paid, I'm still fighting fire. And, sometimes you get called into work because of something like a fire I was on that was forty-one days straight. It was called the Butte Lightning Complex fire. The first day it happened, a big huge thunderstorm came through and made over four hundred different fires in the county. I was on my day off when that came in.

So, I went to work the next day at eight in the morning. There were fires out there just free-burning because we didn't have enough resources. It took us three days before we could have every fire staffed with people. We had firefighters from Southern California, we had firefighters from Colorado, we had firefighters from New Mexico and Arizona, and about thirty days into the tour, we had firefighters from Australia and New Zealand. It was the coolest thing ever, to see everybody come together. It was the peak of the fire season, and we had about thirty-five hundred people, in just Butte County, fighting these fires.

About the first week into it, we're working so hard that it seemed like we had been there a hundred days, but you get into that rhythm where I know I have to wake up, fight fire, wake up, fight fire. We worked twenty-four-hour shifts on the fire line, and the next day we supposedly have twenty-four hours off, but it never happens because by the time you get off the fire line, get into camp, have breakfast, and restock the engine, you have to get all your hoses, all your gallons of water, and get all your tools sharpened—all that before you can be ready to be available again. So by the time you get to a hotel or back to the station, you go to sleep, then you have to be there again.

With this fire, we had a problem with brown bears for some reason. We actually had a bear cub chase a fire engine and then the mom came out chasing after the cub, so that freaked out the firefighters. I'm thinking there were so many fires that the bears were displaced from their homes and they had nowhere to go.

Not this fire, but I've encountered bears many times, especially on little lightning fires. When we spend the night on a fire, everybody will take turns sleeping, get an hour here and an hour there. Basically you keep a little bit of the fire going in one area so that you have light during the whole night. You just sit and you watch it; it's kind of like a campfire. But I won't sleep, because if I hear something, I think it's a bear. I'm just kind of paranoid about something coming up in the middle of the night. You've seen Hollywood movies where you're thinking the worst. I've even had bears come up when I'm using the bathroom in the woods. They come up on you, just wondering what's going on, peek their head around. You walk away slow until you can't see him anymore.

I've seen a lot of snakes, never ever had any close calls with them, but they're definitely out there. I'm not really scared of things like that, just the bears and the mountain lions kind of freak me out. Once, a mountain lion walked up to me. We had a little campfire going, it was almost dawn, and here comes a lion, just walking, wondering what was going on. I go to my captain like, "Wake up, wake up." He wakes up and throws a rock at the lion, and it goes away.

In the early stages of the fire I was talking about, I remember driving up a road. There was a driveway, a house on the left-hand side of the road, a house on the right-hand side. We didn't see the fire on the left-hand side, we saw it on the right and that's where we were focused on. We jump out and we start putting the hose around the fire as fast as we can, and then my captain is screaming, "We have fire on the other side!" You *never* want to have fire on both sides of an engine, because it cuts off your escape route. I'm thinking we need to go, we need to get out of here. So you go back to the engine, cut off the five hundred feet of hose that you just deployed, and get to a better vantage point because we were in a narrow canyon. We left the hose because we needed to get out of there and because the fire wasn't close to the house yet, it was mostly burning their yard. Our job was to get in there to save those homes, but we didn't see that fire on the left-hand side, and so we need to get to either the top of the road to put the fire out or to the bottom of the road to fight it a little bit better. I was afraid a little. The four of us jumped in the engine and went back up the top to fight the fire that was coming down this way. That's what we had to do. We then deployed five hundred feet or so of hose that we had left. We saved that house and a barn.

In the Butte Lightning Complex, seventy-four homes did not survive the fire. We were in the area, we had engines specifically there ready, but the wind came through hot and fast. We were working so hard to save those homes, but you just physically can't when you don't enough firefighters and you have the wind at forty-five-plus miles an hour. I mean you just can't.

There was a time when I almost had to deploy my fire shelter, which is the only thing that you have on your back that can keep you safe. The fire shelter basically is one of those Shake'n Bake bags that you bake chicken in. It's aluminum foil in a compact little square on your back, and it is a last-chance effort to survive in a wildland fire. You shake it out really fast, wrap yourself with it, lay on the ground, and then you stretch out your arms and your legs to hold it down, and you stay there. You carry that with you everywhere. They say that you can survive up to an hour with the fire going over you at like 1,500 to 2,000 degrees, and they say it's extremely uncomfortable.

Nope, I never had to pull it, but the one time I almost had to pull it was my very first job as a squad boss. There were eight on that squad. I was leading them down a canyon, into a fire. We knew that there were people below us fighting fire and they were on the way back up, so our job was to meet in the middle. While we were working down, the people below decided they were going to set a backfire, but they didn't communicate that to us. So, here comes the fire sounding like a freight train. You don't hear it at first. The first thing is you feel the heat, like all of a sudden your lips feel chapped and you feel like, wow, it's really hot, and then you can hear it and then you see the red glow. Because it was so steep, I just remember saying, "Everybody. We got to go. What I want you to do is drop your gear, grab your fire shelter and water, and start running up the hill, back to the engine." I'm thinking we'll be okay, we're good. I just made the decision. Being squad boss, you have to be the last one out. I didn't want to be the last one out, but I'll be damned if I leave my firefighters there. We made it to the engine. About ten minutes later the fire came through there.

You say to yourself so many times, "Why do I do this job?" For me, one reason is when you see the look on somebody's face when you're the first on the scene and see in their eyes, oh thank God, the fire department is here. It's just so awesome when you see their face and there's the sense of calmness, it's like, I'm gonna be okay. And then, also, when you're driving around town and you see "Thank You Firefighters" signs. I'll almost cry when I go by one every time. It gives you goose bumps because you know that you're making a difference in someone's life.

I know some firefighters say it's just a job, and do it for a while and see what happens. I've never felt that. To me, it's a lifestyle. It's not like I'm going to work. It's like I'm just going home to hang out with my family. I'm so lucky that I can say I love getting up and going to work. It's like another exciting day to get to help somebody. You got to really have compassion to be in this job. You have to love it or you couldn't do it.

It makes me happy that I achieved the thing that I wanted the most. When I was little, that's all I wanted to do, and I became that.

Photo Courtesy of: **KIERAN RUNDLE**

BRAD JONES

SKYDIVING INSTRUCTOR

*A*s *the seasons change, Brad Jones travels from Australia to Fiji to the United States to teach tandem skydiving: "I follow the sun, I don't do cold." At twenty-nine, he has more than 3,200 tandem jumps.*

★ ★ ★

I'm a professional tandem skydiving instructor. For people who come in for their first jumps in doing a tandem skydive, I basically guide them through the skydiving process. It's like an introductory to skydiving so they can experience it without having to worry about all the stuff that you need to know to make sure it's done safely.

I did a bungee jump on my seventeenth birthday in Bali after a family holiday and I had a ball. I was just buzzing all evening after that and then said I'll go skydiving on my eighteenth birthday, but I had a car accident and I didn't quite get around to it. Later on, I did the tandem skydiving course and got addicted to it.

I started in '97 to basically make extra cash on the weekends. I was working for an ice cream company, but it was the middle of winter, so it was very quiet and I was hardly getting any hours. I thought if I'm not going to make any money, I might as well have fun, so I quit that and took up skydiving full-time.

In training to become an instructor, you need to know the rules and regulations and then learn the skills that you need to look after someone when they're learning to skydive. You need to be pretty good to be able to deal with anything that happens relatively quickly. You have to concentrate on the student and what they're doing and get to the stage where you're not having to think about how you're flying.

Most instructors I know do have a little bit of ego; there's not too many timid instructors. There might be quiet ones, but you need confidence because if you're not confident, you cannot respond to a dangerous situation. I think I'm a pretty good instructor, but in saying that, I know that there's always ways to improve.

I was quite shy when I started skydiving and still think I am to a degree. I've learned how to interact with complete strangers. It takes me awhile before I feel comfortable with someone and to start revealing anything about myself, but skydiving has helped. I think it has brought me out a little bit. I tend to joke a lot with my customers, and I think that relaxes them a little bit, but if there's someone who is really scared, then I can be serious.

I've got just over 3,200 tandem jumps. I've taken fourteen-year-olds, and I've taken eighty-one-year-olds. We usually say if the people who are a little bit older and they want to go skydiving, go talk to your doctor. If your doctor is happy for you to jump, then we're happy to take you.

I think guys usually try and act a little bit more macho, where women are more willing to say, yes, I'm scared, this is terrifying me, and be open about it, where guys try and hide and act all tough and brave when you can see that they're not really. You know they're scared.

Some people are pushed into skydiving by someone else. It's normal to be scared; it's just that some people are more scared than others. A lot of people have a fear of heights, fear of flying, all sorts of stuff. I've had people who—when we're all clicked up ready to go and we're quite close to do a tandem—you can feel them breathing heavily. I've had people where you can feel their whole body is shaking because of the fear. They're the ones that I love taking, because they get so much more out of it.

There's two types of people that say "no." There's the ones that say "no" who really mean "yes," and there's the ones that say "no," who really mean "no." The ones that say "no" that really mean "yes," you can keep them moving into position and moving to the door of the plane. You're talking to them, and they'll let you keep moving them. I will not take anyone who doesn't really want to jump. The ones that say "no" that really mean "no," you can't move, it's as though all of a sudden they weigh a ton. I've had one-hundred-and-thirty-pound girls who have said "no," and I can't move them; that's when you know they mean it.

When they say "no," I go come on, let's do it, it's all right. I explain that I've been jumping for many years, to try and reassure them everything is going to be okay. If they still say "no," then you throw in that financial thing like, if you don't jump you don't get your money back. That's an incentive. It may be not a positive incentive, but you are also making sure they understand the consequences of "no." I've only had three people not jump with me, including an Italian guy who didn't speak much English, but I could see he looked pretty disappointed more in himself than anything. His girlfriend had jumped a couple of days before and I think she pushed him into it, but he didn't really want to do it.

We have three jump altitudes for tandems: nine thousand feet, thirteen thousand, and eighteen thousand feet. Qualified sport jumping skydivers usually go to thirteen thousand, that's the standard height. The people that go to nine thousand feet usually are the ones that just can't afford to go any higher; it's a cost issue. The higher you go, the more freefall you get, so obviously the higher you go the more expensive it costs to get the plane to that altitude. I think it's like a $149 for nine thousand feet, $190 for thirteen thousand, and it's $349 for an eighteen-thousand-foot jump, which also includes a video by a cameraman who's jumping with you.

Students wear a tandem skydiving harness, which is basically like a canopy harness but without the canopy. Their harness has four attachment points: two on the shoulders and two on the hips. The instructor wears the tandem canopy system, which clips to each of the attachment points so that when you skydive, the passenger is in front and the instructor is behind.

There are two canopies: the main canopy, which is the one we use on every jump, and also our reserve canopy. If the main canopy doesn't work properly or it's not safe to land, we disconnect from the main canopy and then use the reserve canopy. The reserve canopy is inspected and repacked every 120 days to make sure it's going to work, and it has to be done by a qualified packer. With skydiving, we try and make it as safe as we can. We don't want to mess around with things that we don't need to mess around with.

The plane will take fifteen skydivers, plus the pilot. Usually there will be maybe two tandems on board, and then other experienced jumpers. When we get in the plane, we're pretty much ready, the harnesses are all adjusted and ready to go, and we wear a seat belt. There's also little benches to sit on.

The seat belts are on until one thousand feet, and then we undo the seat belts and I'll attach the bottom two clips of my canopy system to the passenger's attachment points, in case of an emergency. At about seven thousand feet, I'll do the top two clips and do any tiny final adjustments to the harness. Then, I'll do a gear check just to make sure all my rip cord handles are where they're supposed to be and to make sure everything on the harness is still fine.

Before we jump, I'll touch on a couple of things, basically going over the exit, saying when it's time to go, we're going to be sitting on the edge: As we go, you get into a nice arch position, push the hips forward, tuck the legs up behind you; when you feel a tap, bring those arms out. Then, when we're closer to the jump, I'll talk through another gear check so that the student knows that I'm doing my checks and that I'm happy that everything is okay. The goggles they are wearing go down, and we start to move toward the door. I get them into the position. Their head is right in front of me. I'm saying to them, as we're sitting on the edge, "Grab your harness, head back, smile, ready, set, go." And off we go.

Once we've left the plane and I'm in a belly-to-earth stable position, I deploy what we call a "drogue canopy" when we're stable. With two people together, we fall at about 180 miles an hour. When we deploy the drogue, it slows us down to about 120 miles an hour, so that we're slowing down rather than to an all-of-a-sudden slowing down very quickly where there is greater chance of risk. Usually by twelve thousand feet, the drogue canopy is out, and then we freefall to between five to six thousand feet, when usually I pull the rip cord on the main parachute, depending on where I am in relation to the drop zone. If I'm farther away, I'll open a little bit high to ensure that I'm going to get back to the landing area. From the time you exit the plane till the time you deploy your canopy, you are falling free through the sky for about a minute—that's the adrenaline rush.

It helps a lot if the students arch, by pushing their hips forward and tucking the legs up so they're curved like a banana. We offer the option that the student can pull the drogue release or the rip cord if they want to, but if they don't want to do it, then the instructor is going to do it. Then, the only other thing the students really have to do is for the landing: lift their legs up out of the way. The beauty of the tandem skydive is there's stuff that they can do, but it's pretty minimal. As long as they lift the legs up, then it's all about them just experiencing what the skydive is like and having fun.

Basically, when we land, the canopy is flying straight across the ground and then we flare the canopy, just like a pilot flares the plane when he lands. If someone is going to get hurt on the tandem skydive, that's where it is going to be: on the landing. With two people connected together, if the front person tries to stop with their feet and the back person is still moving, the instructor is going to come over the top of them. There's a good chance one or both of us are going to get hurt. I've had one lady break her ankle on landing because she didn't lift her legs up. So, if they can't lift their legs up, then it's greatly increasing the chance that they're going to get hurt.

Wind, clouds, and rain are our big three concerns. If the wind gets too strong, like above twenty-five miles per hour, the canopies could end up going backward, which is going to increase the danger. Actually it's the consistency of the wind; I would rather jump in twenty-five-miles-per-hour consistent wind than something that's gusting from ten to twenty miles. At our landing area here, if it's a strong northerly wind, it comes over some trees so it can get a bit turbulent. But if it's still within our limit, we will move farther down into our student landing area, because the air is cleaner there.

With clouds, we like to be able to see the ground when we're going to jump. Planes do have a GPS to help us, but you still stick your head out and look to make sure everything is okay where you want to exit the plane. If you can't see the ground, then how do you know you are in the right spot? So, if it's all cloudy, then we're not jumping.

And then the rain. If it's raining, then it's cloudy, and rain is not pleasant to be jumping through. It's actually quite painful. When you hit raindrops, especially going through a rain cloud, it stings. I've jumped and got caught in rain, and my neck is all red from where the rain has been pelting me. There's no point jumping in rain because then the students are not going to see anything.

We try not to jump in rain but sometimes you just get caught out in it.

There's countless things that can go wrong. The main canopy might not open safely or well enough for us to safely land, so you got to use your reserve. Or, if you're tumbling on the exit, then instead of getting the drogue canopy out nice and quick, it takes a while, which increases the chance of when you deploy the drogue it's wrapping around something. People can get motion sick and pass out. I haven't had anyone full pass out on me yet, touch wood, but I've had people go pretty close to getting quite faint. And I've been vomited on. And I've been bled on. With the pressure change, people get nosebleeds. They've got colds. All their snot comes out of their nose. I've been peed on when a lady peed her pants.

It's not all glamour in skydiving. I always say you are not a tandem instructor until you've been vomited on. You could have millions of tandem skydives and until you've been vomited on, I don't count them. It's not a fun part, but it's just part of the job.

I've had five tandem malfunctions where the main canopy hasn't been safe to land and I've had to use the reserve. On my first tandem malfunction, the canopy opened and the canopy was turning when it shouldn't have been turning. I couldn't get it to fly straight, so I said to my passenger to grab your harness, head back, feet back. I didn't really exactly tell them what's going on, only to just get them in to the body position that I wanted them. I disconnected from the main and pulled the rip cord for the reserve. I'm looking up, checking to make sure everything is right. My heart is going a million miles an hour. I'm sorting everything out and my student was like, "We just had a problem with our first canopy didn't we?" And I was like, "Yes." He was like, "We had to get rid of it didn't we?" And I was like, "Yes," and he is like, "This is our second canopy isn't it?" "Yes." And he goes, "We don't have another one do we?" "No." It was pretty cool that he was aware of it.

On another jump I was taking a Japanese fellow whose English wasn't so good. I know a couple of Japanese words, just for skydiving.

Basically there was something wrong with the main canopy and I couldn't fix it so I used one word that means "be like the prawn," and somehow they think that's like that banana position. So I started yelling in his ear, and I deployed the reserve. Once we landed, I was trying to explain to him what had happened, that we had had to use the reserve canopy, and I'm like, "First canopy no good," and it was obvious he wasn't understanding. Afterward, we got in the bus to go back, and we picked up the main canopy from where we saw it land, and as we're picking it up he just looked at me with an understanding that registered all over his face. He was like, "First canopy?" I was like, "Yes." He was like, "Ohhh." The look of recognition and understanding that came over his face was amazing.

The landing zone here is a pretty big field with pea gravel, probably about twenty to thirty meters long and thirty to forty meters wide. You can see it well enough from the air. Sometimes the wind is stronger than the way you thought or not as strong as you thought, so you might land short or you will go over it. There's plenty of room to fix errors. Sometimes you're not going to make it back to the landing area and you recognize that fact, so you pick another suitable place to land. The other day we did a jump and we had a cameraman with us. We were a long way away and I had opened a little bit higher, to allow for him. We landed in one of the farm paddocks around here. I probably could have made it back to the landing area, but I chose to land with the cameraman because the student is paying for the video. If you're not going to make the landing area, you want to recognize it early so you don't get into a situation where you're going to end up in water or in a tree.

One day last year—it was a hot day and the ground was rock hard—I got caught by a little bit of sink where the wind sort of disappears and you start dropping, and I impacted hard and tore my ACL on my left knee. I was out for four months, but the student was fine. Luckily he had his legs up, so I took most of the brunt. I had sickness insurance, it wasn't much, but it was enough to get me through.

You can only do so many jumps in a day. At the end of day, you're pretty tired. It's physically draining and mentally draining. You're always performing—not actually performing—but you always are up and trying to be happy and cheerful with your students because they've paid money for an experience. I'm no athlete and I've got a bit of extra weight that I can probably get rid of, but for skydiving fitness you use muscles that you probably don't use in normal life: your shoulders, back, triceps, that sort of stuff. There's not too many tandem instructors with tiny shoulders.

I definitely don't do this job for the money. I do it for the lifestyle. If I wanted, I could make a lot more money doing something else for no way near as much work as I do here. But, I get to travel the world. I get to skydive out all the time. Very rarely do I get unsatisfied customers. You get people who jump up and give you a hug afterward. I've made some really good friends from people I've taken tandem skydiving. It's not just a skydive. We're giving an experience, and you're part of such that huge experience. I love doing what I do.

Though it's good lifestyle, it's also not very good to set yourself up for the future. We get paid by the jump, so if you get a week of bad weather, then you don't make any money for that week. And my lifestyle of moving around isn't conducive to settling down and having a family at some stage. Plus it's taxing on your body, so I don't want to get like into my late forties, or whatever, and end up having my body being too old to start something else. It will probably be easier to get out of skydiving in the next year or two, but at the moment I'm having too much fun, so I'm not really sure what I want to do.

JEFF GAMMONS

Storm Chaser

A *native of southern Florida, Jeff Gammons is thirty-four years old. His videos of severe storms and hurricanes often are shown on The Weather Channel and other national television networks. "In a hurricane, you smell things. You smell vegetation being shredded, like someone's been wood-chipping trees. You smell wet fresh wood, like if you went into Home Depot in the lumber section, because of all the roofs snapping and 2x4s breaking. You smell fuel from cars that have been flipped. Raw sewage. It's like the combination of all these smells in a hurricane, plus the smell of the moist tropics. The stronger the wind, the more smells. There is just so much mixing going in the air, because the winds are so violent in every direction. It's really unique."*

★ ★ ★

I chase storms. I chase weather—mostly severe thunderstorms and hurricanes. The pay isn't always steady, because weather is not always steady, but I'm happy.

I'm thirty-four years old. I had to have open-heart surgery at twenty-six. I had a leaky valve, and it was replaced with a mechanical valve. After that, I looked at life a little bit different, and I was sick of working in the corporate world. After my surgery, I never went back to the corporate world. I went straight into weather full-time, and it brought me the most joy. I was sick of being stressed out and working sixty-hour weeks.

There's many types of storm chasers. There's some who do it for universities. There's the ones that do it for making a living, which is what we do—maybe a half dozen that sell the video. There's the standard amateurs that like to just chase for the fun of it. There's the fly-by-night chasers that see it on a documentary and they want to try it and will do it for a season and they realize, wow, this is expensive spending all this time, hotels, and gas on the road.

I've had a huge passion for weather ever since I was a kid. I grew up in South Florida with hurricanes, severe weather, waterspouts, so I've always had a lot of unique weather around me. I had very amateur stuff when I was a kid. Today, I have a lot of expensive toys that I use.

It started off as a hobby in about 1997. I was working in the Internet industry, Web design. I financed my expeditions through my employment, but over the years I learned I could sell video to the Discovery Channel, weather channels, markets like that. Severe weather is a big industry. People like to see destructive weather on television. I think people are fascinated by the power of Mother Nature. People will sit there for an hour and watch a destructive hurricane wipe out a town, and then they'll gossip about it.

In 1988, something clicked with me when Hurricane Gilbert was in the Caribbean. It was a Category 5 hurricane, and it was recording the lowest pressure ever. It had just hit Jamaica and was headed for the Yucatán. The Miami news stations were all covering the massive size of the storm. I just had to experience one.

Florida had a big dry spell with no hurricanes for almost twenty-five years; just little pitiful storms, but nothing major until Hurricane Andrew hit in 1992, which was a Category 5. I think some fifty people were killed in that massive storm. That was a sobering experience, and it fueled my wanting to get into the eye of a storm like that. I lived about forty miles north of the worst damage path, so I wasn't directly affected like a lot of people were in Miami-Dade County, but we still had one-hundred-mile-an-hour winds where we were and it was still pretty impressive. I was seeing steel structures on television down in Miami completely leveled, and I wanted to see winds that would do that.

I remember that I wanted to see more. There was something about how nobody has control over the weather and how wind can be so destructive. I'm fascinated by it, so I wanted to breathe it, smell it, and see it. I've gotten to see that now. I've had some scary moments chasing storms, but it all started with Hurricane Gilbert, and then experiencing the fringes of Hurricane Andrew.

After Hurricane Andrew, I wanted to see how wind can rip a roof off or take down a wall. If you want to compare wind with Andrew, it would have been Hurricane Charley, Friday the thirteenth in Punta Gorda, Florida—August 2004. That was a Category 4 hurricane with 145-mile-an-hour winds, a compact eye wall, and only five miles wide. The tinier the eye wall of a hurricane, the more the hurricane contracts, the pressure drops, and the winds increase about six hours later. It's kind of like the ballerina effect: When the ballerina brings in her arms and tightens up, she spins faster.

Charley was an intense storm, a buzz saw. It came ashore in Punta Gorda, a small fishing community. We got over to Sarasota thinking that the storm was going to come in there as a Category 2. By twelve o'clock the National Hurricane Center released a special advisory saying that they just found 145-mile-an-hour winds. This changed the strategy because at first we thought we were going to be dealing with a Cat 2, which we can drive around in and film. At Cat 4, you're trying to survive while you're filming. You're talking about debris flying everywhere. Once we found this out—we have radar in the car and laptops and stuff—we noticed the storm started making a hard right turn, which was going to bring it in about sixty miles south of where we were, so we blasted south on I-75. We were nervous because about six to twelve hours before the storm, we like to scout where we're going to chase. We want to know what's going to go flying and what could possibly kill you. Is the cabana going to come up and smack us? How bad is the surge going to be in the area? How close are we to the water? We didn't scout anything out and now we had to blast south. This thing is going to be coming ashore in three hours. So we get down there.

There's six of us. We get there, and the storm is intensifying. It's a violent storm with confirmed winds possibly gusting to 160 miles per hour offshore. We have no structure scouted out. We're pretty much out on the street. So we kind of all split up in the little downtown area. Chris Collura, Jason Foster, another chaser with us, and myself find the Charlotte County Courthouse. It's got these little court-yards with bricks and stuff. We pulled our vehicles in there thinking, okay, this will shelter us from the debris. They didn't have parking garages in Punta Gorda. This is not a big metropolitan area. So we're worried.

We made sure we're far enough back from the water that we wouldn't have to deal with a surge, but the debris was a whole different story. We were out filming like we normally do, but then it became survival because there was debris and violent projectiles everywhere. Then the worst came in: We went from 40 to 50 miles an hour to 150 miles an hour. There was a trailer park that was about three blocks from us; the whole thing was torn, destroyed, and thrown in our direction. We had sheet metal smacking into the building where we were. We lost windows in the vehicles. We were on the floorboards while holding cameras up to make sure we got the shot but at the same time not lose an eye or something. The air would get up underneath the front of the vehicle and it would bounce like people were messing with it, but it was just the wind interacting with the building. It was really sobering, because I had never experienced winds like this. This was what Hurricane Andrew was like. I'm thinking, is this what happened in 1992 in Miami? This is what they must have heard.

That was a very sobering storm. Forty-six people were killed around Punta Gorda, most of them in the mobile home parks. A lot of these people thought the storm was going to go forty miles north, but it made a turn at the last minute, so a lot of people weren't prepared. They should have never been in the mobile homes to begin with. They should have been gone. We all said, "I don't know if I want to go through a storm that strong again," because there were points in the storm where we were really scared. I was scared. There are parts in our video where we're saying, "What are we doing? This is violent weather. This is insane."

We were on the right-front quadrant of [Hurricane] Katrina, which was the strongest and where the most surge came ashore. We were one block from the Gulf, between Gulf Port and Biloxi. We were in the Mississippi Coliseum, which is about a three- or four-story structure for things like concerts. It is completely symmetrical. There's ramps on the outside of it where people can walk up, and large enough for a car, which we learned later we needed. We got invited to stay in the building by the management when they found out we were filming and they knew we had radar, computers, wireless Internet connection, and they liked that we knew exactly what's going on with the storm.

The worst started about nine in the morning, and I would say peaked by about lunchtime. Katrina came in with her full force. We were about twenty-six feet above sea level. Thirty minutes after the eye came ashore, the water was thirty feet deep and the ocean was a half a mile past us up the I-10. Our situation went from filming and documenting to survival, because the surge was a lot higher than we thought. Luckily we were in a structure that was able to handle it. All the surrounding homes and businesses around were completely wiped out.

Chris, and Jim Edds, have been chasing hurricanes and tornados with me for over a decade. When we got there, we scouted out the building and we knew we're going to see some surge. We're really close to the ocean and this is an intensive storm, but we weren't expecting the surge that we saw. With Katrina, it wasn't the wind that we were after. That part of the Gulf Coast is famous for having deadly storm surges, so we were really looking for storm surge shots, and we got them. It was more than we were expecting. The water came in so fast that when you look at our video, it looks just like tsunami video from over in Indonesia. It was just a wall of water that came in with the eye. I was not sure if the building that we were in was going to fail. We're in trouble because the casino boats, two-story motels, and houses around us were completely being swept away. You could feel the coliseum we were in vibrating with all the water and the debris and the cars and the boats slamming into the walls below.

Inside with us were about fifty-three residents that lived in the houses around the coliseum. These people didn't have all their family members with them. Some had stayed in their houses and refused to come over. When the water came rushing in, a lot of the residents were up on the second level with us where we were filming. They wanted to know what was going on. They saw this wall of water take out all these homes, knowing that they have family members down there. You could hear people screaming.

The situation went from us just trying to film Mother Nature at her worst to now there is all this emotion that's around us, too. We didn't know that all these families were taking shelter in this building until after things started getting rough. They came out from little hallways or somewhere else in the building. It was really sobering. The water started rising so fast that my partner had to run downstairs and move his car up one of these ramps on the outside of the structure. He got it up to almost the third level and there were like these concrete posts that won't let you go past it, so he couldn't go any farther. The water came up to the back bumper of his car.

The water is full of automobiles, poker chips from all the casinos, debris from homes, and this is where I got worried for two reasons: One, how high is the water going to get and is our structure going to survive? And two, all my dialysis supplies are still in the car and I've been separated from it. I'm looking at a sea of water and debris keeping me from my supplies. I didn't think beforehand about getting them out of the car and bringing them into the structure with me. I just didn't think about it. I was still new to doing my treatments.

This was the first time we were put in a situation where we had all these people around us where their lives are being destroyed and the possibility of losing family members right in front of their eyes. Usually when we chase hurricanes and tornados, everyone is gone. They are evacuated. We usually never see anybody except for law enforcement and some other media, but we were stuck. We're in a structure where people were taking refuge, trying to survive the storm. They knew they couldn't survive it in their little houses.

Once the storm brought in the surge and the winds peaked out, it took about six to eight hours for the water to retreat back out to the sea. Between, I would say, the peak of it where we did most of our filming to when we were able to get back outside by about six o'clock, we got to know these people. We were stuck in a building with them trying to survive just like they were and giving them information. They would come up crying, "How long is it going to last? Is it going to get any worse?" We would say, "No, this is the worst. The eye is inland now. The water is going to start retreating."

After the surge, I did a quick dialysis treatment in the car. I was supposed to have a treatment every four hours. I did a treatment probably at six in the morning, and the next one wasn't until about eight o'clock that night. I went the whole day without a treatment. I retained some fluid, felt a little heavy and puffy, and toxins built up in my body. I think the adrenaline kind of overpowered a lot of what I felt, because I didn't feel a lot until we stopped and had time to settle. Then I started to really feel it. But I could have been in a really bad situation because if the water didn't retreat as fast as it did, or the vehicle was lost, I would be without a solution. It was a little risky.

We also are ham radio operators, so we started communicating with emergency management in Biloxi, letting them know there's people in this building and that they're going to need help after the water retreats. It was sobering, because when it was time to come out of the structure, it was time for them to see how their families were. By then, law enforcement was moving in. We filmed some of it, but we gave them respect. We all three agreed that we were not going to go film them at their houses and follow them around. There was just too much damage and there was so much emotion.

We stopped filming probably by two o'clock that afternoon. The winds were still screaming, but we realized that this had turned into a deadly event and we were starting to hear on the ham radio about people finding bodies in the water, so it changed the whole atmosphere. We were there strictly to film Mother Nature at her worst. We're not the news media and we're not there to get a story of somebody who has just lost a mother. We've thought about it, because we know that it will sell video, but that wasn't our point: We want to show how bad it is on the weather side of it, not how people were affected emotionally. That's not what we do. We're storm chasers.

Well, we get back to South Florida and rested for a day. The next day we started splicing the video. We are being bombarded by the media. Now, this is a huge international story with Katrina. A lot of the media we've worked with know our Web sites, follow our blogs, and they know when to start calling to ask for video. So I wake up the next morning, my voice mail is overfilled and my e-mail inbox is out of control. By now the levees in New Orleans have collapsed and people have drowned, so it's a lot bigger than we thought it was in Mississippi. I've got every major media market wanting to do interviews with us and wanting video footage of the storm surge in Mississippi because they know we were there. They want footage of debris, buildings being washed away, buildings deep in the water, 125-mile-an-hour winds, the surge rushing in tsunami-type of waves, cars in the water, and cars smashing into the wall below us.

When I look at the video, I look at it as how did we survive. And when you look at aerial shots of the building we were in, everything was wiped out by the twenty-five- to thirty-foot wall of water that came in, except for that coliseum building. Everybody that was in that building survived, but most of the people around us did not. There was an apartment complex across the street from us that had twenty-seven people in it. They all drowned. Some of those were related to the people that were in the building with us.

Yes, there's been a few chasers that have been killed, but storm chasers don't die from the weather itself. The biggest hazard for my profession is hydroplaning. The three storm chasers that have been killed have all been killed hydroplaning in car accidents.

And because you're out in the open—usually in a field with a tripod—you are the tallest object. I've had a lot of close calls with lightning. I've had lightning hit trees right next to me. I've had lightning hit in the field in front of me. A lot of people say, "Aren't you afraid the tornado is going to hit you?" People who die in tornados don't know the tornado is coming and get caught off guard and get leveled. When you're chasing a storm and there is a tornado forming, you can see it. You can outrun a tornado even if they tell you not to. Tornados in the northern hemisphere usually move from southwest to northeast. So, if you move south you will be fine, if you can get out of the storm's path. Storm chasers always have an escape route to the south when we're chasing tornados.

When you're trying to keep up with a storm, especially in the Plains where they move thirty to fifty miles an hour or so, you're definitely chasing it. Hurricanes, I wouldn't say you are chasing. You are intercepting it. You're waiting for it to come to you. You can't go out to the ocean to get it; you have to wait for it to come ashore, and then you place yourself right there. Also, with hurricanes, your biggest threat is storm surge if you can't get up high, and also flying debris. But most of the time, you are in a structure, so you're protected.

When a storm starts organizing three thousand miles away off the coast of Africa, I get chills down my spine. I think, in fourteen days, is this storm going to be on one of the coasts here in the United States as a Category 4 or 5 storm? We're getting jazzed. We're predicting. We're pretty good at it. I do better forecasting storms that come out of the Caribbean than the ones in the Atlantic. It's the way the steering currents are in the Atlantic; they're tricky. Another thing is, in the mid-Atlantic, there's not a lot of weather data, so it's hard to know exactly what the upper atmosphere is over the central Atlantic to steer these storms. In the Caribbean, there's reports all over. So, yeah, forecasting can be really tricky, but it's part of the fun of chasing, because it leads up to the chase. You'll get up at three o'clock in the morning going, wow, the National Weather Service just released new models for the six-hour period.

Most storm chasers are not meteorologists, but we have an education almost as if we had a degree, because it's important to know what you are chasing and to get in the right place at the right time. I couldn't sit at a desk and wear a suit and talk about the weather. I would rather be out in the field with stickers and spiders and baseball hail smashing out the window and filming it. I have interviewed TV meteorologists and a lot of them are just book educated. They've never seen a tornado. They've never experienced a hurricane. I have a strong feeling that if you are going to sit there and educate people about weather, you got to experience what you are talking about.

In the early spring, I chase severe weather here in Florida. Mid- to late spring, we travel to Texas to be in Tornado Alley. Tornado Alley runs from Texas northward to the Canadian border, and it includes eastern Colorado, eastern New Mexico, Texas, Oklahoma, Kansas, Nebraska, South Dakota, North Dakota, and Missouri. We start wherever Mother Nature is going to start the show. We spend almost a month out there, fifteen to twenty thousand miles on the road, lots of hotels, lots of small towns, lots of wheat. We're hunting water vapor, what we call the "battle of the seasons": the cold air from the Rockies spilling out over the Great Plains and the warm water and air coming in from the Gulf.

We return back to Florida for the summer, which is the lightning season here. June starts hurricane season, and it peaks in September. Most of the hurricanes that we end up chasing happen from late July through early October. In the fall, we try to pitch all of our video for the year. That's when a lot of the documentary companies like The Weather Channel and the Discovery Channel start production for their spring and summer productions.

Some people like my work. They love my time-lapse photography and video. My family, at first, thought I was nuts; that I was wasting my time. But now they support it. They've seen that I love it. It completes me. Chasing weather helps with my dealing with my health problems. It lets me release energy. It lets me focus on something to keep motivated. A lot of people on dialysis get depressed and just are surviving. I look at it differently. I look at going through dialysis three times a week allows me to stay alive to chase storms. The more I can chase, the better.

★Author's note: *Months after the interview, Jeff received a kidney transplant. He continues to chase wind, rain, and lightning.*

JEFF SHINER

COAL MINER

"*When you walk out at the end of your shift—how the heck can I explain it to be polite—you spit a honker that looks like an oyster, because of the dust you breathe.*"

Jeff Shiner is a proud member of the United Mine Workers of America. He lives with several other coal miners in a house in western Pennsylvania. He and a friend, Barry, are outside around a fire pit, drinking beer and preparing pork chops for dinner. They invite me to join them. Jeff says, "I'm fifty years old. I have thirty-two years with the union. The money is not bad; the money can be better. But we have a pension, and we have medical when we retire, which *means a lot. We can get by. It's keeping my ass alive. When I turn fifty-five, I'm out of here."*

★ ★ ★

I'm a union coal miner. This is the way I make a living. I'm proud to be a UMWA member and I'm proud to be an official in it, too. It's pride, ask any coal miner; they are ~~fucking~~ proud to do what they do. All coal miners are brothers, regardless of whether you're union or not.

I grew up in a coal patch town called Sagamore, Pennsylvania. My grandfather was a coal miner, my father was a coal miner, and I'm a coal miner. I'm the last one in the line. I started right out of high school. When I was eighteen years old, I needed a job, so my grandfather took me to the mine. He made me wear a suit and tie because you got to be respectable. No problem; I'm just a kid. So I walked into this big fancy office and the big cheese, who is running the coal company, knew my grandfather by name. He goes, "How you doing, Whisky Joe?" "Oh, not too bad. It's just the grandson, he needs a job." So I talked to this gentleman for a little bit and he says, "What are you doing now?" I say, "Washing cars." Well, he says, "I'll hire you. When can you start?" I said, "I have to give at least two weeks notice." He says, "You start tomorrow."

I had to go to school for a week, you know, for training, and then I went to work with like eight hundred people. This place was like Grand Central Station. There's a lot of guys there. The boss would come up and say, "You go with me," so we went with him and they took you underground. You weren't afraid; you were more intrigued than anything, because you've never been in that environment before.

I remember this one old guy, he says, "Where you from?" I say, "I grew up in Sagamore." He says, "You know a guy named Whisky Joe?" I said, "Yes sir I do, he's my grandfather." After that, those people took me in and taught me everything I needed to know. These guys were good. They started in the forties and the fifties and didn't take no ~~shit~~ from nobody. They were a tough breed of people.

When you go underground, these guys would teach you how to do everything that there is, because there is a whole other way of doing it. Like when you work where it was only forty-eight inches of height, they teach you how to handle things and move things around so you don't get hurt. They'd say, "Don't listen to the boss, he'll kill you. You listen to me." These were all Polish people, Slavish people, Hungarian, Italians. The bosses used to get mad, because they'd speak Hunky or Italian, or whatever, and the boss couldn't understand them. Those old guys were tougher than we'll ever be, and they had a camaraderie together. I mean, they got treated like slaves for a lot of years, and they fought long and hard for their rights and the laws that we have now. I will not let what my grandfather and all these people fought for go down the tubes. I'll stand there and fight for the same rights.

I'm on day shift now. We have three shifts: eight to four, four to twelve, midnight to eight. Every week is a different shift. As long as I've worked there, they've rotated shifts; that's just the way it's been. I hate the afternoon shift—four to twelve—because you get off at midnight or at one or two, whatever; it just ruins your day. When you get up in the morning, you can't start anything or really do anything because by then it's three o'clock in the afternoon, and you got to get your stuff together to go to work. I'd rather work midnight to eight, then I have all day to do anything I want or just hang out.

As a kid, you didn't play on that yard or that street of whoever worked the midnight shift because you were brought up to have common courtesy. You knew these guys were sleeping, and you didn't piss around. Coal miners are tough old bastards. They are the grumpiest people you ever met in the world, and if you wake them up in the middle of the afternoon, they are mean and will cut you no slack.

We have forty-six miles of track underground here at the 84 Mining Company. The coal mine I work in is right over the hill. We're sitting in the best pocket of quality coal in the whole United States. We're the people that turn the light switch on for America. Everybody envisions coal miners as working in little tunnels in the ground. Our coal mine is bigger than the city of Pittsburgh. I mean, the area that this place covers is amazing. This coal mine has been here for over one hundred years. We have met coal—metallurgical coal. Met coal is used mostly for high-quality steel production and aluminum production; steam coal is used for power plants to generate energy. We load a lot of coal, about a million tons a month, though we used to load a lot more.

I worked in the mines for almost twenty years and then got laid off, so I went to a culinary arts school because I like to cook. I did that for a little while and liked it, but I couldn't make no money out of it. If I had been eighteen when I had started that shit it would have been really cool, but I wasn't. I got called back to the coal mines, so I figured I needed to finish my pension off and get my benefits for when I retire. I've been back ever since.

When you go to work, you get into the elevator, the doors close, you go nine hundred feet underground, the doors open: Welcome to hell. We walk where the devil dances, that's what people say, because you're so far underground and you travel two or three miles in. When you go underground and that elevator door opens, shut your light off, hold your hand out, you can't see your hand. You've never seen anything that dark in your life. The sun has never ever shined underground. There's people that just can't take being underground. You put them in that situation, they can't handle it. I mean, just by even going in there it will scare the ever-loving shit out of you. It's not being a sissy, it'll just scare them. To work underground, it takes balls.

When you go in the mine, you check your Solaris: It detects the atmosphere—methane, oxygen, the whole nine yards. You wear it all the time. If you get into any kind of bad atmosphere, this thing will tell you that you're in it. Normally, the oxygen level is like 20 percent. If you get in like 18.5 percent, this baby goes ballistic, and it tells you don't go no further, and you don't. If you're in low oxygen, you may get so far into it you'll pass out, but a Solaris will let you know a hell of a lot quicker.

I wear bib overalls, metatarsal boots, gloves, a hard hat, light, a battery for my light, hammer, wrenches, my rescuer—a rescuer is a device that . . . I'll show you one of these in the house; they've changed over the years. It's a device that has oxygen in it, so if you get into a situation underground, like a fire or an explosion or something like that, you take the rescuer off your belt and you put it on. You have oxygen for fifteen minutes. There's also places in the mine where there are other oxygen tanks; you can be there in fifteen minutes and pick up a bigger one that has about an hour of oxygen.

The mine generally is seven feet of height at the mine face [which is the exposed area where coal is extracted], but a lot of places will be from three feet high to eight feet high, depends on where you're at. Whenever you advance, the bottom could come up and heave, because the pressure breaks everything up. So instead of the roof falling in, the bottom comes up, and that takes away your height.

You always add on as you move the mine face forward, then everything else goes forward. We drill holes in the roof for the hangers, and then we put three-eighths-inch chains to hold that structure, because everything has to stay off the bottom of the mine. You're constantly mining forward and you're taking coal out. While you're taking coal out, everything behind you has to advance up behind you so that you can get more coal out of the mine. Sometimes you have bad roof conditions, so as you're going forward, you got to keep this roof above your head from falling down on top of you and killing you. You got to keep a constant vigil to keep this from happening. Then there's everybody that's working behind you who still has the same damn problem, because it can happen anytime, anyplace, in a mine.

Usually, your crew is pretty much the same people all the time. You see these people more than you do your family; they become family. You're inseparable. You're more than friends, you're more than buddies, you're more than pals. Your life is in his hands and his life is in my hands.

You don't speak a lot underground because it's noisy and the machines and belts are running. The average coal miner has a language that has no words; all he uses is his hand: If we go like this, it means "come here"; if you go like this, it means "no"; if you go like this, it means "yes." [Shiner demonstrates by drawing his hand toward his body, side to side, and up and down.] I can understand him, and he can understand me. Everybody knows what you're doing.

Right now, I'm a repairman on conveyor belts, underground. We have twenty-two belt drives, covering seventeen miles. If something breaks, we take care of it. These conveyor belts are like an inch and a quarter thick, made of six-foot-wide steel fiber. If you cut a piece of that belt to put in the trunk of the car that you drove in here today, you and I couldn't pick it up; that's how heavy this stuff is. We transfer a lot of coal over a lot of miles on those belts.

Sometimes the rollers on a belt could dry and burn, or the belt could break and pull apart from the weight and cause a fire. One time, we had a belt fire in the mine. I went to work and went in the mine. The belt caught on fire from rubbing and friction. We had a cement block wall in there that was so hot you could see through it. When you catch a coal mine on fire, everything is a fuel source, because everything around you is coal. The more intense that fire or that explosion gets, the bigger and bigger it gets. It never quits until it gets to a certain point, and then it backflashes where it comes right back and totally destroys everything.

What we do sucks. I mean, it's a different environment working underground. It's tough to explain. Anybody who thinks like, if you're an ironworker one hundred feet in the air, that is really cool. Go underground and see what happens. Life is different, life is cruel, life is tough. It takes a beating on your body, and it beats you to death. It's not easy. I'm not claustrophobic, but we're all afraid of the dark because you don't know what's going to kill you. That's what the dark is.

When you mess with Mother Nature, you can't call your shots. Ninety percent of the time you're okay, but there's that 1 percent that's gonna nail you. One time, it was just a normal day; I was running the miner—that's the machine that cuts the coal. We used to do what's called "retreat mining," where you have a planned cave-in behind you where you take out these blocks of coal that keep your roof up. I went in there, did my job, and when I started backing the miner out, boom! Shit happened. I had made it maybe ten feet, then solid rock caved in on top of me. I'm sitting inside this miner and I couldn't go anywhere. It's made out of one-and-a-half-inch solid steel, and I watched the paint inside the machine crack from it taking the weight of the coal. Everybody that was with me, like the buggy runners—the guys that load the coal—they're gone; my helper, gone. I don't blame them a bit. If I had been in the same position, you're not going to catch me there.

So I'm sitting in the compartment of the miner and waited about ten minutes for the dust to clear. Then I heard the guys behind me. They dug a little hole about the size of a briefcase, which makes me a little skinnier back then. I took my hat and my miner belt off, and I shimmied right through that hole. They said, "Are you scared?" I said, "Yeah." I shit myself. I did. I ain't lying.

They took me outside and I got showered up, and they said, "Are you okay? You want to go to the hospital?" "No, I'm cool. I was just scared." I mean, I got really frightened. The very next day I get back to work and they said, "What do you want to do?" "I'm running that machine," because if I don't do it now, I'll never do it again. I got a little gun-shy on it but got right back into it.

We've been lucky as far as explosions. We've had ignitions, and we've lit the mine face up with methane and it came right back over the top of the machine, like poof!—a big explosion. But everything stayed right there because we did our job. It didn't get the chance to go any further out. When you have an explosion, and if there's no more forward in the mine to go, the more force and the more rock, the bigger and badder it gets. The explosion goes to a certain point and it has to quit, then it comes back and it will pick up more dust and everything with the more force it gets. It's going back and forth and back and forth, picking up more and more force as it goes until it blows itself up. If you get in an explosion, you ain't coming out alive. That's just the way it is.

When you go to work every morning, you get in that elevator and them doors shut. You can hear a pin drop. When you come out [at the end of your shift], them doors open, it's like, "Yeah, you're out of here." You're out in the sunshine, whatever. Even if you're on the midnight shift, it don't matter, you're outside. Most coal miners don't spend a lot of time indoors; they spend their time outside like we're doing right now, in the yard, barbecuing and stuff.

If you get the opportunity to come back, give me a call. We'll take you underground and show you where the bear ░░░ in the woods.

We done with the interview? Let's eat.

JOAQUIN PEREZ

Pizza Delivery Driver

*J*oaquin Perez holds down three jobs: He's a maintenance man at two apartment complexes, he's a supervisor for sign shakers who stand on street corners advertising for restaurants and housing developments, and he delivers pizza.

"I don't have a gun in my glove box for two reasons: Number one, the likelihood of me being able to utilize that weapon if something was to happen is rare, and secondly, I've learned that in the long run you don't want to bring a weapon, because you're gonna have to defend against it if it ends up in the hands of the wrong person. I'd rather get beat up than stabbed, so why should I bring the element that might very well become my undoing; it just doesn't really make sense. I mean, I'm delivering pizzas. If I have to start thinking *about an arsenal, am I really in the right profession? I'm already killing you with calories."*

★ ★ ★

My third job is with Round Table Pizza. It kind of occurred to me that minimum wage had already gone all the way up to eight bucks an hour and so you're like, wow. Even if I'm only working four to five hours Monday through Friday it adds up, and then the tips came into effect, which blew me away. I'm going home sometimes with twenty-five to thirty bucks a night, which when you get a twenty-dollar bill, you feel something. I mean if you're used to just going every Friday and cashing a paycheck, that extra money feels great. Everybody knows what the famine part is like four days before payday; you're scrimping, that's how it is. But when you make a little extra, you're just kind of like I got it in the pocket, I'm okay.

I'm thirty-three. You don't think about a guy being thirty-three getting a pizza delivery job. People sometimes look at me and you just know behind that flat poker face they're giving you that the wheels are going, what the hell is wrong with this guy? He's thirty-three years old and he's delivering pizza? You're always thinking delivery guys are gonna be nineteen- to twenty-year-olds, but now with the economy, that's kind of changed.

I've worked fast food my whole life. I was hitting the pavement for the pizza job because I wanted to find something that was going to be flexible enough to give me about twenty hours a week. I've had some weeks where I end up with about thirty-two hours, just because. Last week I went in from five to ten thirty, which means you don't get out till about eleven. When you start figuring four of those days you've worked six hours, you're already at twenty-four. Then you figure about six hours at the apartments—we'll say five at Round Table five days a week—so you're talking fifty-five hours. And then on the weekend I'm out supervising the sign shakers for three hours each day, and then I come back in and deliver pizzas for about another six hours or so. You're talking about seventy-three-some hours a week.

I've gotten to a point where I pretty much do just about everything inside Round Table: keeping the salad bar up, helping bus the tables, folding pizza boxes, and making a little care package, you know, plates, cheese, crushed peppers, napkins, just stuff that you throw in when you put the pizza in the carrier. Me, I wanted to get more hours, thus I wanted to be a little more helpful: learning to answer the phones, learning what to say, learning how to handle the hustle and bustle inside the kitchen, learning how to properly remove food from the oven, know where to put the hot dishes as compared to the cool ones, how to basically do the register—except you don't take money, that's the only difference between you and the cashier.

There's really no training for being a pizza deliverer. There's just things that they will tell you about, you know, like you're told to be aware of your surroundings, or if there's a problem like you're having a hard time finding the address, and carry a cell phone so you can call the resident or whoever. Or, if you're robbed or if somebody is demanding money, you give it to them. Any store is gonna basically tell you that it's not worth your life; you should give them the twenty bucks.

On a slow night, I would say I'll deliver zero to three pizzas, and on a regular hustle-and-bustle normal night, you could get anywhere from seven to eleven. The busiest I had I ended up with like nineteen or twenty deliveries.

When you're going on your first delivery, you're thinking to yourself, I've seen where it is on the map, did I get everything, did I make sure I got the ranch dressing, did they have breadsticks? Okay, I think I got everything, and then when you leave, your brain goes into a secondary mode of now trying to remember what the map looks like so that at least you've some sense of the road. When you start to get close to the customer's area, especially when it's dark, you're trying not to get into an accident while you're looking for the address, and you got a flashlight if you're smart, and so you've got a lot on your mind. You're not really thinking that anything is gonna happen, but you kind of look around, so nothing seems out of the ordinary because it's a residential area. You might be a little more scared if you're out in a dark, wooded area, but who's gonna be eating pizza out in a wooded area, so you really don't think about it. When you arrive, you're like, okay, no guy with a hockey mask or a chainsaw, I'm good, and there you go.

We do get the occasional small order where it's probably an elderly person who just didn't want to get out, or maybe a medium pizza from a guy coming home from work. When you've got a decent order, it's kind of as if you don't even have to look for the number of the house, because you pretty much know it's the one with the four cars in front and you can hear the commotion going on in there. At that point, they pretty much are just opening the door kind of waiting for you. For fun, you can say something like, "Dinner is served," or if a little dog is barking you're like, "I've got pepperoni on the pizza that's bigger than you." With kids, I'm like going, "Ta da, the pizza man!" You try to have that superhero attitude like I've saved the day. It's just something that you kind of have fun with.

And, there are deliveries where if they don't answer the door, I'll call them like, "I'm at your door," and they're usually like, "Oh, I'm sorry," and they come. But there *are* situations where it's a fake call and I end up at somebody's home, like what happened three weeks ago from this coming Thursday.

It was my day off, but one of the managers calls me and wants me to help out. It turned out it was really slow, and then we got the call for a rather large order of about four or five pizzas, but then the caller was like, "I think our eyes are bigger than our appetite, let's stick with three." Someone else took the order, and there was a lot of laughing and commotion in the background, which means one of two things: either a prank call or a legitimate party. Then they ordered wings and two liters of Sierra Mist.

So I headed on out. This was around nine thirty at night. It was probably about a mile, if that, from the restaurant. For the most part, that area is getting into the heart of a solid residential area, but if you go a little farther down, it's you know—I don't say it's the ghetto—run-down older homes, so it's a mix, and it's a multiracial area. It goes from whites to Indians to blacks to Mexicans; it's just a melting pot of everybody.

I arrive at a legitimate address, pulled up in front of the house, got out, looked around, everything was quiet, went up, rang the doorbell, a kid answered, he looked at me like what are you doing at my door, and I'm like, "Hey, you ordered pizza." He turned and spoke to the family in their language, and you could just tell they're obviously not the people that made the phone call, because I've got an All Meat Marvel pizza and I'm looking at a Middle Eastern family. The pizza's got sausage, ham, bacon, and they're full turban, they're fully in their traditional clothes, and I'm thinking there's no way these guys ordered the basic swino special—I'm not trying to stereotype but, you know, the first impression you get. They looked at me, "We didn't order it," and I'm, "Yeah, I'm getting the feeling you didn't order this."

So at that point I'm kind of walking away and make the phone call back to work: "Hey, a prank. They got us." It's not a big deal. I got back in the car, put the pizzas back in the warmer, went back to work, and my cell phone rings and I answer it and they're like, "I ordered pizza and it never got here. I gave you the number to the house across the street." You then get the feeling they're having a party and he just gave the wrong address, this is a legitimate call, let's head back out there.

Now, I'm driving and I'm speaking to him on the phone, "I'm coming down the street, where are you," and he goes, "I think you just passed me." I turned around, and as I'm driving up I see him standing across the street, maybe a house or two down from the first house where I went. You're still thinking (not to upset any pizza people reading this book, but as a person who has dealt with the public, you realize that not all customers are exactly that bright sometimes), oh great, I got one of those.

I pull up thinking, thank God, finally I'm gonna get to deliver these pizzas, maybe salvage a tip out of this, and go back and finish my night. I get out of the car, I'm making small talk, take the food out of the car and set it on the trunk. Then I reach back into the car to get the two liters of soda, and I turn back around just kind of looking at him, because he's gonna ask me how much. Now instead of paying attention to him, I'm fumbling with the receipts so that I can say this is what you owe. At that point, there's a guy with a hoodie over his head and a bandana tied around his face—like an old-school train robber—coming out of the shadows from behind some bushes and he's got a rifle pointed at me. But he's holding the gun pretty close to his head. I'm thinking it's gonna have some type of a kick because he's holding it close to his face. The first guy has his face exposed to the world.

The first thing in my mind is, "This is dumb; these guys are robbing me." But I'm kind of thinking to myself if this one of those situations where I'm gonna be able to call their bluff. I'm trying to feel them out just like I would if they were answering the door to me, but the one guy is obviously angry, he's trying to portray dominance over me with the rifle. They don't look much bigger than me, so I'm still not really feeling that I couldn't take them, but, unfortunately, with there being two of them, reality kind of sets in.

The first thing out of his mouth is, "Hand over the money," with the derogatory slang, "nigger." I just said, "I'm a pizza delivery guy. I've got twenty bucks. What do you think I'm walking around with, stacks of cash?" Yeah, I said exactly that. I'm not coming off as threatening, but in a way I'm trying to kind of reach out to these guys by saying they are picking the wrong way to go about doing it. Times are tough, and in my mind I'm going, you guys are placing yourself in all kinds of crap.

I'm surprised and I'm a little taken back, but at that very moment, I wasn't afraid. Just to be straight with you: I think one of the things is that because I do have faith and believe in God, I was looking at these guys, honestly, with a sense of sympathy and kind of sadness for them. I'm working three jobs; I'm not sitting on money. I've got bills to pay, and in my toughest times I would have never thought of robbing somebody. For whatever reason, they're driven to this desperation. I'm talking at this guy and looking at him, and I'm like, "Dude, are you really going to this extreme?"

While we're talking I'm handing him the twenty bucks. Meanwhile, I had about $350 in cash, in my front pocket. I just had gotten paid from one of my other jobs. I probably shouldn't have been carrying it but, you know, you work three jobs and go around without money in your wallet for a little while, and then slip some twenties in there and tell me how you feel; it feels good. I did a total bluff. They're looking at me and they're kind of taken a little aback that I'm not just shaking out my pockets.

The reality of my life before this was I had nothing. I've been on the streets. I bought stolen merchandise. I was the drug dealer's best friend. They would call me up, "I got another crackhead with three DVD players, you want one?" Now here I am, years later, working hard for my stuff, and I've been blessed. So I'm trying to relate to these guys that there's an easier way.

Then, I got hit in the head. At this point they're realizing they've now only gotten twenty dollars. I'm looking at the guy with the gun, talking to him, because obviously he's one I want to pay attention to, and all of a sudden I just get hit full bore in the left side of the head by the guy without the gun, right around the temple area. My glasses fly away and my Bluetooth flies out of my ear. I didn't fall, I just took the hit, looked right back at the guy with the gun—I didn't want to look at the guy that hit me, because I didn't want to give any indication that I was gonna retaliate. I still had my wallet and, at this point, I still had my life, so I pretty much felt that I wasn't gonna say anything more. I was hoping that they would just leave.

Then they say, "What kind of cell phone do you have?" They're still thinking they're gonna get more out of me, and I'm telling him I've got an old phone, "Seriously guys, what are you gonna do with an old phone? Let me keep the phone." He steps closer and puts the barrel about a foot and a half from me, and he's still hunched over as if he's making a long-range shot. At that point you're starting to feel angry; there's a part of me that started to think, you know what, I've been nice, and I'm gonna take that thing from you and I'm gonna beat you with it, but then I'm thinking, I'm no Jackie Chan. I'm not just gonna flip the rifle around on him. So I let well enough alone, and I finally handed him the phone, but I still wasn't gonna be scared, so I just looked right at him like, "That's done, now what?" The guy is like, "Are you gonna call the cops?" I said, "Come on, what am I really gonna call the cops with?"

Then they took off running. They didn't take the pizzas. I looked around, and while I'm gathering myself, I said a little prayer to be thankful that I didn't get shot, I found my glasses and Bluetooth, and I still got all my money. I put the pizzas back in the car. Then I could kind of tell that the eye is starting to swell up, and I would end up with a black eye.

It wasn't until the following day that I had found out another robbery happened in the same area and that delivery driver had been shot in the leg. Everything sounded the same, and it was probably the same two guys. When I realized how it played out for me, I certainly knew that had he pulled the trigger it wasn't gonna be my leg, it was gonna be my face.

There were a couple of times since then where you're taking a phone call for a pizza and they're telling you where they live, and you get that apprehensive kind of fear. I'm not one that normally takes to being afraid, so it was kind of a weird feeling that all of a sudden I was like thinking to myself, I don't know that I want to do this. You realize what could have happened, and you're thinking, "Am I really gonna put myself back in that position again?" I'm not gonna say it's changed me in ways to where I'm more scared, it's just made me smarter. I still like the job. I'll probably keep doing it to get my savings back up again, and when I stop doing it, it wouldn't be because of the robbery. I would stop because of the fact that I think I'm working too much and I don't want to end up burning myself out. I have a family, and I want to spend a little more time with them.

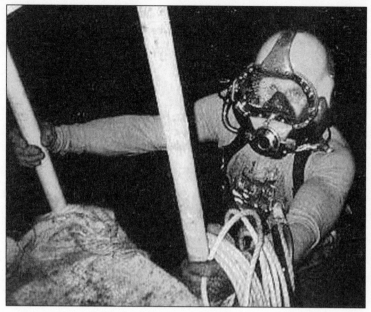

CHRIS MOYER

COMMERCIAL DIVER

As a little kid, Chris Moyer liked the television program Flipper so much that "I used to pull my socks half off and swim around my grandmother's living floor where she had this Victorian blue carpet." He is forty-two years old and still likes the water.

He has been a commercial diver since 2000. "When you have zero visibility, you have to do everything by feel. Maybe you're putting this thing that weighs six to seven tons on another thing, and you're clamping it with a hydraulic jaw. That's probably one of the more dangerous things that I have done: working with heavy loads and hydraulic jaws in zero visibility. You don't worry about it, you just do it."

★ ★ ★

I'm a commercial diver. A lot of times when I tell people I'm a commercial diver, they ask, "Oh, you dive in commercials?" I say, "Yeah, you know the one where they're changing the Pampers underwater? That was me. They used Brad Pitt in the wide shots."

Basically, what I do is underwater construction. It's not a whole lot different than a topside construction worker other than the fact that we're doing it with our head underwater. I once described commercial diving as taking a cross between a biker, an astronaut, and a lowland gorilla; it's a combination where a lot of these guys have kind of a free-range spirit. It's a lot of second-chancers. A lot of them are into Harleys and have that blue-collar roughneck construction mentality, but you have to be able to think your way through things, too. You have to come up on a problem and solve it in a relatively short amount of time, with limited resources, like maybe a guy will send me down a piece of rope, and you rig up a crank with it and a stick. But then there's times when finesse won't work and you just have to be able to muscle things. They say that the smart divers are strong divers, but sometimes strong divers aren't smart divers. A smaller guy who can solve a problem by rigging something up and do it with a minimal amount of effort and strength usually beats the guy who goes down there and muscles it.

In 1995, I got my basic PADI certification—a sixty-foot sport diver certification. That was neat, because it introduced a whole new host of reading material to my magazine stack, along with magazines for model airplanes, cars, and motorcycles; now, I have dive magazines. I was in the Air Force at the time, and a few weeks away from getting out, and I didn't know what I was gonna do. Up until that point, every job I'd had was a job I needed to have because I needed to have a job. I had worked at a department store, a restaurant, and a Gas Town. So, I was turning the pages of this scuba magazine and here is this ad for a College of Oceaneering: It's got this picture of this guy climbing up this ladder coming out of the water, and they have got all these pink and blue lights on the water and he's got this cool yellow helmet on and, as best I can tell, he has like a grappling hook and a laser gun on him. I'd never seen something like this before, and the ad said, "Come Up a Winner," and I'm like, hmmm.

So I gave them a call, and when I got out of the Air Force, I got into this dive school and finally was on a track to do something because I wanted to do it. It was something that interested me, and it had potential and a decent income. I went, applied myself, graduated, and tied for first in the class.

The first company I worked for was called Epic. It was a general kind of commercial diving company down in the Gulf of Mexico, doing all kinds of work. My first working dive was in a little dock in a channel. A tug, or some kind of vessel, came in and hit something with the prop, so they had me go in the water and do a sweep search. I pulled out a couple of tires, a piece of galvanized pipe, a little section of an engine, a cover for a lawn mower, and a couple of other things. When I'd find something, I'd hook it to a crane and they'd haul it out. It was probably only in twelve feet of water, but it felt like I was on the right track and things were gonna be good.

I also hadn't worked any kind of construction before, so I figured I'd go out sea where you work twelve-hour days, in two shifts: noon to midnight, midnight to noon. The time went by pretty quickly because you're not worrying about your commute, you're not worrying about getting home. When you're done working, you take a shower, eat, relax, sleep, get up, and go to work. It's really not as monotonous or onerous as one would think; it's kind of a nice pace. And you find out that there's a camaraderie. You don't worry about if there's gonna be somebody who is a real hard-ass or a jerk. People generally get along pretty well offshore. They tell sea stories, joke, and have a good time. And, sleeping on a workboat is one of the most restful, peaceful things that you ever do. The one that I was on a lot was called the *Midnight Dancer*. A couple of the rooms had cheap paneled walls and the bunks were made out of plywood instead of steel. You get in this little bunk, close the curtain, you get all rolled up and tucked in there; it's like you're in a cocoon, and the boat is rocking. It's great, you sleep like a baby.

We work with an umbilical—a hose—supplied with air from an air compressor on the surface that comes down to us, which plugs into our dive helmet. The helmet has a regular scuba regulator on it, but the advantage is that the helmet is enclosed so your head is dry and stays warm. We also have two-way communications through a wire that runs along the hose; that gives us the advantages of speaking to the dive supervisor so he can tell us what he wants, and we can tell him what we see or what we're doing. Say, if there's a crane involved—for when you're working with heavy items underwater where you have to lift them or place them—we have to give directions because all the crane operator sees is his wire going into the water. He has to go completely by our voice command.

The rule of thumb for diving is, at a hundred feet we can work about a hundred minutes. If you were at 140 feet, you're probably cut down to forty-five minutes, maybe thirty minutes, and then you have to leave. In a typical dive, you go down as quickly as you can, hit bottom, work as quickly as you can, secure all your tools, leave bottom, tell your dive supervisor you're off bottom, then he starts your decompression schedule. You climb up, as he watches your depth. If you're in the Gulf of Mexico, you usually will climb a leg of an oil platform. They're really the only structures out there in the Gulf; they're really neat, because they're teeming with life and it's real great visibility.

Below 150 feet but less than 200 feet, OSHA mandates that you have to do saturation diving, which is a different kind of diving where divers live in a bigger chamber—I call it a Winnebago—it's like six feet in diameter and twenty feet long. They have a diving bell that mates to this chamber and the bell is lowered to the work site. When the bell gets to the depth of the site, the pressure equalization causes the hatch on the bell to open. One diver then goes out and can work for five or six hours, then they switch to another guy, he works for five or six hours, then they bring the bell up. Then those two guys eat and sleep in the chamber. They found that with really deep diving you can't stay long enough to get enough work done and also be on a decompression schedule that's practical, otherwise you would have to spend all your time decompressing. So they leave the divers at that depth.

There's a second air hose on your umbilical called the "pneumo-fathometer." It's basically an air hose with an open end on it where they run air through it and it's hooked to a gauge on the topside where the supervisor is. That gauge measures the amount of air pressure it takes to push air out against the water; they can watch your depth that way. [When ascending,] I'll stop at, say, seventy feet, wait there for like seven minutes; move up ten feet to sixty feet, wait about fifteen minutes; then keep moving up in ten-foot increments until you come to the surface. What that basically has done is, it bought you decompression time to give you about four minutes to get out of the water and get over to the hyperbaric chamber where you begin your real decompression. In the Gulf, you're decompressing in a dry chamber under pressure, and you have an oxygen mask, because when you breathe pure oxygen, it pulls the nitrogen out of your body quicker than just breathing regular pressurized air. That speeds up the process of decompressing, and it's safer.

What happens in the chamber, which is about four feet in diameter and about eight feet long, is you start at fifty feet worth of air pressure. Then you begin a cycle of twenty minutes breathing oxygen, with five-minute air breaks, so that you don't get something called "acute oxygen toxicity" where you can have seizures and stuff. You're there probably for about an hour and a half to two hours, maybe a little more. That is your decompression process. Then you're done with your dive.

Because of the physiology of diving, the air you and I are breathing right now is about 20 percent to 21 percent oxygen, about 78 percent nitrogen, and 1 percent of trace stuff. Nitrogen is inert; it moves in and out of our lungs with the oxygen our body uses and when we expel carbon dioxide. When you dive, your body begins to absorb the nitrogen into your bloodstream. The deeper you go, the more the air is compact and the tighter the gas molecules are, and the more your tissues pick up the nitrogen. If you ascend too quickly without taking what's called "water stops" then you can get decompression sickness, or what people call the "bends."

Also, there have been studies that suggest that if you do a lot of surface diving, where we do decompression at the surface and a lot of up and down in the water, it can start to affect the bone density in your long bones, like your thighs. You can get off-gassed to a certain extent, but inevitably there's a trace amount of these gases left in your bones.

When I worked in the Gulf of Mexico for this company called Torch, we laid and buried oil and natural gas pipe between production platforms. Usually the pipes are six to eight inches, but they could be as small as four inches or bigger like ten to sixteen inches. If you're shallower than two hundred feet down, you have to bury them into the bottom because the shrimpers will come by and snag their nets on them. This process is called "jetting" where you take pressurized water in what looks like a fire hose, and you dig in the bottom with that. The water pressure comes out real high to where you have to be careful; if you sweep it under your helmet, you can blow it off your head.

The water is so warm in the Gulf that 140 feet down you can wear a sweatshirt and jeans. In the summer, it's actually too warm to wear a wet suit. You stay out of wet suits as long as you can because they get torn up on the barnacles, and a $20 pair of jeans is a lot easier to replace than a $200 wet suit. The surface water temperature there, in August, is probably on the high side of what your pool would be; I'd say maybe close to eighty degrees. What happens with water is as you're descending, the temperature changes gradually where there are layers of water, like say when you drop down thirty feet, your toes and shins can be in water that's ten to twenty degrees colder than the water that your shoulders are in. You actually go through a layer and you feel it.

Once in the Gulf—I think it was a 140-foot dive—I was coming up and the supervisor on top said, "Hold on a minute. We can't get your air hose up," because the hose got snagged on barnacles on one of the legs of a platform, and they couldn't pull it. They said, "Are you all right?" I said, "I'm fine. I can move. I'm not stuck in anything." So I'm just sitting there, and they said, "We're gonna try and figure out what's wrong with your hose," and they got the standby diver ready—he's the guy that's always on standby in case you have problems—but the standby hose hadn't been used in so long, and it had been out in the hot Gulf of Mexico sun so long, that the rubber had deteriorated the inside of the hose and it flaked away. When the standby diver jumped in the water, rubber flakes blocked his airflow and he couldn't get any air. I'm at like seventy to a hundred feet, and I'm just hanging out. They then somehow got the hose cleared, and I came up.

I think I had about thirty-five working dives in the Gulf, but I had been there long enough. I then was talking to this guy who asked if I wanted to dive in the Bay Area, but he said I had to join the Pile Drivers Union. So I moved, made some calls, talked to people, ended up joining the union, and started working. Pile driving is predominantly aboveground so, initially, I only had some diving interspersed with working on land, but then the diving got more steady.

We had a fairly lengthy project in Benicia at the Valero refinery wrapping the piles that hold up their fuel dock—where the tankers come in and pump the fuel out. That dock is held up by steel piles that were starting to rust and degrade. They weren't gonna last much longer, so our job was to wrap these twelve-foot-long sheets of PVC-type material around the piles and then secure them with stainless steel bands. Underneath that, you put this heavy cloth, which is almost like a cheesecloth that's impregnated with grease that is a corrosion inhibiter. The purpose is to protect the piles enough to make sure you get enough of a transition to where the steel below the water is never exposed to air, and the steel above never gets wet.

Depending on the tide and the current, the depth there was maybe twelve to thirty feet. But there was a lot of current. On the outflow, the current would get pretty strong because you have got the inherent evacuation of tide on the ebb tide going out of the Bay, plus with the river coming down, you get a pretty good current. You have to hang on there real hard. What you do is, you set yourself up underwater to work on the upstream side and you straddle this thing to keep yourself balanced, because it's pushing against you. You also have to have your hands free to work the tool that tightens the stainless-steel bands. If you lean too far to one side, the current will catch you and try to pull you off. When you come out of the water after working that job, your thigh muscles are pretty tired.

If you have to cut something underwater, we use a Broco torch. It has a torch head with like seven or eight little self-consuming steel rods that come out about eighteen inches long. You blow pure oxygen through it and the steel burns at such a great temperature you can cut with it. It's almost like an oxyacetylene torch. When you're burning with Broco, you're heating the water around it so much that you're separating the molecules of oxygen and hydrogen. What happens is, as I'm burning, if I build this gas up, eventually that hydrogen is gonna ignite and it can be a pretty violent explosion, especially underwater, because the concussion is magnified. That's the major risk with using a torch.

On one job, I used a hydraulic chainsaw underwater to cut off a little retaining wall. I couldn't see because there was zero visibility, so you have to get your chainsaw and punch-cut this wall, which means to stick the chainsaw straight through the wall. You have to put your hand where the tip of blade meets the wall—and you keep your hand off the trigger. Sometimes I close my eyes if it's zero visibility. I don't know if it's psychological or physiological, but it's easier to visualize what you're doing. You can't see with your eyes anyway. So, get the tip of the chainsaw set against the wall, fire the chainsaw up, punch-cut it. Then you got to get through the wall, and then you have to cut a fairly straight line horizontally without cutting the hose to the saw and without cutting your air hose, and without chopping your leg half off. Sometimes there's that kind of an inherent danger to the work.

I've also done work cleaning potable water tanks up in the hills for a municipal utilities district. They have water tanks that gravity feeds all their water down. This is drinking water that has been already processed through the water treatment plant. It's very clean, but there's a little bit of finite amount of silt in it and the silt settles in these water tanks, maybe a quarter-inch layer on the bottom. Every ten years or so, the tanks need to be cleaned out. So we go in there and we vacuum it out with a three-inch suction hose. It's basically three hours of underwater Tai Chi in forty feet of water vacuuming this silt. You have to move really slow to suck it up, because if you move too fast, you stir it and, because it's so fluffy and light, it will come up into a cloud. The only time that job gets a little difficult is when you're in a dry suit. The primary reason to wear a dry suit is to seal you from the water—this is people's drinking water—because they don't want some guy in a wet suit peeing away. So you have to hold it, where in a wet suit you can pee and it's great: You're warm for a second, and then you just rinse it out later. But in a dry suit, anything you put inside the suit stays with you for the whole dive. So the night before a tank dive, I'll stop drinking fluids after like eight o'clock. I'll get up in the morning with the driest mouth in the whole wide world. I might swish something and spit, but I will not drink anything.

I like my job because it's interesting and you meet a lot of the challenges physically, which is kind of fun for me. It's also fun telling people you're commercial diver. I like saying it, because you say it differently than you would say, "I work at Gas Town." You don't have to make up a title like, "I'm a junior commodities associate." Being a commercial diver is something to be proud about because not everybody does it.

There are days when you get in the water and just nothing goes right, it's so hard. And when you come out, you wish it hadn't been your dive and that someone else had dove. But there are days when you get in there and your stuff goes right. It's really rewarding because you're like, "Yeah, *I* did that." Plus, I can say there's places on this earth that I have walked on that no other human has, and no other may ever walk there again. That's kind of cool.

ULA THE PAIN-PROOF RUBBER GIRL

KNIFE THROWER'S ASSISTANT

*U*la asked that only her stage name be used in the book. She sits in her *small New York City apartment, where she trains students in various aeri-alist skills, and where she spent this Friday afternoon talking about her work as a knife thrower's assistant for The Great Throwdini. "You know, there are a lot of things that you just can't predict. I would say the probability is higher against knives hitting me than against things that I can't see or control. There are so many things that you just have no idea what will happen."*

★ ★ ★

I was told that I was recommended to The Great Throwdini because I was thin, so I would make a smaller target. I'm five foot, five and I weigh anywhere between 110 and 115 pounds depending on the time of the year. The Great Throwdini is a modern-day knife thrower. I believe he was inspired by the movie *Girl on the Bridge*. When I first met him, he had had two other assistants. I think they were both actresses and they didn't work out, or they freaked out at some point. I'm not sure what happened. And, he and his wife used to take turns being at the board, but I guess you could say his wife didn't have any crazy dreams of performing. She is actually an excellent knife thrower herself, but she had a good job, so she didn't want to be his assistant.

I was the third assistant he had. Todd Robbins, an old sideshow guy I worked with—not old, I'm sorry—he has been around for a while and had worked with Throwdini. I think he suggested rather than use an actress, maybe Throwdini should try using a circus person, because they are a little bit more familiar with the danger involved, and it might work out better.

I thought it would be something interesting, because knife throwing is an old circus tradition. Wild Bill Hickok used to have a traveling circus, and they had knife throwing back then. Around the Civil War time, it was pretty big. Knife throwing wasn't just for killing people, it was an art form in Wild West shows and all the circuses. You don't see it very often anymore and I thought Throwdini was a talented knife thrower, and if I could help him carry on a tradition, I would like to do that. I did it so that people of my generation could see an old-time act that they've never seen before. It's not like it could even pay enough for putting yourself in danger like that. You really can't put a price on that. How much? It could pay anywhere from $100 to $1,000 depending on the event. I did it purely because I thought he was a very rare individual and I wanted to help carry on a circus tradition. It wasn't something that I needed to do and it wasn't something that I wanted to do. Why would I look for something like that?

I watched a few of Throwdini's shows, and I actually asked him to teach me how to throw knives. Once I understood it and saw how skilled he was, I agreed to do it. What I did is controlled danger. I know how much danger I'm in. I know anyone can die instantly, even as a knife thrower's assistant. Sometimes you can't see danger underneath you like cancer attacking your cells, but I knew I could see knives coming at me.

I knew Throwdini for a year before I actually worked with him. I knew he was the world champion, the fastest knife thrower, and the most accurate knife thrower. I knew he was an incredibly intelligent individual on top of all of that. I would have never worked with him otherwise. And he is just an exceptional person. I can't imagine finding another knife thrower that's as talented as Throwdini. For me, it was always a job and a tradition. I'm sure I see it much differently than most people do. I don't know what it is. There is definitely something psychological happening there, but you would have to ask a shrink about that.

A lot of Throwdini's assistants wear a bikini, but I would always wear a dress, heels, two pairs of stockings, two pairs of undergarments, padding on my head, and a wig. I also would wear a lot of stuff under the dress. I was raised horseback riding and I knew that when you're trying to saddle up a horse, the horse always blows itself up with air so that the saddle is looser. I thought, you know, the more I put under my dress, the bigger I would be and the farther away from me he will have to throw. I did a joke once when I came out in a suit of armor, but he didn't go for that.

There would be a red board behind me. Pine. It's always stationary. For the point of the knife to stick in a board for a half turn of the knife, he would have to be approximately seven to eight feet away from the board. A knife turns as it goes through the air; it is not thrown like a dart or a bullet. So you have to calculate the length of your arm and the speed that you throw the knife to determine how close to the board you should stand. You just keep calculating half turns, because when you throw a knife, you hold the blade in your hand and you want the point of the blade to be sticking in the board. For a full turn, it's a few feet behind that. For a turn and a half,

I think it's somewhere around fourteen feet. I can't remember how many knives he throws a minute, but it's the world record.

[*Author's note:* The Great Throwdini claims the world record for throwing the most number of knives around a human target in one minute: seventy-six fourteen-inch knives.]

I was on a wheel just once, at his house during a practice, but I've never been on the wheel for a show. The wheel is huge. You're not going to haul a wheel somewhere for one night unless it's like some huge extravaganza and a company can afford the liability of having a knife thrower. It's also probably not the most politically correct thing to have at your dinner party. So when you're getting on the wheel, you have to practice it, and there was no reason for me to practice it if we weren't going to do it. I'm not sure how I would have reacted if he had asked me to do it.

Like I said, a knife is not a dart; it's not a straight shot like a gun. It rolls. You really can see the knives turn. Throwdini's hand-eye coordination is so good he can get it very close. Or, as close as I let him, meaning I could say something like, "Come within two inches of me and this is my last show." But he could easily control whether it was a quarter inch from my skin or two inches. Usually it was about an inch away from me. But if I had told him he has to throw it two inches away, which I think I did when we first started, he was respectful of that and he did. I guess you have to have trust in the other person, but I think you also have to have knowledge of what that person is doing. The big cure for fear is always knowledge. If you know how to throw a knife and if you can see a knife coming toward you, you're not going to run and hide.

In the course of an act, he would throw at least forty knives, in different combinations. Each act would have about six sections, and each section he would throw approximately seven knives. I didn't like it when he threw axes and machetes, but he did. I cheated a little bit then. I mean, some assistants would just stand there in the center of the board. But if I knew he was throwing to the left of me, I would step to the right and raise my right arm. If I knew he was throwing to the right of me, I would step to the left and raise my left arm, not enough that anyone would notice. I wouldn't, though, let him throw them between my legs, but some assistants do. I didn't, because, like I said, it's controlled danger. I'm not out to get hurt. I don't have a death wish. I refused to do a lot of the different tricks. It's a job for me and a tradition and I have respect for the tradition, but at the same time, I respect myself and I'm not going to do anything I perceive as putting me in a danger zone. There's a line that you don't cross, I suppose.

I guess I've been aware of my own mortality from a very young age. There are so many things that you can't see coming. You can't see death coming. You can't see Mt. Vesuvius erupting. The probability [of avoiding danger] is higher with knives than against things that I can't see or control here in New York City. The carpet could be pulled out from under you at any second and you'll never see it coming, but I'll see a knife coming if it's going to hit me.

Been hit? Well, once on a stunt the point of a knife hit a knot on the board and it fell out on my head, but it didn't stick in my head, obviously. It just skimmed the wig a little bit. If hadn't been wearing the wig I might have been hurt a little bit.

You're definitely in the moment. I wanted to be as calm as I could be because I would feel that my worry would translate to Throw-dini. When someone is nervous, you tend to make other people nervous, so I wouldn't want to be nervous before a show. If something happened when he was throwing at me, I could see that and I would react.

Why did I leave the show? I never made a decision; he never made a decision. I went with him to Brazil for the circus festival, but I think I was really busy with aerial work after that and he needed to find somebody who was more reliable. He has a few other people he can work with regularly. I became a lot busier and I couldn't do a lot of the days he needed and it doesn't pay as much as my aerial work. I never had any problems with him. I was happy. There was never a deciding factor like, oh, I'm not going to do this anymore.

There were certain shows that I didn't understand why he had taken them. If there was a show I really didn't think was an important show to be doing, I would question why he needed to do, but he has a love of performing and he really needed to do it. I believe he is still throwing and I think he's doing something with *Guinness Book of World Records*.

If somebody was actually looking to be a knife thrower's assistant, I would think there was something psychologically wrong with them. I would just give them Throwdini's phone number and not want to get involved. Honestly, if somebody is looking for that, I don't want to know why. I wasn't looking for it. I mean, if there's some person who is, you know, a crackhead off the street looking for a couple of bucks to be a knife thrower's assistant, then I don't know what their deal is and I would just give them the number. But if somebody was involved with the circus, I would say, "Break a leg. Knock them dead."

Photo Courtesy of: **BUBBA BLACKWELL**

BUBBA BLACKWELL

MOTORCYCLE DAREDEVIL

*B*ubba Blackwell broke all of famed daredevil Evel Knievel's motorcycle ramp jumping records, and he has at least forty-two broken bones to prove it, including a life-threatening crash at the Del Mar Fairgrounds in an attempt to jump over twenty-two cars. "The impact knocked me out. I was in a coma. What happened was, it shattered my pelvis like a spiderweb, broke six vertebrae in my back, one in my neck, broke every one of my ribs, crushed my right shoulder, punctured both of my lungs, ruptured my spleen, but the worst part was I had a major head injury. I was bleeding on the brain. You can die from that. It was amazing that I survived."

★ ★ ★

Bubba Blackwell

I was raised in a little bit of a tough neighborhood where a lot of the kids went on to get in trouble and do a bunch of things that they shouldn't have done. I credited the fact that I never got into trouble because I was always busy riding my bicycle and motorcycle for fun. What really got me going was whenever I would see Evel Knievel on television, I was real impressed with his charisma and his presentation, and how he could sell you on what took him about three seconds to accomplish, yet he turned it into an attention-getting show that you pretty much had to stay tuned in to see. I always enjoyed his showmanship. Then I would go ride my bicycle and pretend to be the same thing.

I knew motorcycles were going to be a part of my life, so I pursued racing as a career. I started road racing motorcycles part-time, and had a lot of success. I actually won a National Championship in 1988 as an amateur, and then got a lot of big breaks and went down to Daytona in 1989 with this real big deal with big sponsors, but I had a crash and got hurt real bad. I barreled into the left turn wide with the throttle wide open and the bike started sliding. I chopped the throttle, the next thing you know I'm flying through the air.

I was in the hospital for quite a while. I'm lying there going through the healing process and kind of reevaluating my career choice. I kind of thought—this is a crazy way of thinking of it—if I was a motorcycle stunt rider and I fell off and I got hurt, at least I still would get paid, whereas if you're racing a motorcycle and you fall off you don't make any money. That's a naive approach for a career, but it's the basis for the way I kind of created my career. And I always knew that I was more of a showman and show-off than I was interested in going out there dogfighting with somebody elbow to elbow, racing at 150 miles an hour. It's practically this simple: I knew what I wanted to do, which was to make a living goofing off and having fun.

My one talent seemed to be on the motorcycle. I simply wanted to make a living riding a motorcycle, and I thought about it and I saw a clear-cut vision for me that I need to start thinking about making money every time I get on a motorcycle regardless of if I fall off or not. I know this sounds like a real bubba from Alabama speaking this way, but I simply thought of Evel Knievel and knew that nobody since him had made any kind of splash in getting the public's attention at riding a motorcycle. And, Knievel proved the fact that you really didn't have to have a lot of talent, because we all know how many times he crashed. He made a large majority of his jumps and didn't crash all the time, but he wasn't that great of a rider. But he was so smart in making sure that you paid attention to him.

Back in the seventies you practically had to give Harleys away because the craftsmanship wasn't there. But, in the late eighties, early nineties, if you didn't have a Harley Davidson in your garage you had to give up your "I'm cool" card because that was the motorcycle to have. My marketing approach was, because there wasn't anyone out there performing on a Harley Davidson motorcycle, these new Harley people really didn't have anyone to root for, and I thought, maybe if I can get that Evel Knievel thought process going again, then maybe this is something I can turn into a career. So that's what I did.

It took me a long time to find a Harley Davidson XR-750—that's the type of bike that Evel rode. Anyways, I hooked up with a guy who saw what I saw. The very first jump that I did on the motorcycle I knew wasn't gonna make me a rich man. I did it real cheap, because this man was able to get ten brand-new Peterbilt semitrucks off the showroom floor for me to jump over at his racetrack, and I knew that it was gonna make for a great photograph and a great presentation. So I went over there that night to do this one motorcycle jump, knowing full well that the little bit of money I was gonna make wasn't gonna do anything for me, but the setup would. I then paid a friend of mine a hundred dollars to come over and write an article on what he saw. I made the jump. It was real successful, and a lot of people came to see it. So my friend wrote this really cool article, and we included a bunch of photographs and sent it to a couple of different magazines. One picked it up and as soon as that magazine hit the magazine stands, immediately my world changed. Anyway, that's kind of the way it all started.

One day the phone rang, and it was a guy who said he's opening the world's largest Harley Davidson dealership near Boston—86,000 square feet under one roof. He said, "What do you think you can do for me?" I said, "I think the world's largest dealership needs a world-record Harley jump." He said, "Well, how much are we talking?" I had never been paid more than five grand for a motorcycle jump at this point; however, I had never done that big of a jump. I said, "Thirty thousand dollars," and he said, "Sounds great, let's do it." I heard through the grapevine that Robbie Knievel had gotten thirty grand for a jump, and I figured, he jumps on a sissified Honda, and I'm riding a Harley, so I just threw it out there.

The guy that was the event promoter must have been pretty darn sharp, because what he'd done right before the jump was he alerted Lifeline; that means every media source in the whole area is alerted. You could have seen this jump on CNN. I made the right inside of the first or second page of the *Boston Herald*. It was on *Hard Copy*. I mean, it was on all these national news outlets. So, not only was it a huge success locally, but this guy could not even so much as think about affording what the impact media-wise was for this grand opening. I jumped twenty cars. That beat Evel Knievel's record of nineteen cars—the same-sized takeoff ramp, same-sized cars. I just added one more car to it. It was very exciting, because at this time in my career, I was a little bit behind on my truck and trailer payment, and I was struggling. I went up there broke, and I came home with a check. I got to tell you, at that point, that was like a billion dollars.

Del Mar was a year later. That jump was over fourteen buses. The effort was to break Evel Knievel's record. He tried to jump thirteen buses in London, and he crashed. A few months later, he came to Kings Island in Ohio and tried to jump over fourteen buses. He made that jump, but in the video footage you can see that he actually landed on bus number fourteen, and he even admitted so in the postjump interview. Del Mar drew thirty thousand people. The jump was very successful.

After that successful bus jump, the *Tonight Show* came calling, wanting to know if I would be interested in doing the only other Evel Knievel record jump I'm aware of that isn't broken. He once jumped thirteen semitrucks; I must go for fourteen. So they flew me out to California to inspect the area that I was gonna jump, and everything was great. Well, a couple of weeks went by and they were having a difficult time trying to find the semitrucks. They call my management back and they say, "We might have to cancel this because we are not getting any cooperation." Well, within one day, we talked to U.S.Express, which is a national carrier. We tell them, "How would you guys like to get your trucks on the *Tonight Show*?" Oh my gosh, not only did they supply them for free, but they cleaned them all up and they gave me stuff. We put the deal together and I jumped over fourteen semitrucks live on the *Tonight Show* in October of 1999.

I think seven and a half million people watched it. The interesting thing is it didn't make the phone ring from people wanting jumps, but what it did do is validate us as being one of the top acts out there. After the show, I'm sitting in my dressing room collecting my things, and I stop for just a split second and thought to myself that this was absolutely the biggest thing that will ever happen in my career. That was kind of sad, but I didn't buy into it. I went on from there.

The biggest jump ever on a Harley Davidson is when I jumped fifteen tour buses in Las Vegas in December of 1999. During the day, the weather was fantastic, beautiful and crisp. We worked all day and we finally got everything set up, and then that night it was really cold. But the interesting thing about it was, it was full-sized-type tour buses. Not only did I not make a practice jump, but it was a brand-new takeoff ramp, which if memory serves me, was like thirteen feet in the air, where my regular takeoff ramp is seven-foot, two inches. But I never used a speedometer. I wanted to break all of Evel Knievel's records the way he did. He never used a speedometer, so golly if he could do it, then I could.

I know the way to be safe is not to change very many variables. I knew approximately how far I can go and the feeling for how fast the bike is going in top gear. Now, I never changed the gearing on the motorcycle and I always use the same takeoff ramp—although the way this one was elevated, all the angles were the same that I was used to. The only difference is, like I said, I never even practiced the jump, because we were kind of running out of time, but I was confident. The other part of that is, you're in the middle of Las Vegas, it's a huge event and it was for a TV show called *I Dare You! The Ultimate Challenge.* The introduction was enormous; they had all this equipment there, the staff, the production trailers, and all the other things that are necessary to make the event happen. I remember riding to the top of that ramp that night and looking at all these people that were there just for me, just for this event, and I thought, man, what did my big mouth get myself into? You know, at that point you realize this is time to separate an amateur and a professional. It was exciting.

That is the kind of the thing where there's that scared butterfly feeling in your stomach, but that's what's exciting. It's scary, and it helps you focus because you could die today. The exciting part about doing something like this is, I have never done drugs in my life and I have no interest in it, so there's nothing that could top the feeling of being totally in that moment. You got to do it. That's what gets you going. Then, you go from total terror in a split second going from ramp A to ramp B, and when it's completed and it's successful you're feeling this euphoria like you have never imagined. You just went from total terror to perfectly calm. It happens fast. You don't get to enjoy the ride because you're so focused on where you're going. The real exciting part is, in some cases, it is something nobody has ever done, and the other part of that is you have held up your end of your bargain. You're a man of your word. Plus, I got paid a lot of money; that's always nice.

On that particular jump, it was for television only, and it was closed to the public, but everybody knew what was going on and they had it all fenced off so people couldn't see through, but it was such a high jump that people stopped in the middle of Las Vegas Boulevard, and were on the top of their cars. The production company got in trouble with the police, and I loved every minute of it because the idea was that I was gonna have a lot of crowd to play in front of. The other big jumps I've done were in front of live crowds, and it's just amazing to go from landing the motorcycle, and you're safe, to then ride back up the landing ramp and you're still onstage. The euphoria that comes over you is a difficult thing to harness because you have to maintain your showmanship.

At that time, I had claimed all the world records there were that Evel Knievel had set. Then the Del Mar Fair paid me a lot of money to come back. I could have bought a house with what they paid me, so I wanted to do something spectacular: I was gonna jump twenty-two cars, to push my own record from twenty cars to twenty-two. I spent $12,000 of my own money to have a laser light show company come out there for my introduction. It was amazing. To be honest with you, I put so much attention into that introduction I had failed to remember that on a horse track, like at Del Mar, the dirt is like powder. You can roll pack it, and that's fine, but when you make several run-ups to the ramp and doing wheelies to hype up the crowd, you chew the track up. I had forgotten to put down a roll of roofing paper, which is like a tar paper, for the run up to the ramp. By the time I made all these speed runs without the tar paper there, it had chewed up the runway and by the time I was going to the takeoff ramp, I was running in, like, sand. I didn't have a speedometer and I'm in top gear. The motor is revving like crazy, and I just simply wasn't going fast enough.

Here is the thing about an accident like that. When you don't use a speedometer, you rely on your peripheral vision to give you a gauge about how fast you're going. I started on the track approximately five feet away from the concert stage. They had a concert stage that fed up on the horse racetrack, and they got it all fenced off so that it can be private back there. I'm going from that fencing to the takeoff ramp, and I'm right up against the fence. When you're relying on your peripheral vision and you're right next to a fence, it feels like you're going ten thousand miles an hour. Plus, the engine was revving really high and the bike wasn't fishtailing and was still going fast forward, so I just assume—because I have no memory of the jump at all—is that I clearly wasn't going fast enough. I think one of the greatest things that can happen to you when you have a major traumatic situation is you don't have any memory of it, because you got to go on. This is my chosen profession, and I just wasn't ready to find something else to do.

I think the jump distance was 137 feet. I didn't go fast enough and I hit the edge of the safety ramp that covered the last three vehicles. I barely made it that far. It could have been, cancel Christmas. The impact immediately ejected me off the motorcycle. I did one and a half cartwheels and landed on my head, which destroyed a Kevlar helmet, and the bike shot way up in the air and did several cartwheels and came all the way down and landed beside me. It was a real traumatic crash. When I impacted the ramp, I flew another seventy feet before I hit the ground. You can go to YouTube; it's all over there.

Normally, when you have an accident in a car, the ambulance is called to the scene and they take care of you. However, imagine if the ambulance and the paramedics are on scene and they are buying into all the hype that you do by pumping up the crowd, doing wheelies and all that stuff and you do in a live event in front of thirty-five thousand people. And then you crash. When the paramedics came over there to work on me, they were all traumatized. They were trying to put a tube down my throat and they were not getting it done. The interesting thing is, when the fire chief saw the accident happen, he immediately called for Lifeline. Within five minutes, they were on the ground. This one awesome guy that they call Braveheart came over, pushed everybody out of the way, and intubated me within seconds. Then they flew me to Scripps Memorial Hospital in La Jolla.

Eventually my wife and all the crew members got there. I was in really bad shape. I was on life support. Interesting thing is, I'm real good friends with a preacher that's on television all the time, and he sent a friend that's a pastor to pray over me. I'm going by what my wife told me because I was in la-la land. She said that he held my hand, then he held her hand and she held my other hand, so they were kind of like over me. He started really getting into his prayer and speaking in tongues and just going crazy. She said the hospital monitors and everything started freaking out and, all of a sudden, I convulsed, arched my back, I let out a big noise, then I completely relaxed. All of the monitors went totally normal. I was out of the coma the very next day. Dig this: Not only did I survive that head injury without real lasting effect, but I don't limp, I'm fine. I'm a very lucky man. I got to share that story, because it's true. I'm Christian and I believe in the Lord, but I'm not a religious guy. I was in the hospital for a month, and then I had to stay out there another week and couldn't fly because of my punctured lungs.

I knew what went wrong with that jump. You can make two choices: You can tuck your tail, quit, and go away and say it was fun while it lasted, or you can analyze what you did wrong and decide you never want that to ever happen again.

I'll keep doing it till it isn't fun anymore. It's still fun, it's still exciting. I don't jump all the time, and they got to pay me a bunch of money to do it because I got nothing left to prove. I think that if you're gonna have a successful career in something like this, you got to know when to say "no," but I'm very fortunate, because I do a stunt riding show and a wheelie trick show that I use as a marketing campaign for Harley Davidson and Buell motorcycles. I put on a real entertaining show that's very family friendly, and it shows what the motorcycles are capable of. So, now, I do a stunt riding show almost every single week. When I'm not jumping, I do burnouts and wheelies, crawl all over the motorcycle, and do something that not many people do: I do all this with a microphone in my helmet. I'm constantly interacting with the crowd. I still love it.

I never give too much credit to a guy named from Bubba from Alabama, because, you know, I look at things from a simple approach:

What I do is nothing more than physics. That is the most boring way that an entertainer can explain what he does, but if you go out there like a nut ball, the next thing they're on the edge of their seats and they're rooting for you. Then you enhance all the senses, like noise, where we microphone the exhaust so the crowd thinks I'm going two thousand miles an hour. Don't explain a stunt to the T, because you'll make it boring.

You know, people like crazy people, but not real crazy people. They like to see interesting individuals, not necessarily the guy next door. But, you know, I'm just the guy next door. I just got a very unique job, and on show day, I'm not the guy next door. It's a heck of a lot of fun and it's real exciting.

TOM MULLALLY

POWER LINEMAN

"*H*abits keep you alive in this job."

We meet at Tom Mullally's electrical power company's shop, then find a table and bench outside to talk. Several younger men training to become power linemen practice on power poles a hundred yards away. Mullally is fifty-five years old. "My heart is in the field. You're up a pole with a guy and the rain is sideways and there's sparks flying and you get the job done safely. You become pretty close. You go through a lot together. There is quite a camaraderie that you get from that."

★ ★ ★

I worked at a grocery store as a bag boy and then a clerk, became a checker, making pretty good money, but it was part-time. A guy that came in all the time at the store was a lineman and I got to know him. He taught me how to climb. We went out on Saturdays after he was off working. He showed me how to climb a pole. When he gave me climbers—hooks that strap on your legs—I just climbed up the pole, and when I was about twenty feet up I looked down and went, "Oh my God, how do I get down?" He was laughing.

Now, I'm a supervisor, and I train young men to be apprentice linemen. I started out as a grunt, or groundman, and did that for ten months. Then I started climbing poles every day as an apprentice, for four years, before I was a journeyman lineman. I like hard work. I like working outside. I like working with trucks and ropes and men and the thrill of being up in the air.

I think it's a natural instinct for everybody to be afraid of heights. You learn to acknowledge it is scary, but if I want this job I have to lean out there and grab that insulator or grab that wire. I had to put the fear behind me and do what I am asked to do. After you get working on a pole you forget the height. You forget that you're way up there and you concentrate on the task you have to do, because if you fall, you'll get hurt or you're dead. People have to learn to trust in their tools and say, I can now forget about my fear, put it behind me, and do my job.

There's also the fear of a heavy strain, where you have a wire up there that's two pounds a foot and there's a four-hundred-foot span. That's a lot of strain on that pole. If you cut the wrong conductor or guide wire, the pole is going down or it's going to break and you're going down with it.

And then there's weather to deal with. Weather is kind of fun and challenging. We call it "storm fighting." We enjoy it actually. You're on call most of the time, but if a storm hits and you're not on call, you know you're gonna get called. Most guys are right there and are ready to go storm fighting. You get up and put your boots on, and if it's windy and blowing outside, my God, what am I doing now? You go to work, you put your rain gear on, you get the trucks, get with your foreman, get your material, and you head out there. The money in an emergency is good, too.

The first time I did a storm I was probably twenty-three years old. The foreman was driving the truck, the lead lineman was on the passenger side, and I was sitting in the middle. We're going down Dillard Road, which is a long flat road, and every once in a while the whole horizon would light up. What it was, is a grounded wire was touching a hot phase of the twelve thousand kilovolts and it would blow up. It would just light up the whole sky with electrical arcing, and as we get closer and closer, I go, oh my God, I'm going to go fix that? So we got there and we watched the phase touch the ground and blow up. The foreman decided we're gonna de-energize it and ground it. I was pretty happy about that. Then we did the repairs.

I had this one foreman, Tom Mansfield, and he was always real creative and real courageous and real macho. We had wired down number-6 copper wire, and he came up with this plan to grab the wire with ropes, bring it up clear off the ground so it's off any second point of contact, then using a block and tackle to bring it up over the crossarm, and then splice it together hot. Yeah, all hot. We would have a lot of people out of power if we de-energized it. I was game for it, but it was raining hard. So we pulled the wire up, got it up to sag, and the blocks starting melting because of the heat and trying to pick up that wire and the load that was on it. It was turning blue and flames were creeping off of it. We had to bump the wire with hot sticks quickly before the blocks melted and the wire went back down. That was kind of hairy to see the blocks turning blue and bumping the wire. The fear of heights isn't even a component at that time; it's not even a factor. The fear is that the hot wire is twelve thousand volts, phase to phase. What if we're pulling this wire and the blocks melt and the hot wire goes down? If the hot wire goes down and hits something, it could energize the pole that I'm on. We were pretty much in the clear, though, because if the wire goes down hot it'll hit the ground, and hopefully everybody on the ground knows what's going on.

[Mullally pauses to point out several men in training.] See those guys over here on that pole? If they fall right now, it would probably kill them or break their back or paralyze them for the rest of their life. They're probably about twenty-five feet up, working energized, with rubber gloves on, low voltage: 120, 240. And the guys over there are working twelve thousand volts.

The deal is, when you're doing a mundane task that you've done a hundred times, say you're just hooking up a service wire or changing out a crossarm, and it's a nice day like this, that's really the most dangerous time, because you lose your focus, you drop your guard. The wire is there. You can't smell it, but it's twelve thousand volts. You touch it, you're dead. Most people are hurt doing the task they do every day. They fall, they touch a hot wire, and they're burned or electrocuted, or they cut something under strain and the pole breaks or a crossarm breaks.

But when a storm is hitting and sparks are flying from electricity, you're in a zone. You're focused because you see everything that's going wrong and crazy. You have to tell yourself to be careful, this is twelve thousand volts, or this wire is under strain and I'm going to lower down, or I'm climbing this pole right now. Stick to my training, stick to my technique, and climb properly.

You do all the things you're trained to do. You check the pole. Is the pole rotten or cracked? You look up the pole, figure out the path you're gonna take through crossarms or telephone wires or TV wires. You pick the safest path. Maybe an energized wire is touching the wood, so now you have a hot pole. You do those things before you go up. You have these certain things you do every time you climb a pole. You have certain things you do every time before you cut wire, every time you're working energized and you never veer from them. Habits keep you alive in this job.

Normally a wire is hot because it's giving people electricity in their homes. It's an abnormal situation for the wire to be dead. So if you're going to touch that wire, have a habit. What are you gonna do first? Are you gonna put your ground on it? Are you gonna look down the line to see if the other guy grounded it? Then, the boss drives by and says, "Hey, Tom, it's grounded." But you don't see it. Are you gonna grab that wire? Hell no, you're gonna wait for somebody else to go on first. You're gonna pull your hammer out, put it on the wire; the head of your hammer will "zzzzzz"—it will buzz if it's hot. Is that legal? No, but the boss just said it's dead and grounded. Are you taking his word for it? Maybe he missed it. Maybe it wasn't grounded. So now you're putting your ass on the line for him. Habits are the last line of defense.

A bad day at work is when somebody gets hurts, you break a piece of equipment, or you have a near miss. I've had a few of those. As a young man, I wasn't that good. I made some mistakes. One time I was go-like-hell into the macho part of it and working real hard and beating the other guy. I was on a rotten pole and I had it tied to a brand-new pole. I cut the top fifteen feet out of the rotten pole and it fell into some phone wire and took it down to the street with me on it. I was probably about twenty feet up, and I thought I was going to be okay, thinking this phone wire is gonna hold it up and I'm not gonna go all the way down. The top of the pole was right at my chin, so I grabbed the phone wire and wrapped my legs around it like I was just going to ride it. I rode it and it smashed into the street and smashed my ankle, and I headbutted the street and rolled off the pole, but I never went unconscious.

A couple of guys came over and cut my safety off the pole. I knew my ankle was bad, and I said, "Take my boot off. I want to see it." So they cut the tongue of the boot—the boots are like $300—and pulled it off. I was worried that it was a compound fracture. I sat up, looked at it and there was no blood, but it was so painful because a joint got crushed. I was out for fifteen months with that injury.

The worst day at this job, though, was when an apprentice on my crew fell off a pole. We were down south near all open country fields. I believe it was right after Thanksgiving. It had stormed three, four days ahead of time, and we had all kinds of damage to repair. He climbed a pole and was doing an overarm jumper. He got up on the crossarms on his hands and knees, and he was making connections with a jumper. I told him, "Hey, Jim, that's not the way to do that. You need to be strapped to the pole. You don't want to be on that arm doing that. Get on the pole and make those jumpers up." I climbed up the pole and told him how to do it, and then I went to work on another wire. He got off the two crossarms and went to get his hooks back in the pole. He missed and he lost his grip. He fell probably thirty-five to forty feet and landed on his back and his head. I think he died as soon as he hit. I started yelling, "Everybody down, everybody down." He wasn't breathing and he had a lot of blood coming out the back of his head and blood coming out of his ears. One guy started CPR and he wasn't doing it right—he was in a lot of stress—so I moved him out of the way and I started doing the breathing. Another guy started the heart compression. A chopper showed up and they, you know, did their thing and then they pronounced him dead. We never brought him back. He was just married and had a wife who was pregnant.

Everybody starts out scared, and you talk 'em through it. You say, "Hey, I know you're scared. I was scared, too. Put it behind you, and do what I'm telling you to do." The biggest thing is overcoming the fear. You can have a big muscular bodybuilder guy out here that can't do it, and then you have some wiry little kid that grew up out on a ranch that runs up a pole like a rat. He's not scared of anything. That's your lineman.

It doesn't take me long anymore to see which ones are scared. They're hanging on to everything. When they get any height under them, their legs are shaking. They're sweating. You need to coach them and tell them, "Let go, you got to let go. Two hands for the company, not one for you and one for us. We want both of your hands working, so let go and do your job." If they can't do that, they can't do it. Sometimes I'll see a guy that's struggling. He's scared, but he won't give up. He is hardheaded. He wants the job because he knows it's good pay and benefits, and he knows it's a good company. But he can't overcome the fear. He goes home at night and dreams of falling. Comes to work the next morning and he's stressed out, but he has to climb a pole again. Finally, I'll tell him, "Look, you know you're not cut out for this. You're not progressing. You're scared." Some will say, "Yeah, I know," and they are relieved. They go home that night and sleep. But they don't want to admit it to themselves. You just give them that little push. Or, I'll give them the old soul-searching speech: "You know, not everybody is cut out for this; you don't need to be ashamed if you are not dealing with the fear; sometimes it takes more of a man to admit I can't do this, and now I'm moving on rather than keep struggling."

There are some guys you could call a "hot dog" that climb really fast. He's completely fearless, though sometimes he can be dangerous because he's going too fast and gets careless. The wild man gets a lot of work done, but you better watch him, because he's fixing to hurt himself or somebody else. The guy you want is the guy that climbs confident, smooth, and graceful. He thinks about his job, thinks about the electricity, thinks about the strains, and is methodical.

Then you got the guys that somehow got through but are not enjoying the work. I tell them, "If you don't get off on this job, if you don't get a thrill from it and enjoy doing it, don't do it. It's too dangerous and it's too hard." If you do get off, it's a blast. We buy excellent trucks, excellent equipment, and we have excellent training, but if they don't enjoy it, don't stay here to be a lineman only because the benefits are good and the money is good. They're not going to be happy.

I was a hot dog at first. I was a wild man. I'd go out drinking with the boys at night and raise hell, go to work, and do it again the next day. Once, I got hit by 6.9 thousand volts, and it knocked me out. I'm not proud of those mistakes. In this business, if you get hurt, you're fucked up. You didn't do your job right. It's very embarrassing to get hurt. I don't really like talking about it, but that's the fact.

I matured after I rode that pole down. It was probably the best thing that could have happened to me. I lived through it, and I'm not a cripple, and it brought me to my senses to slow down and think about what you're doing. I then volunteered to be a trainer, and when I started teaching, I started learning the correct way to do things, not the hot dog way.

I started in '76. I'm getting older. It's hard on the body. It's a tough job in the heat and then in the storms. I love working outside and sweating and working harder than the next guy. Now, I love passing down the trade to young men, especially in the world today where a lot of them want to play Game Boy or sit at the computer and eat chips and cupcakes and Coke. There are still young men around that will come outside and work and bust their ass and are thrilled to learn the trade. I just love those guys.

JOEL HELGEVOLD

COMMERCIAL FISHERMAN

A light snow falls on Kodiak Harbor this early morning. Joel Helgevold is on the deck of his father's Arctic Dawn *while a welder fixes a hole in the bow that was caused when the boat hit a rock two days earlier.*

"Superstitions? Well, here's one: If you whistle in the wheelhouse, you're going to whistle up a storm. I don't know where the origins are, but I've heard it since I was little. Another one is—see this big hatch on the deck, we move it to off-load the fish—if it was flipped upside down on the boat or moved or whatever, there's a superstition that your boat will roll or turn upside down. I'm not saying I so much as believe it, but it is a superstition. I've never seen a boat turn over, and I hope to God I never do."

★ ★ ★

I'm a son of a son of a sailor. My dad's dad owned a boat, my dad owns a boat. I'm gonna own a boat, and that's how it is.

When I first went out, I was only six months old. I credit that to me never getting seasick in my whole life. I've been in some seas, too.

I grew up with my old man, so I'll stick with him. We're going broke or making billions, that's what I know. You better have your heart into it, because you're going to be busting your ass. I've seen a lot of people quit just because it was too hard. They say, "I'm done with this. I want to go home. Bring me back to the dock." Come on, man, we all signed up for the same reason: to make money. I don't know why else I would be in this frigging Alaska. If I just wanted to live life doing something else, I would live in Acapulco. I want to make big money.

To tell you the truth, man, I just like being with my dad. He knows his shit. If we're out on the ocean, I don't have a care. Like I said, I grew up in this. The ocean is what I know. I know a little bit about mechanics and stuff and what it takes to run a boat, but we're not a one-man show. It takes a team to make this run.

I'm going to live on the ocean and I am going to die on the ocean. I feel more at peace on the ocean than I do on land. It's like serenity. It's peaceful. All you see is water, and if it's a nice day you're at peace. I'm with my family. There is nowhere else I would rather be. I can't explain it.

A good day is making money. My dad owns the boat. I don't know if he's making a whole lot of money, but he wouldn't be here if he wasn't making money. It ain't nothing like the old days, when we used to just catch crab and would gross six to seven hundred thousand dollars, and I'd get 7 to 8 percent of that. That's a lot of money, but that was a while ago, man. It's not like that no more. For some people it is, but not for this boat.

It's a bad day when nothing goes right. We break a hose. We break a board. We break a piece of metal. On any day that pump over there could turn around and take a shit on us. That thing is so big it can pump more fish than we can handle. Sometimes it doesn't want to work; sometimes it does. That's a $30,000 pump. We got it for a thousand dollars off of a boat called the *Cleo* that burned up about two years ago.

We got a big ninety-six-foot boat, twenty-eight feet wide. It was built in Hood River, Oregon, in 1982. This boat is seaworthy, I tell you. It weighs 250 tons. We've got three times as many ribs in the front as normal boats. This boat was custom built for somebody. Good thing it was, because we got ribs peeled from the ~~fucking~~ we took two days ago. It was nighttime and the wind was blowing about forty miles an hour, and it was snowing. We couldn't see in front of our hands. We bumped into a rock on the north side of Kodiak Island, and we had about a five-inch gash in the bow and we were taking on a little bit of water, not a lot, maybe a couple hundred gallons. It takes a lot of impact to do something like that. We have what's called a "crash void." If you hit something, the water goes in there and doesn't go anywhere else.

I woke ~~the fuck~~ up, right away, hearing and feeling it, almost like it was an earthquake. It wasn't nothing nice. I knew right away we hit something, so I ran up to the wheelhouse in my boxers and socks. My dad was up there, but he had went down to grab a pack of cigarettes—that's as long as it took. I see nothing but a big mountain right in front of us. Then I ran on the bow to look and see where we were at, and the port side had a big rock shooting up higher than the bow—that's about forty or fifty feet. Our aft tank was full of water, so we pumped the aft tank out, put the boat in reverse, and we're off that rock. That rock is now a gravel pit.

When the boat starts rocking, you gotta get your balance. I've been knocked over by waves, and that's not a good feeling. You're talking about standing right there by that rail and the boat takes a roll this way, a roll that way, and the next thing you know a roll comes and you got waves crashing over the bow. When you're out fishing, you aren't tied down. The water is coming up so fast you can't even place your feet. You have to spread your legs to where you can balance yourself. The way boats are built these days, you have more shelter. You're eating the weather, but you're not eating it as bad as people would think. But fuck, when those waves out there get to be twenty to thirty feet, that's not a joke.

I've never gone overboard, but I've rescued a couple of people. I've had to pluck people out of the water when they're crossing between boats. People try to cross as we get into town, because when we get into town everybody parties and has their girlfriends and stuff. I've had to pull two people out of the water with the crane. You're talking about steel bumpers between both boats, and if the boats want to come together they're going to come together. One guy—his name was Hector; he passed away about four months ago—all he cared about was his watch that he's holding out of the water. He's in the water in between the boats, and the boats are coming back and forth, and it's shitty weather. His head could get crushed at any minute, but all he cares about is his watch. I had to rescue him.

Another memorable time was a couple of years ago when we had the Discovery Channel people on the boat. What happened was, I was running the boat, and we're moving crab pots on the back of the boat and all of a sudden, everything went down. The lights went down, the pots stopped hauling, and we're like, "What the hell is going on?" We open the engine room door, and white smoke was so thick you couldn't see one foot in front of your face. A hydraulic clutch for the winches to bring the crab pots up had burned up somehow. We were about two hundred miles from any nearest land. Well, good thing we got three generators and two Caterpillar engines that propel us, so we have a backup for a backup in case something like that happens. When you're two hundred miles from the beach, that's off-the-wall shit.

We used to be crabbers, but I wouldn't call us crabbers no more. We're fishermen. Crabbing's been changing since back in the day. The seasons are getting shorter. The last season we fished for three days and caught eighty-five thousand pounds. Crabs are down three hundred fathoms—that's eighteen hundred feet. That's deep. They're down there, but if you don't find them within those three days, you're screwed. When we were crabbing, we had five guys on deck and my dad, who's the skipper. The government made the quota so low some boats didn't even have a crab to eat. The government took what crab we had. It used to be a derby. If Fish and Game says the quota is twenty million pounds to catch, then as soon as they think twenty million pounds of any kind of crab are caught—king crab, red king crab, brown king crab, blue king crab, opilio, you're talking about all kinds of different crab—then everybody is done. Basically, our family business got snuffed out. We used to live off of the crab. My dad knows where they're at, and we catch a lot when we go, but if the government is gonna give us a certain amount and give every-body a certain amount to kind of equal it out, you know . . . even the lazy people and the fucking people that don't know where the crab are, they're allowed to fish. It used to be a free-for-all derby, but it's not that way anymore. It makes me mad talking about it.

Crabbing is hard. On my first trip—probably when I was like fourteen—we were out for like two and a half months. After that trip, I never wanted to eat or see or touch another crab again. I was so worn out. I said, "Man, I'm tired, I want to go to sleep." Then an old guy told me, "You will sleep enough when you're dead."

Fishing is for a different breed, for sure. It's hard to explain, man. You've got to have heart, I guess. I brought one of my friends from Anchorage out and he didn't like it at all, because sometimes you just work and work and work. But the whole time you're saving money. It's not like you're working in the city, buying a coffee every day. On a boat, you're saving your money. You got your food. You got your warmth.

If someone says they want to put in the effort to do it, you put them to the test to see if that's what they want. This is fucking hard, for years and years and years. We're talking eighteen to twenty hours a day in the wintertime. You might work for two months straight every single day. But when it's done, when the fish is caught and you're back at home, you get your time off.

You could make a lot of money. It could be bust or it could be lucrative, it's hard to tell. Fishing is wishing, that's what my dad told me, and that's what my motto is. You could catch a lot and make it rich and never have to work for the rest of your life, or you could catch something and wish that you caught more. That's just fishing, you know. You don't get paid by the hour, you get paid by the pound. If you don't catch a pound, you don't make a dime. If you catch a hundred million pounds, you make a lot of money.

There is no doubt in my mind that I'm going to fish again. I'm going to fish from here to China if I have to, but right now I'm looking forward to getting the hell off Kodiak Island.

KATIE ROWE

STUNTWOMAN

*K*atie Rowe has a black belt in mixed martial arts, is a master scuba instructor, and is a certified lifeguard. She can kickbox, handle tactical weapons, bail out of cars, and surf, and she is willing to be put on fire. "We have a kind of a phone directory of stuntpeople, the Stunt Players Directory. I'm always the biggest girl listed, so normally any time they need a prison matron, a biker, a thug, a giant lesbian, or a girl to get in a fight with a guy, that's me. I get a lot of that. Apparently those people are all really big in the real world."

★ ★ ★

Katie Rowe

I'm a professional Hollywood stuntwoman. I work in TV and movies and commercials and videos and everything else under the sun. It's always something different.

Sometimes when I say I'm a "stuntwoman," people kind of say, "You're a stunt what?" I think they think, "She couldn't have said stunt*woman*." I guess if you say stunt*man*, people would probably recognize that more easily. And then they are like, "Oh, you work in film and movies," and then there's always the, "What can I see you in?" Normally, I say that you can't see us. The stuntperson will do the stunt, and then the actor will do the walk up—the "cowboy switch" as they call it where the actor lies down where the stuntperson has fallen, and then carry on with the scene. Normally, you don't see the stuntpeople because they are very adaptive in turning their shoulders and dipping their heads so they can hide their faces.

I'm either doubling for actresses, which is pretty rare for me because I'm tall at six foot two, or playing my own character, normally as the big-mean-bad person. I'll do almost anything risky that either the actor wouldn't want to do or the production didn't want the actor to do, knowing that if the actor—especially a well-known actor—gets hurt or cut or scarred, it would bring production to a halt, which obviously would cost them a huge amount of money and time to replace or repair the actor.

I think people always assume stuntpeople have some superhuman *Matrix* powers, like all we do is fly off buildings all day long and karate chop people. There's always a lot of duct tape and bubblegum and mirrors and wires behind all of it, not to say some people can't do phenomenal things, because they absolutely can, but combined with a little of dash of movie magic, it's really pretty amazing.

Sometimes, stuntwork is sitting around all day, and sometimes it's very specialized, like crashing a car or jumping off a building. Like if the character falls off of a tall building or jumps off a building, that's a very specialized skill to be able to land without snapping your neck. Usually, people who are high divers, or people that are very comfortable with heights, end up doing those types of stunts.

Growing up, I swam the whole time and did a little bit of modeling. I always liked being the center of attention—I guess you could say, being loud—but I never wanted to be an actor. I was never one of the kids that, you know, said, "Since I was five years old, I knew I wanted to be a stuntwoman." I didn't even have a clue what stunt-people were, and I don't think I thought about it during college. When I got out of college, I had a lot of friends that were athletes because I was on our national swim team and the varsity swim team at UCLA. A lot of them were getting into sports modeling, and at that time, sports commercials were becoming really popular.

I got hooked up with this sport agent who would send me out, and, of course, I would only get sent out for things like basketball and other sports that I was obviously horrible at. I did some swimming things and a couple other things, and then from then on I just knew I wanted to do something along those lines. And, I was too big to model—like probably fifty pounds too big. You have to be about as big as a pencil, obviously, and I was obviously not fourteen years old anymore. So I kind of started working as an extra, just to kind of see what the movie business was about. That was fun because it's like playing dress up every day, and you get to go somewhere new.

Eventually, I worked as a stand-in, which is kind of a higher step up in the extra universe. A stand-in is the person who stands in for an actor, while they're setting the lighting. The actor may be making up their hair or just resting. You're paid more relative to the extras, which I think at the time minimum wage was four-something, so I was making eight dollars an hour, which was a huge raise of course. I actually got a job standing in for John Corbett, the actor who was on *Sex and the City* for a while, because he thought it would be cool to have a girl stand-in. I had to wear this little brown wig and I would pull it on and stand there in the lighting. You may have to stand in a little pose for, you know, five or ten minutes, mimicking whatever the actor has to do.

Then, on a show about twelve years ago, the stunt coordinator said, "You should get into stunts." I was like, "Okay, I'll do stunts"—still really having no clue. As much as I love being on camera, I know I'm just not an actor. I just am not that dedicated to studying acting, and I don't feel I come across that well on camera to talk. He then was kind of my mentor, because in the stunt world, you need somebody to kind of take you under their wing and say to others like, "She's okay." He kind of pointed me in the right direction.

Having grown up being an athlete, I had great respect for their skills. I never remembered feeling awed in a sense of, oh wow, that's just phenomenal, although I've certainly seen phenomenal things and still do to this day. I have an athlete's respect. It's like seeing Brett Favre throw a pass—not that you think you can do it—but it's like you understand the training and work that has gone into it. Stuntpeople struck me as being very disciplined, hardworking people.

The stunt universe is very small, and there's just not a lot of room for people who think they are just gonna skate along. Stuntpeople tend to be diligent and precise about what they do; also, because you don't want to get killed and you don't want to kill someone else, they tend to be kind of methodical about what goes on.

Obviously the younger you are, generally the better condition you're in, and you're more resilient. You might have a case where an actress always wants some stunt double who is tiny and not a pound heavier than they are, which is very difficult when you have a very nonathletic actor or actress with no muscle on their body, and then you have to match them to make something very physical. So we get these really tiny little stunt-double girls who then start thinking they're kind of invincible.

And, I've seen this with the guys who think, "I can do it all; I don't need to listen." A lot of times it's not so much their physical skills, it's more of their on-set behavior that ends up maybe costing them their job. Or, maybe they mouth off too much or they try to get too chummy with their actor or just kind of hinder production—they start thinking it's all about them. There's no doubt they can do amazing things, but then they start feeling like, let's everybody pay attention to me. Well, when you're spending hundreds of millions of dollars on the movie, it's not really all about little twenty-one-year-old Sally. Those are the kind of the people who get washed out.

I was mentored by somebody who's kind of old school, you know, show up, shut up, do your job. You show up, bring all your gear; directors don't want your opinion on how to do it. You basically do what you're told to do. If they ask your opinion, you give it, or they are like, I need this pad moved here. That's fine, but they don't want your opinion on why don't we do this or what if he came this way? The director obviously has a reason that the actor has to come from this side, or the person has to jump from here. They don't need you rewriting the scene or resetting the set.

You always have to be prepared, have your bag right at your side, and be ready to carry or move stuff without being asked. A lot of the really old-school guys would insist that you always have a knife in your pocket at all times in case there's some rope or rigging that needs to be cut. I normally have one in my bag.

People really don't like—especially on TV—tiny women getting abused by a man, especially by a much larger man, although it seems to be okay for a really big and attractive woman to get knocked around by a man. I guess it probably strikes a lot of people as really not fair when you have some six-foot-five hulking guy beating on this five-foot-three average housewife woman. I've actually done fights on TV where it's supposed to end with the guy grabbing me and killing me, and then all producers would rush in and have this twenty-minute meeting and they'd decide maybe the actor would just like give me a stern pointing-to and let me go instead of killing me.

Also, I tend to get called for the side gag with, you know, the tiny little guy. I remember doing one scene in *Numbers* where the guy comes up—I'm sitting in my car parked at a light—it's like, "Give me your keys!" Well, of course, the guy is five foot three. So I get out of the car and I stand up and hulk over him, then I grab him and clock him.

I try to make my niche in water stunts and anything having to do with water, from scuba to rough water swimming. For instance, I trained all the actors for the *Poseidon* remake. We did a little bit of scuba training and then, because a lot of people are very uncomfortable in water, we had them swim long distances, maybe breathe off a regulator underwater and then drop it, so they can swim while on camera. We did it so that the actors didn't panic.

I love the water, but sometimes not after soaking in it all day. For *Poseidon*, I would get to work maybe by seven, be in the water by seven thirty, get out at one o'clock for an hour-long lunch, get back in the water at two, and stay in the water till nine or ten at night. It was in an enormous multimillion-gallon tank at Warner Brothers where they filmed *The Perfect Storm*. I mean it's a huge tank, they could build an airplane in there. Sitting in the tank all day, every day, day after day, is a little uncomfortable. I was never dry, and I ended up getting a yeast infection in my ear, which was really nasty. Of course the actors have to get in for *three minutes* and they complain about how cold it is, and you're thinking, I've been in here for *four hours* and I haven't gone to the bathroom yet and I haven't had a bite to eat. There are plenty of actors that I've wanted to actually hold underwater until they stop breathing, that's for sure.

I'm a water person, but you usually kind of try to become a jane-of-all-trades, because you never know, you may get a call to do that. I've gotten calls to do smaller high falls, so you want to be prepared and know the drill. It's like you want to taste everything so you know what you're up against. I kind of get the tiptoe-up-to-the-edge feeling. I've seen people run backward, break out a fake window on fire, and fall down 150 feet. I wouldn't even think of doing that.

But I've been on fire, and have done a couple of explosions. We wear Carbon-X fire suits, just like race car drivers do under their clothing, and then put gel over that and on any exposed skin. It still usually gets hot. You look at your arm and notice that it's on fire. Doing full burns requires you to hold your breath, because the fire is consuming all the oxygen. The stuntpeople doing those will precisely time out the explosion again and again. They'll have a bunch of guys in full fire suits and hoods, like NASCAR guys, standing there with fire extinguishers. The stuntperson will be running, and as soon as he drops to the ground and signals if he's suddenly in trouble, they put out the fire no matter what. It's kind of a claim to fame about how long you can do a full burn. It obviously becomes quite dangerous after a time. People do get burned, and they don't usually realize it because severe burns will burn the nerves.

I'll tell you what normally happens: The stunt coordinator will call you and be like, "I've got this job," and it kind of all depends on how much they need you. If there's an actress at six foot two and they can't find anybody else, they're gonna have to either train me to do it, or get me to do it, or hope that I can do it, or they're gonna have to hope somebody else is relatively close who can do it. For instance, they may call and go, "I've got this full burn on a show. Are you comfortable doing it? What's your experience?" I may say, "Well, I've done a partial burn, but if you give me a couple of days I'll practice it." They may be okay with that or they may not, depending on how risky the job is. They also may say, "This is a really crazy situation: You're also falling over a banister and five feet to the ground." So then immediately you'll call up all your stunt friends that specialize in fire and say, "I got to do a full burn," and they rush out and they're like, "Okay, come out to my house this afternoon, we'll work on it. We got the gel, we'll light you up."

Same with high falls. I have friends that have fifty-foot towers built in their backyard to practice high falls off of. Everybody will go over there and you say, "I really need help." Or, I'll have friends call me and go, "I need help because I'm doing a scuba thing." I will be like, "Come on over, we'll hop in the pool this afternoon and I will tune you up." You know they will do the same thing. Everyone benefits. It's kind of almost your job to like help and pass along your knowledge, because these are people that you're going to be working with some day, and if they're not safe, they could end up hurting or killing you. It's your benefit to have everybody be as knowledgeable as possible.

In my stunt bag, I have a full Carbon-X suit, two hoods, two pairs of gloves, two pairs of socks. The joke is that you buy expensive stuff like that, then you'll never do another burn again. Then I also have shin guards and all sort of different types of knee pads: hard knee pads, soft thin ones and thicker ones, elbow pads, four different back pads. Trying to think of what else. I also have a mouth guard, hairbrush, deodorant, four different bras, a white T-shirt, and a little pair of bike shorts to wear under a fitted harness—for when they hook you up to fly, or to pull you, or drag you. I would say that's kind of the common stunt bag.

The young stuntgirls always want to be wearing something sexy, and you see the older stuntgirls are always like, "No, I'll take the long sleeves and the jeans," because you want to be able to fit on all your pads. The young people are always like, "No, I don't need pads," and the old people are like putting on every single pad they have, because that's how you preserve yourself. If you don't preserve yourself, you don't end up with much of a career.

I've trained a lot for movie fighting, and I've always liked it. If you're fighting an actor, you don't want to be anywhere remotely close to them. In movie fighting, you're kind of faking the punches, or you're filming them at an angle where it looks like you're hitting somebody but you're really six inches away. But the problem with actors or untrained people is they don't know how to fight, or they get excited, or they jump in six inches closer than you planned. Then the actor has a bloody nose, which of course comes back to you, because you're supposed to be the one that knows what to do. But sometimes you can't prevent it. I have seen stuntpeople lose their jobs for doing so.

Fighting stuntpeople is great, because you know they can take it, and even though you're not really fighting, sometimes you can hit them in the stomach. Actually, I would prefer being hit in the stomach, because then you don't have to fake your reaction and it's easier to "sell the hit," which is what we call it; you can just gasp and groan through it. We get paid really well for what we do, so they expect you to sell it and give it everything you can. If it means you hit the ground extra hard or throw yourself onto the concrete wearing just a tank top and shorts, then that's what you do. Those are the ones that you just know are gonna hurt, and the worst part is when you finish and you get up and they go, "Okay, let's see it again." You feel like, "Oh no," but you got to do it, though I would rather be punched in the arm than drilled in the face.

A lot of the fighting motions on camera are unnatural, but some-times that's what you have to do to make it look right, or you might have to cheat a little and turn your body extra or kind of cheat where I may be looking 10 degrees off to the side. A lot of times we have the biggest trouble teaching real fighters how to do on-camera stuff, because their instinct is to do fight correctly, but we're like, we can't have you do it correctly because it doesn't work like that on camera.

A lot of people think we're daredevils, which makes stuntpeople furiously angry, because we really try to disassociate from anyone who claims to be a daredevil, like the car crasher guy at the fair who does the daredevil show. What we do is very rehearsed and practiced and controlled to the ultimate degree we possibly can. Obviously, there is risk involved and things can go a little awry, but we go out of our way to ensure that every detail is considered. We rehearse and rehearse. Like for anytime they do a big car chase scene, the coordinator breaks out little matchbox cars and lines up all the little cars on little lines drawn on the road, and he goes, "All right, Bob, you're gonna be in this red matchbox here and you're gonna chase this one. Katie, you're gonna be in this blue one and you're gonna do this," and we'll work our set in and then we'll all line up and we will walk through it like we're in the cars. We practice those things again and again to ensure that nobody gets hurt. It's not just "let's put on a show in the barn" kind of thing.

On *NCIS*, for instance, we did a fight where five of us storm into this room and grab this guy and beat him. There's all these different fights going while I'm standing outside the door peeking through the crack, and then I bust in. You hope that this group didn't get too far ahead of this other group, because then everybody kind of has to fake something until it can all comes together at the end. You hope that everybody is exactly where they need to be. I certainly have been in things where I've been the one to mess up; it's not a good feeling, and you get yelled at. Like one time I was supposed to grab a girl and punch her across the face, but where the camera angle was it looked like a miss—that's where they can see that your hand is obviously not going across the face—so I hear, "Damn it, Katie."

You always want to know where your "out" is, because it's better always to stop and regroup if you need to. We usually have a preapproved signal, especially when you're with other people, like I'm gonna just raise my arms or something. I remember once there were five of us sitting in front of a window that was supposed to explode toward us. We all discussed it, like Jeff says, "I'm gonna go to my left," and I say, "Okay, I'm gonna go straight back," and another person says, "I'm gonna duck under the table." You don't want two people both thinking that we're gonna go under the table, and then knock each other out. You also may be at the point where we abort the stunt, like if I get to this particular point and Bob isn't right behind me, then I'm gonna just say, "Cut." Yes, I've cut scenes where I've seen us, say, start an underwater scene but I see somebody isn't prepared, or is starting to freak out.

I worked on a movie called *Dance Flick*, which came out in 2009. It's a spoof of different movies, kind of like *Scary Movie*. In it, they're spoofing some music video where a beautiful young girl is frolicking on the beach, and she is out in the water when a shark drags her out to sea and eats her. My boss was like, "Go put on a bikini, we're gonna use you," and I'm like, "Oh great, I had extra lunch today." So, I'm in the water, and they dump me into this big foamy shark. I rigged this tiny regulator thing over my head with literally not an inch to spare. They are slowly dragging me out to sea, and I'm in this big shark that's filling with water, and there is no way to get yourself out. You have to hope that your safety people are there to grab you out. I'm supposed to be thrashing in this thing, so we made up signals, that once I tap my legs together side to side, they would come and yank me out. The coordinator is like, "Hold your breath as long as you can and thrash around, and hopefully we will be right there!" But it takes seconds after you start doing the signal to have people actually come from off camera. I made it, but I would not want to get in that sucker again. You know, I'm extremely comfortable in the water. But this was probably the most terrifying thing I had ever done. It was quite unpleasant, but it was exciting.

I also worked on *Wild Hogs* [in the scene] where John Travolta blows up the bar, and we're standing outside. They built this bar in the middle of nowhere in Albuquerque, and they had the whole bar set with miles and miles of primer cord and explosives and fuel and whatever else they used. I remember they had all these Harleys set to blow up fifty feet in the air and then come down. So the gas trickles, and all these fire lines start going past us, and we're supposed to stand there looking around cluelessly, like we don't know what will happen. I remember the bar explodes and I'm standing wearing my leathers and Nomex, totally coated in gel, and it's 110 degrees outside. I remember the wave of heat washed over me, like it happened in slow motion, and I thought, I'm literally on the face of the sun. I also remember looking up and thinking, it's raining Harleys, like things that big should not be falling out of the sky. But we're supposed to hesitate, and then give the "Oh, no!" and start running. They wanted us to stay as long as possible. It had been rehearsed over and over with about fifty people. I got a couple of blisters on my hands, because afterward we had to go back in and get the bikes and push them out, but we hadn't thought about how hot they had gotten from the heat. That was just one of those things you couldn't plan for.

I wouldn't say I'm a seasoned veteran. I never have felt like I was that agile of an athlete. Swimmers aren't necessarily agile, but I've always felt powerful as an athlete, just not particularly flippy and bendy and floppy like the aerial gymnastic people are. So I've been always cautious of what I did. I was certainly willing to take the big hard hits; we call it "groundpounds." Groundpounders are the ones where you're gonna get knocked on your ass and it's gonna suck, and that's how it is. That usually tends to be my deal, because I'm a big person. So, if an actor has to knock me down, I'm gonna grab the actor so they land on *me* and people are gonna be tackling *me*, meaning I'm normally on the bottom of the pile.

The job is fun. You get to play dress up every time you go to work. I've been everything. Like a couple of weeks ago on *NCIS,* I was a prison guard. They gave attention to every detail of my little military uniform and my gun, and how I'm running down the hall. And the next day I can maybe be a biker in a gay parade and riding a Harley. And the day after that I'm a bikini girl doing whatever. There is always something different.

Most stuntpeople I know spend their free time training or practicing or going out with other stuntpeople. And I would say that most stuntpeople I know either date or are married to other stuntpeople, because they understand the business, or learn to adapt to it. I've been on vacations where I've had to fly home early because I don't want to pass up a job, because in the long run it could be great earnings. But it can be very hard, and people outside of the film industry don't understand; it looks like just complete chaos to them. I could get a call right now at two o'clock for an audition today at five, which means I'd be running home to grab my stuff and drive there. But I guess that's kind of what makes it neat, because I know Monday morning at eight I won't be at work, or I may be in an airplane or on roller skates.

I'd like to do it forever. I just love every day at work, so I guess I'll do it as long as my body holds out.

BOBBY BURRELL

NASCAR RACE ENGINEER

*B*obby Burrell is thirty-seven years old. In the shop of Robby Gordon Motorsports in Charlotte, North Carolina, he talks about the past thirteen years working on NASCAR pit crews. "It's entertainment for people who are watching at home or in the stands. To us, it's life. It's a tough job. This is what we do year-round. There is no off-season. You're building cars to race in Daytona in January, and you're still trying to build cars to go race when November comes around. You might spend Thanksgiving with your family and then you maybe have a couple of days off before Christmas, and then you get ready to go to Daytona. I just can't take a week off during the racing season and go spend a week at the beach with my family."

★ ★ ★

Bobby Burrell

I'm the race car engineer for Robby Gordon Motorsports. I work on the engineering part of race cars from the aerodynamics to the kinematics, which entails the way the car handles and performs out on the racetrack week in and week out. These race cars are not like passenger cars. They have a lot of science built into them.

Back in the sixties and seventies, when NASCAR was just really getting up on its feet, they actually used passenger cars. They basically threw the interior out and tried to lighten the car up as best as they could, and then they went racing. Nowadays, it's totally different. We build the car from scratch. We assemble what we need to assemble to make the car go round and round.

I grew up around racing in a little town called Hot Springs in Virginia. I'd build street rods with my father, and go dirt racing, if I wasn't playing sports when I was in high school, or I'd go drag racing with my buddies. The mechanics of a car was just one of those things that I grew up around.

After high school, I went to college at Syracuse University and couldn't really make up my mind what I wanted to do, and then as time went on I kind of decided to be an engineer. I majored in mechanical and chemical engineering, and then kind of got tired of school. It took me a little bit to get out of school, because I couldn't make up my mind if I wanted to party and have fun, or be serious and get an education, but I got it. I graduated in mechanical engineering in '95.

I started in NASCAR thirteen years ago as a team engineer. The way the team was structured was you were an engineer and you were a jack-of-all-trades. You learned how to set the car up, you learned how to build shocks, you learned how to build crush panels and windows, you learned what it takes to completely put one of these cars out on the racetrack. You need to know everything about the car that makes it run, from the hubs to the brakes to the motor to the aerodynamic side of the car to the shocks to the springs. If you don't, then you're limited in your value.

Over the years, I've worked for guys like Dale Earnhardt, Ricky Rudd, Casey Mears, Reed Sorenson. I've been here with Robby

Gordon since January. It's kind of a soap opera with guys bouncing around and drivers moving from one team to another, crew guys moving from one team to another, sponsors leaving, sponsors coming. It's a dog-eat-dog world in this industry.

Here, we are a small team. I'd say we have fifty people. We have unique people that do unique jobs. You can't come in off the street and say, I want to go racing. That's fine, glad you have the heart and desire, but what knowledge do you bring to the table that you can make the car go faster? Time is the essence, it's all about time. How fast can the car go? How fast can you get done with pit road? Money buys speed, it helps make the car go fast, and it helps get fast pit crews, but money don't buy time.

On race day, you get up before the crack of dawn and go to the racetrack when most people haven't even rolled over. You go in and start doing race preparation. What I do on race day is that I make sure our timing and scoring is up so that we can track the car and how it's going on the racetrack, what our position is, how fast Robby is going. I'll get my fuel mileage programs up and running to know how many laps we can make on a tank of fuel. Like last weekend at Richmond, you could probably go a hundred laps on a tank of fuel, which is roughly right around four miles per gallon.

During a race, when the driver comes in for a pit stop, say for fuel, I'll stop doing what I'm doing on top of the pit box where I am with the crew chief, and I'll run down to change tires. The pit box is where the crew chief, race engineer, and some other people sit to observe the race from a higher level. I'm watching for time and scoring, kind of to see where we stand next to the other competitors and if the car is losing speed or why we're losing speed. The crew chief is sitting right next to me so I can tell him what's going on about what I see.

The crew chief is essentially like the director of the team: He is the leader, next to the driver. How it works is, there's the driver, crew chief, car chief, race engineer. You also usually have a couple of mechanics, and the pit crew that are the guys that go over the wall, which ranges from a front tire changer and tire carrier to a jack man, a rear tire changer and carrier, the gas man, the catch-can man (the catch-can man goes to the back of the car to catch excess fuel that could come out of the car so it doesn't spill all over). Sometimes they'll allow an eighth man that services the driver, for like cleaning the windshield and handing the driver a drink.

I'm thirty-seven years old, and I've changed tires and been over the wall for twelve years. I've changed both front and rear. I used to change rear tires many years ago. The front to me is easier on your body, because you're not chasing the car. In the front, the car is coming to you.

When I started in the industry, they said I was big enough to be a jack man. I'm like, no I'm not. I'm too short. I'm five foot eight. I tried it, but it just wasn't my forte. It's a technique, not just all brute strength.

Fuel guys need brute strength and good eye-hand coordination to hit the gas hole. Catch-can guys have got to have some strength just so you can hold the gas can if the gas man steps back to get a second can or to make adjustments.

The tire carrier is finesse and strength, because tire weight will range anywhere between forty pounds to eighty pounds depending upon if it's got inner liners. The tire changer needs hand speed, eye-hand coordination, and overall body strength. You're carrying a four-pound air gun and you're running out there and you're dropping down on your knees and you got to go from the right-hand side of the car to the left-hand side of the car right in around two seconds to do a thirteen-second pit stop. Your mind has to be sharp.

Changing a tire takes about four and a half to five seconds. It takes quite a bit of time in your passenger vehicle compared to this, trust me. This takes a lot of athleticism. It's not the kind of job that any Joe Blow Shmoe thinks they can come do. That's not being negative, it's the reality of life, because not everybody can go out and play football, not everybody can go out and play basketball or baseball, and not everybody can drive a race car. There again, not everybody can be a pit crew member. You can go to a training school to learn the skills of the trade, but it still doesn't replace real time.

For me, going over the wall means thirteen seconds of pure madness. What I do is I jump across the wall and change both front tires. A pit stop usually takes anywhere between twelve and a half seconds to thirteen and a half seconds. I've done eleven seconds top.

What happens is that you will see the car coming down pit road, and when he crosses the back line of the pit stall behind you, you jump off the wall and I'll run to the right front tire and knock the five lug nuts off with a Ingersoll Rand air gun. This air gun is not like an air gun you'd see at a Penske Auto Center when you go get your tires changed; it's an air gun built on steroids, because it moves fast and it moves hard. When you squeeze the trigger on the air gun, that's when you hear these great big whines on pit road.

The speed that the car is coming at you ranges from thirty-five to sixty miles an hour. You go run in front of your car and sit down. The jack man will carry the jack over, and when the car comes to a complete stop, he'll jack the car up. My tire guy is running behind me with a tire. What I do is I'll start hitting the lug nuts before he jacks the car up. Then I'll pull the tire off. As soon as I pull the tire off, the tire carrier puts on the tire to replace the one I just took off, and then I'll hit the lug nuts and tighten the tire out. As soon as that gets done, I'll jump up and run to the left front side to repeat the process. Somebody is in the back of the car doing the same thing.

When you go over the wall nowadays, from what it was seven years ago, you have to have a helmet on. Underneath your helmet you usually have a set of headphones that's molded to your ears so that you can hear what's going on. You also have to wear a double-layer Nomex fire suit, which is mandated by NASCAR, all the time, all day long. And you have knee pads and gloves and, of course, your equipment that you're using, like the air gun or jack.

The height of the wall varies from track to track. I'd say like Richmond International Raceway is probably two foot, and Homestead-Miami Speedway is probably about three foot; it just depends on what track it is and when the model was built. Miami is the hardest place for me, because it's so tall and wide, and I'm so short. Basically I got to crawl over that wall; it's not just step up on the wall. It's pretty bad.

Yeah, I've been off. You go out there and instead of hitting five lug nuts, you start stabbing at it and you look like you're trying to cut a cord of wood. If your body is trying to go faster than your mind is going, you're gonna mess up. You always hear, "slow is fast." Well, fast is fast, but in between you got to find a happy medium, and that is how fast can you do it right and not mess up.

There's a lot of variables that play in how many pit stops you're gonna make. Last week we did, I'd say, eight pit stops. It depends on conditions, like tire wear, what kind of fuel mileage we're getting, if you're involved in an accident and you had to come in for body damage, and if you have a flat tire. We are somewhat limited on the amount of tires that we can have depending on how much money you have to spend, but then NASCAR also dictates that you can only have say ten sets of tires. A set of four tires is about $1,400.

There is no stress out there. Now this is me and my thinking: The only stress that's there for a pit crew person is the stress you put on yourself. If you've done this job for X amount of time, it's like second nature. If you're on the right-hand side of the car, you got cars coming down pit road beside you, but I'm not thinking about getting hit. I've been hit. I've been hit several times, but you don't think about that. You think about, I will go there and I will hit five lug nuts, pull the tire, put the lugs on, go to the other side of the car, and how fast can I do it and can I do it right? That's all you will think.

The risks in this job are that you can get run over, get your leg broken, you can break your hand inside a wheel, you can get hit by a tire that gets away, another car maybe hits the tire and it comes flying back at you and hits you. I've been hit by a car going by. I had my ankle run over in 2000, at Martinsville Speedway. I was on the right side of the car changing the front tire. I dropped down to the ground and a car comes in too close and drove over my ankle. It stretched all the ligaments and stuff. I went to the infield care center, they taped it up—like football players get their ankles taped—put my shoes and socks back on and went back up and finished the race, including more pit stops. At the end of the day, my ankle was black and blue and I couldn't get the shoe back on. On the Monday after the race, I had it looked at and they put an air cast on it, and then went right back at it again. I blocked the pain out. I don't want that to sound like it's blood and guts out there, but it's brutal, let's put it that way. You'll see guys go out there and they're banged up from week to week. Same with drivers. They might be in a bad accident, but the doctors will release them, and they'll go drive with bruised ribs. It's one thing after another. I can give you a good example. I've heard stories of Ricky Rudd—I mentioned I used to work for the man. Once, he was in a bad accident and then he drove the next weekend with his eyes so swollen they taped his eyes open so he could drive.

Having that ankle run over was one of the worst ones that had ever happened to me till the accident in November 2001. We was at Miami. The race was going on. Was working for Ricky Rudd, number 28, Texaco Havoline, Robert Yates Racing. We come in for a pit stop on lap 111. We're sticking spring rubber on the right front tire—that's a piece of rubber we stick inside a spring to increase spring rate to help the car handle better. I was tucking it in the right front and was putting the tire back on when another car—number 22—was pulling out and was hit by another car—number 19—that was going at probably fifty miles an hour, and it shot it into us. Yeah, the 19 car hit the 22 car, which got slammed into our 28 car. When all that went down, there was a jack man, a tire carrier, myself, and a NASCAR official all on the right-hand side of our car. All four of us got wiped out by the number 22 car. The front of that car hit so hard it flipped me over, snapped my neck back, and I landed on the back of my head on the concrete. The momentum shot me through the air and into a concrete wall, headfirst. I probably traveled a good fifteen feet. I remember the entire day except for that. I was out.

When I got done flipping, I was lying on my right shoulder up against the wall. The safety workers and my teammates were trying to get to me because they seen the severity of what it was, and when they seen me finally stop flipping, they seen I was bleeding from my eyes, my ears, my nose, my mouth. The only part they couldn't see was the back of my head. They put me on a stretcher, took me to infield care center. From the infield care center, they life-flighted me to Jackson Memorial Hospital in Miami. A lot of people were in shock because when everybody got to the hospital, the prognosis wasn't good.

When they revived me, and I knew where I was brought to, I was freaking out and pulling IVs. My first intuition is like I got to get out of here. I got to get back to the racetrack. I got a job going on. The prognosis was they gave me like a 20 percent chance of living. It fractured my skull from the top part of my eye across my temple to the back of my head. The biggest thing that they said saved me is it ruptured my eardrum, because it relieved the pressure off the brain. That's why I was bleeding from my ears. I've probably lost 10 to 15 percent of hearing in my left ear and I've no sense of smell whatsoever. I can still taste, but no smell. It doesn't bother me. When we had my little girl five years ago, my wife told me I always got to change the diapers, because I can't smell them.

I was there in the hospital for about a week, and then they transferred me to CMC Charlotte, where I spent another half a week. The crew chief that I had at that time pretty much wrote me off, but I told the owners I've been hit, I've been hurt, but I'll be back. So from the beginning of December, I worked out five days a week. When the doctors finally released me to get back to work in January, I never skipped a beat. Did I think I still had my game? Well, I probably had to prove it to some people who probably had some uncertainty, but not to me.

After that accident, NASCAR mandated helmets for everybody that goes over the pit wall. It bothered some people, because it's a rule change. It took some adjustment, but it didn't bother me. If I had had a helmet on, it would probably have dissipated half of the energy from the car that hit me, and it would probably have just knocked me out.

It's not a job for the weak-minded. You have things hitting you so fast you got to think in a split second what to do, what to do, what to do. If you don't, you're gonna mess the whole stop up. I mean, you have forty-three teams up and down pit road every Sunday and they're trying to accomplish the same thing that you're trying to accomplish: have good pit stops, have fast pit stops, put your driver in the best position he can to win the race. You have to focus on your position, your driver, your team. If you're worrying about which other cars are coming in front of you or leaving behind you, you're gonna mess up. It's like extreme athletes that do motocross or skiing or skydiving; they're adrenaline junkies. This is kind of like that; you got to have a little bit of adrenaline junkie in you to go do what we do. Fear is not an option. If you're scared or have just a hint of fear, you could get yourself hurt or somebody else hurt. I think about nobody else. I do what I got to do.

How long can I keep doing it? If I stay in shape and stay healthy, I could probably do it till I was about forty. How long do I want to keep doing it? I could retire today and it would be hard to walk away from, but I could do it because then I could spend more time with my little girl and my wife. Whether they're gonna let me keep doing it depends on whether I'm on top of my game. I'm one of the oldest tire changers out there on pit road. I've been around longer than half of these young guys have been around. Can I keep doing it? Yeah, I can wear half these guys out every weekend. The races are long and the races are hot, you have to be competitive, you got to be on our game for four hundred, five hundred laps, four hours, 30 degrees to 110 degrees. You're racing from February to November, week in and week out. You got to be on your game, you can't just stay in the game. Does my body physically let me do it? I hurt, I don't lie. My knees hurt, my ankles hurt, my hands hurt, my shoulders hurt. I've been beat up anyway you can think of, but I keep on plugging.

Author's note: In 2009, Bobby left Robby Gordon Motorsports to work on the pit crew for Mayfield Motorsports.

Photo Courtesy of: T. LEBARON

JEFFREY MARSH

Special Effects Pyrotechnic Operator

"*I get a phone call: You want me to do what? It can be a bullet hit or it can be fire on water or it can be a naphthalene bomb that some guy wants to do. You know what mothballs are? That's naphthalene. It makes one big, nasty, black orange cloud, and a great fireball. You use it for car explosions, or just explosions out in the field. I tell everybody that I can't stand the smell of that stuff, but it's the smell of money, boys. I charge an arm and a leg for one of those, and they'll pay it.*"

Jeffrey Marsh is a talented guy with a lot of projects underway. "I've got Dancing With the Stars coming up next week, where we have to do some pyro flame projectors with Michael Flatley, and then other stuff in between that keeps popping up. I do a lot of 'one-offs' where you go in and you do one show, like I've been working on Bones *and* House *this year, and a couple of other TV shows; maybe do a small explosion for a car wreck when the driver loses control of the car, or little things like sparks shooting past an actor in a machine shop scene." Also, he is the only special effects operator to create a pyrotechnic display in a New Year's Day Rose Parade while the parade was moving, including the award-winning Honda float in 2009 that opened the parade with explosions and streamers coming out of the hat of a forty-nine-foot tall humanoid robot.*

★ ★ ★

While in college, I started poking around, not really knowing where I was going, just taking general classes. Thought about teaching but just never really came up with anything. Then I was doing fireworks shows in the summertime. Whether the fireworks were a very small device or a huge thing, when you get the whole thing together and shoot it off, there was an immediate audience response. I wouldn't call it glamorous, it was grunt work like digging holes, but it was exciting.

Then, I started picking up theater work, and eventually became the stage manager at Fullerton Junior College. I was twenty-one years old and I'm running the spotlight, working in an air-conditioned building in the middle of the summer thinking, this is not bad, you know, dance concerts with pretty girls in tights. My first job there was to cover the floor with fog when the curtain rose for the musical *Brigadoon*, except they wanted the fog about two feet thick for the entire stage. In the old days, you had these oil foggers, which is basically a machine with a heating element and you had to push a button and walk around the room to lay the fog down. Well, the curtain is down, the orchestra started, the curtain opened up, and all the fog rolled down into the orchestra pit and across the audience. The first ten rows couldn't see diddly for the first ten minutes of the play.

I got out of college and kept doing some fireworks stuff, just stumbling around trying to find a job. I was doing construction, I was doing electrical work, I was hanging drywall, and then I got a phone call from one of my former teachers who said, "There's this guy looking for somebody to do a fireworks show, go talk to him." Well, I went in and met this gentleman and he offered me a job running the nightly fireworks show at Knott's Berry Farm. We were a two-man crew, and I was making the grand sum of thirty-five bucks a day, eight to ten hours a day, seven days a week, one hundred days straight. So I snatched it up, and because of that I really got into the business. At the time, it was really the only big fireworks thing going on. Nobody was doing stage fireworks at that time, but it started coming around, and I got a chance to be part of it, like when I did the Rolling Stones' Steel Wheels Tour, and stuff for the Who and Journey.

For the Stones, they opened on a darkened stage. Across the front of this wide, 350-foot stage, we had thirty-five red flame projectors every ten feet. There's ninety thousand people; people are packed in. On the opening note of "Start Me Up," the lights hit, then all thirty-five flame projectors go off all at the same time. I got the first fifty rows to climb over one another heading for the exit, because it was like, oh my God, what's that? The audience doesn't realize that was the opening shot, and they're going nuts. I don't want to say this like I'm bragging, but I upstaged the band for just that five seconds. It was the biggest kick every night on that tour. That was an adrenaline rush. On the other hand, one of the worse things in the world is to have other cues in that same sort of show, and have that Englishman, Mr. Jagger, look across the stage at you in the middle of the show with a look that says, you just screwed up, and I've had that happen.

I also did some stuff for Bette Midler, worked at the Hollywood Bowl for almost fifteen seasons, and started meeting more and more people. I ended up working for Thaine Morris, who worked on *Star Wars*, *Raiders of the Lost Ark*, and a bunch of other movies. He started getting me involved in more effects stuff, and I did a lot of jobs dealing with explosives. I'm still with Mr. Morris today as my day job, but about ten years ago I got together with my lawyer, and we put together my own company on the side.

People like to see things burning. If you're doing special effects in a movie, there's wind and rain and fog and glasses breaking, or chairs that fall apart when the fat guy sits down. I don't do a whole lot of that. If you want the chair to fall over when the fat man sits down, I'd use balsa wood legs on it and precut it, but I'd rather blow the chair up. Explosions and fire are what I know the best.

My office is my truck. My tools are whatever the job needs, ranging from having a birthday candle lit magically in a TV show where the candle goes *poof* and comes on, to putting a blood pack on somebody and blowing a hole in their chest, and to how far we can throw that BMW across the street and how much powder we are gonna need to do that. When there's an explosion or something is on fire, I'm usually the guy pushing the button when the explosion goes off.

Earlier this year, a lady called for a TV show and said, "I want to do a nuclear bomb creation out in the desert, can you help me?" They wanted to see what a nuclear bomb would look like. It was supposed to be for one of these reality-based shows that are so big right now. So, we went out to the High Desert, got permits, and I brought out twenty-five pounds of black powder, five hundred gallons of gasoline, and some detonating cord, which burns 22,000 feet per second—you don't light it, you basically shock it to get it to go. This is all happening in milliseconds. We created a scenario that when the inner bomb goes . . . if I get too technical here, just stop me. Okay, I took fifty-five-gallon rubber trashcans and I wrapped the detonating cord around them, and then I put black powder charges in the bottom and then lined them with trash bags. I filled the trashcans with gasoline and put a cap on. We did three cans in the center, formed a ring of five more cans five feet away, and then put the rest of the trashcans in an outer ring. The look is supposed to be: *boom* the center goes, then the next ring goes *Boom*, and then *BOOM* the outer ring goes. This is to force shock waves to get that mushroom look. You only get one chance at this.

We had been up all night to prep, and we shoot it at seven in the morning. The sun is coming up, we start loading the gas from a fuel truck I brought in—it's wintertime, so I don't have to worry about static, which is always the fear—and then this camera guy walks up behind me and sticks his head in one of the fifty-five-gallon trash-cans, and I hear him mumbling. I turned around, "What the hell are you doing?" He says, "I'm just looking." I said, "Get the hell out of here! You don't know what's going on here," and he huffed off, and even though they were told to stay out of this area he decided to walk right in anyway. My partners said, "You sure pissed him off." All right, I'm a little guy with a big attitude: a big attitude for safety. I have no tolerance for other people around me when I'm dealing with explosives. I'm an asshole about this. My mantra is "Safety first, show second." I don't care who you are, I'll pull the plug on it right now. I'm scared to death of somebody walking up behind me with a lit cigarette or something that's going to cause me severe harm, because they don't know what they are doing.

So we go to do the shot. They've got four high-speed cameras shooting one thousand feet per second, and they want to catch it from different angles. I'm on the button six hundred feet away, I pushed the button, and the explosion was perfect: A great big ball of fire. That sucker initially was a hundred feet high and about a hundred feet wide, and it rolls out from there. One camera caught the shock wave going across the desert floor.

You can get killed doing this. I've been very fortunate. I've lost some facial hair now and then, but nothing serious. I do not have enough fingers on my hands, though, to tell you how many friends I've lost in this business. I lost a really good friend, a guy named Kenny, and four other acquaintances in 2003, down in Florida. They were off-loading explosives from trucks, and Kenny made a cardinal mistake: He put the trucks ass end to ass end, almost bumper to bumper, instead of side by side where he could have a path to get out if there was a problem. We don't know what happened, but one truck went up and so did the others, and all five guys were killed. Here's a guy who was very safe and had hundreds of shows and he was a good operator, but he made a mistake by allowing that to happen. That was pretty tough.

By itself, a bomb or pyrotechnic device is safe. It doesn't get you into trouble until somebody picks it up and starts handling it. It's human error that usually gets you killed. You just got to be safe, absolutely sure, and you got to have a good crew around you. I make sure I hire good people. You do get the occasional guy who is in it just for the explosives and fireworks, but you get rid of those guys; they will hurt you.

You recall the *Twilight Zone* movie accident? John Landis was doing the movie. Vic Morrow—from the old *Combat!* TV show— and two kids were killed by a helicopter that crashed. A pyrotechnic explosion caused the tail rotor to come off and the helicopter went into the water. That accident sort of changed the pyrotechnic rules. Mr. Landis, because he was going through all the aftermath of the *Twilight Zone* with lawyers and stuff, hadn't worked in a year. The first movie he did after that was the *Three Amigos*. We had a fireworks sequence in that where we had to set up this big fireworks display, and his attitude was, "You guys handle it. I'll be over here. Anything you want, let me know. Fire engines, hoses, whatever you need, you'll have it."

In this business, if you do an explosion and you burn an actor or somebody, you're gonna hear about it for the rest of your career. It will hang around for a long, long time. You won't be called back. So I'm a safety Nazi about this stuff. Don't come near me five minutes before I got to shoot something or I'll take your head off. I get really intense and really focused. I'm thinking about what I've got to do, at precisely what moment. That involves hand movements, foot movements, where that actor is gonna be.

We're just cocky enough that we think we can do it right and do it safely, and that's where the fun lies. If the guy is on a motorcycle going through a wall, and I'm blowing that wall up, if I don't blow that wall right, it's gonna crumple into that guy and he's gonna get hurt. We've rehearsed this, but you can rehearse a live stunt only so far. These productions don't always allow you three or five or six takes; you get one, or two, if you're lucky, so you got to make sure you do it right. I got to make sure that I'm being dead-on.

A lot of the stunt guys that I work with get set on fire, jump out of buildings and out of cars, or they get thrown in the air. People like to see buildings on fire, or things burning. Say I'm supposed to blow a car up. What we do is, take a standard telephone pole, cut it down usually to three feet, slide it like a bullet into a steel gun—usually half-inch steel tubing with a bottom welded on it—and you put screws in it to hold it in place. Then, I'll use up to a pound of a standard black powder charge on top of that gun. You take that and weld it to the bottom of, say, a BMW. So now you got a bomb on top of a piston, and you got wire coming in where you're gonna put a charge to it from a 12-volt or 24-volt battery. When you hit the battery, that piston is driven down. The ground below is not gonna give when you do the explosion, but the car is gonna give.

Now, what do you want to do with the BMW: Do you want the car to flip nose to ass, or flip it passenger door to the driver's door, or cartwheel it? Where you put the telephone pole gun depends on what you want the car to do. I've done them where the car will go straight up, flip it, and it lands it right where it started. But, if you do it wrong, the car will go up and come right back down to earth. You never really know until it goes off.

We also do what's called a "body burn": It's from the shoulders down to the backside. They pay me a good amount of money to do it, and they're paying the stunt guy more money. We use a special gel. The guys ice themselves down with this special formula that keeps their skin protected and creates a barrier so that the heat can't get through, but it lowers your body temperature so that most of these guys, when they are doing a body burn, are freezing their butts off. They put this gel on their clothes, their hat, arms, everywhere. Then you tell everybody: "I'm gonna light him." The cameras are ready; you walk right up to the guy, light 'em with a stick match or with whatever you've got, you step out, and let the stunt guy do his work. Let's say it's thirty seconds, then we use CO_2 to extinguish the flame. If something goes wrong, the stunt guy hits the ground and taps his hands in such a way that the crew knows there's a problem and to put him out right now. I've been very fortunate and usually don't have a problem. The stunt guys don't want to screw up because they want to get rehired to do another one.

Part of my job is to be the camp counselor and make people comfortable with what I'm doing. Some actors don't want anything to do with fire or explosions. They don't want to be near it, so they bring in stunt doubles. When you get a big enough star they can pretty well dictate what they want to do and how they are gonna do it. Other actors will walk up and start asking you questions. Depending on the magnitude of the star, you try to get them away from it if it's a big explosive device, but if it's a small device you take the time and talk to them. Some want to learn. If they are comfortable, that's makes your job easier. Like Dennis Hopper, we did an award show and put some charges on him. He couldn't care less, he's just fine: "Is it safe? Okay. Knock yourself out. Let's have a good time." So it depends on the actor.

One of the worst things in the world is to push the button and nothing happens, and now you're causing everybody else to stop; all the focus is on you and you got to find out why that device didn't go. The pressure is severe because you just stopped an entire production company that is filming at some ungodly amount per hour. So, what happened? Usually it's human error. Like I said, the device by itself usually is no problem. Then you got to walk to a live device to find out why it didn't go, and that's when the pressure really is on you. You can't send your crew to do it, because you're the one that hooked it up and set it and had the final say on it so, in my book, it means I personally have to go take a look.

You know, actors can flub a line, but you can't flub an explosion. If you're off, the director and the producer and everybody else is gonna go, "Oh jeez, he was off about a second on that. He ruined the shot."

They are that demanding. They expect you to be dead-on with little or no rehearsal. You're forgotten the next time a show comes up.

I'm harder on myself than I am on anybody else if I screw it up. The nice thing is, in a television or motion picture setup, I've got complete control of the situation and we don't have to go to live till I'm ready. They can push me timewise, and I can say, "Give me another minute." But with live shows, you don't have that option: "Curtain is at eight o'clock, Jeff. Your first shot is at eight-oh-five." Well, you can't say, "I got to go have a cigarette, I will be right back." No, you have to be ready. You can't have an excuse.

I think this craft is one of the last unwritten apprentice programs left in the country. Everybody tends to keep their tricks to themselves, so you have to get the trust of other effects guys to learn the tricks. You got to be on time, show up with your tools, and work your butt off harder than anybody else so that you gain that trust. Then they'll share their secrets with you, or maybe they'll drop them in conversations.

I still get a big kick out of doing this, whether it's a fireworks show or pyrotechnic display or blowing a car up or setting a guy on fire. A good day at work is where everything goes as you planned and it all went *boom, boom, boom*, exactly like you wanted it, and they got it on the first take.

TYSON RININGER

AVIATION PHOTOGRAPHER

*T*yson Rininger is thirty-three and has been a full-time aviation photographer for seven years. "I hate takeoffs and landings. I can't stand them. They make me nervous because you're close to the ground, you're doing a hundred miles an hour, there are crosswinds, and you're putting a lot of faith in the pilot, as well as the airplane. I get butterflies every time we go flying, because, gosh, what happens if my equipment breaks down, or what happens if something goes wrong with the airplane, or maybe this is my last flight. I know that if I ever do fall out of an airplane, it's gonna hurt a lot."

★ ★ ★

I'm an aviation photographer, which means I basically hang out of airplanes for a living. My clients are engine manufacturers, aircraft manufacturers, and aerobatic pilots looking to put together a portfolio for a sponsorship. And I've had magazine clients who want to do a story on a particular type of flying.

There are about somewhere between nine and twelve full-time contract aviation photographers in the world, but there are a lot of aviation photographers who have jobs that work for a single magazine where that's the only place where their photos go. And then you've got the weekend warrior guy who has a regular job and who just likes to go to air shows on the weekends for fun. They don't hang out of airplanes quite as often.

We find whatever platform we can: helicopters or fixed-wing planes. We take off whatever doors, windows, and panels that would allow access to be able to shoot without shooting through something, and without causing aerodynamic difficulties for the pilot. You can't just walk up to a plane and take a door off, so we do it according to the *Pilot's Operating Handbook*. Then we harness ourselves in with a five-point harness that fits around your body and has a strap on your back that you wrap around either a seat or some solid platform in the airplane.

I'm a navy brat, and I lived a pretty exciting childhood through my parents. I remember going on my dad's ship, but my real love was wanting to be a pilot. At a very impressionable age, *Top Gun* had come out, and I thought I wanted to fly fighters. I did try, but it didn't work out. My eyesight was 20/25, so the recruiter told me, "Unless your eyesight is perfect and your nickname is God, it's not gonna happen." So, during high school, I went to work for a local camera store and started to learn camera equipment. I went into medium-format and large-format photography, and I also learned that it doesn't matter how beautiful your photos are, you really do have to make a name for yourself—that's just how the fine art world works.

I was living out of a trash can pretty much, so I started doing motor sports photography with a huge camera lens I had wound up buying, but I just didn't like the egos of race car drivers. I'm sure when they're alone they're really great guys, but they've got a different ego than pilots, as it's more about their income, whereas pilots want to share their craft and they're willing to take you under their wing, pardon the pun.

The motor sports thing lasted about three years. In 2000, I went to an air show, and it was like 120 degrees, or something, and I was able to compose images differently than anyone had seen. The photos kind of started to make their way around, and my name started to get known.

Then in 2001, after September 11, when the FAA had imposed the no-fly rule, I went to an air show not expecting anything to fly, which is exactly what happened. But there was a wing walker performing her act on top of a tractor that was being driven, a helicopter demonstration team doing their routine on golf carts, and other routines on the back an elephant and the back of a camel—it was all these things on the ground rather than in air, just for the community. There was not a dry eye in the house. It was at that point that I got a true understanding of aviation.

The first time I tried taking photos from a plane, I was fifteen years old. I was working with a guy at an air show (I had shown him my portfolio of images two years earlier, which was absolute crap, but he saw it and he gave me a chance), and we drove to where a helicopter was waiting for me, and I said, cool, ran over to the helicopter and sat down—first helicopter ride ever—started strapping myself in and this guy all of a sudden takes the door off. I asked, "What are you doing?" He goes, "We're taking the door off so you can take pictures," and I went, "You know I'm only fifteen, right?" And he goes, "Well, don't fall out," and walked away. It was the most exciting ride ever. We flew out to the Malibu Canyon Hills, and the pilot was doing 90-degree banks and you're looking straight out seeing nothing but ground. I was mortified, but the adrenaline was pumping. I was having a good time. It cemented in my mind that that's what I wanted to do.

I like in-your-face photography. I'll crop off the wingtips, and I'll possibly crop off some of the tail, and I'll concentrate on the pilot's eyes, because it's their eyes that tell the story. I've shot a lot of photos that are very stunning as far as the aircraft, but unfortunately you can't see the pilots. It just doesn't convey the human aspect. I don't think I've ever seen fear on a pilot's face, which is a good thing. You see concentration.

For the photographer, we've got technical things to watch, like shutter speed on the camera. And you got to get that sense of action, so you've got to somehow try and blur out the background because you don't want the background to be too distracting. When you're flying, you're constantly looking around, not only at the aircraft, but at what could potentially finish the photo. Say, if you fly over a city and you got nothing but suburbia in the background, it looks horrible. It doesn't sell photos.

I don't know all the pilots I'm flying with. A lot of times a story for a magazine will involve flying with certain types of aircraft, and if you can't find a pilot that you trust, then you've got to see if you can at least know what that pilot's qualifications are. They've got to be comfortable with a photo plane flying on their wing. Sometimes that doesn't always happen. You get a lot of these guys that are new to the industry, and you got to brief them very clearly to make them feel comfortable. You want them to know where you want the aircraft positioned and how they're gonna get there so that the pilot understands, in layman's terms, what they got to do, because they don't know what looks good to a photographer. Even for some of the pilots who have gone through training to fly in formation with other airplanes, that training doesn't necessarily relate well to photography. Sometimes you got to teach them how to fly in a slightly different manner than what they're accustomed to, which now you're introducing elements of danger and unfamiliarity.

You've got to have hand signals in case your radio breaks down so that there's always a backup way of doing things. And you've got to brief them on how you're gonna separate so that everyone separates safely and we can all land.

There was one flight where I was flying with some Chinese warbirds, like a Nanching CJ-6, and there was an incident where two of these warbirds were joining up on two other warbirds. I was with the pilot in the lead, we had another friend of mine on the wing on our left side, and the other two guys were gonna take position on our right side. What happened was one guy had too much power, and in order to bleed off that power, he did a high bank kind of a swoop over the right side of us, eventually gaining altitude and leveling out on top of us. Well, if he is on top he can't see where we are and he immediately started to go down in altitude, and in doing so he's basically gonna land on top of us. So the pilot I was with noticed this, looked straight up and saw nothing but wing, and he immediately pulled the stick forward so we can go down. I then went straight up and banged my head into the canopy; it was kind of a negative-G feeling. I was scared out of my mind because I'm at the control of these other pilots and they are new pilots to me. We were able to separate safely and then we landed. I don't think I was upset or angry, because I didn't have near the skill that these guys do, so I've got to try and understand their position. Everyone makes mistakes. But there's that risk factor of putting your life in the hands of people who you don't know.

We lost six photographers that went up in an Aztec about two years ago. It was a simple mistake. There was a Mig that they were gonna photograph, but the Mig had a landing-gear issue, so this Aztec pulled up to double-check the Mig's landing gear, and as the Aztec pulled underneath to check, the Mig's exhaust ripped off the tail and the Aztec and all its crew went down. Again, sometimes you're putting your life in the pilot's hands.

There was another time, I was flying with Jim Cheatham, a helicopter pilot who I trusted. We were gonna photograph a pilot named Sean Tucker, who wanted to do what he calls a "harrier pass," which is when his helicopter is flying at about thirty miles an hour. I'm basically sitting backward out the door of a R44 Robinson helicopter, and Jim was kind of going sideways so that I can shoot straight down at Sean to get this great head-on type shot. After a little while, the helicopter's engine starts to get hot, because there's not as much airflow as there is at normal speed, so Jim has to get the nose level and then build up air speed to cool down the engine. Well, what happened was Jim decided that it would be best if I maximized my viewing time of Sean, so Jim rotated the helicopter 180 degrees—basically going sideways—with no warning, no words, no nothing. He just flipped the helicopter around and I'm of course looking through a little tiny viewfinder, which means I have no bearing of my horizon—I got just what I see in front of me. All of a sudden, the G-force of turning the helicopter is wanting to throw me out and I start flailing around inside the helicopter and I can't, of course, let go of the camera, so I've got one hand on the camera and am looking for anywhere I can grab with the other hand. That was a very scary moment of almost falling out of the helicopter. I did have a seat belt, but I didn't have a harness, which was probably not the brightest thing in the world.

Usually, I'll stick my head out of the plane to take photographs. When we're doing 120 miles an hour, there's a decent amount of wind. For the most part, your head is exposed to the elements and you've got to hold on to the camera, and you can't have a strap on it, because if you do it's gonna whip around and lash you. You're holding it for dear life. You do have a headset on so you can communicate; however, many times what I'll do is I'll just tell the pilot I'm going with no radio and I'll take the headset off, because when you stick your head outside, the headset is gone. The only thing I've lost out of an airplane was flying in an open cockpit with the Red Barons, who were doing aerobatics, and the wind ripped the lens hood right off a friend's video camera. So far, that's it. I've been lucky.

I think it's safe to say that I'm afraid of heights. Like climbing a ladder to your rooftop, the scariest transition is going from the ladder to stepping on the rooftop. There's a disassociation, however, when you get in an airplane and you can no longer discern individual people or cars or buildings on the ground. In an airplane, you're so high up that your mind doesn't realize that if you fall, it's gonna hurt. When you're on a roof, if you fall, you're gonna break a leg, it's that simple. When you're in an airplane, if you fall, you're not gonna feel a thing, hopefully. It's that kind of disassociation. Unfortunately, the lower you fly, the more your disassociation goes away, and then I start getting a little bit nervous. We fly an average of 1,500 feet above ground level. Depending on the terrain, we may fly up to three thousand to four thousand feet, but we try to keep it somewhat low, because we want the ground in the background to make the photos more stunning.

For a typical photo shoot, I'll usually fly for an average of about forty-five minutes to an hour. I take an average of four hundred to six hundred images within that flying time, but a lot depends on what we've got set up. If it's a very difficult shoot—like there was one where I was flying with Wayne Handley and we were in an Extra 300 aerobatic airplane—it's a two-seat aircraft. Wayne was flying above Bill Stein, who was in an Edge 540, which is a single-engine aerobatic aircraft. What we did was we flew inverted above Bill—basically I'm shooting straight up, which is technically straight down—and Bill was flying really low over a riverbed. It was actually a very dangerous shoot and it's not something that I would trust with a whole lot of people, but Bill and Wayne are two of the best pilots in the industry. So they were very low and Bill is watching Wayne, and Wayne is watching Bill, and I didn't see anyone looking straight ahead, which is not a good thing. We were so low that the entire background is just a complete blur and there's negative G-force, so I'm being forced into the canopy while hanging by the shoulder straps, which, because of the difficulty level, makes the photo. I'm just basically pushing the shutter button and firing away as long as I can, because you don't want to try and do it again.

One time, we were flying and doing a photo shoot of a three-engine seaplane over Lake Winnebago, in Wisconsin, and it was one of those times where you know the pilot wasn't too comfortable with the formation, but he wanted to do the shoot anyway. When my pilot started approaching the seaplane, he is flying straight and level and really doesn't know what's going on because he is looking forward for other aircraft in the airspace. As the seaplane is coming toward us, that pilot had way too much energy and instead of banking and then pulling to the left, he decided he was gonna go over the top of us. You just never do that! It's one of those situations where you look straight up and all I see is this huge float on the bottom of the seaplane and I yell, "Photo One down, down," and we wound up doing this whole weightless routine. I've got the harness on, which is great, but I'm not belted in, so I immediately fly up to the roof of the plane. We still have our lives and we got some fantastic photos, but it was one of those things that can happen.

A lot of my friends think I'm insane to get into these small airplanes and put my life in the hands of pilots, but then some of my friends have a hard enough time getting into a commercial airliner let alone justify flying in single-engine "putt-putt airplanes," as they call them. I keep trying to convince them it's safer to fly than it is to drive. Granted, we add that little element of danger in there by flying with other airplanes in close proximity when even the FAA doesn't really like us doing the formation stuff. Flying in a formation involves airspace and confusion, because when you fly, there's different airspaces depending on the size of the airport and the type of traffic that it receives. A lot of times we'll fly to an area that doesn't have airspace constrictions, but sometimes you can't avoid it. For example, one time we had to do a photo shoot of an airplane landing, but we had a commercial airline coming in behind us. I was flying in a Husky, which is similar to a Piper Cub on steroids, and we're shooting a Piper Cherokee. Basically we have to get a photo of the rear of the Cherokee in front of us as it's landing. So you have to take this Cub and you have to do what is called a "slip" where you put in a lot of left rudder to make the plane point to the left, which exposes both you and pilot to the full brunt of the wind, because we got our doors open. You got to sit there with your camera, and the really hard part about this is there's a vacuum that's created between the viewfinder on the camera and your eye, so your eyes just start watering like crazy and your vision is like 20/1000. You can sort of make out something, but you just got to trust in the camera that it's focusing, and you keep shooting away. We were flying sideways, and it was in the winter, so we've got probably thirty-degree air that you're getting blasted by and we've still got that airliner coming behind us, so we've got to hurry up, get the shot—which always adds an element of danger—and then break off and not land in order to let the airliner pass us. That's a lot happening in a very short period of time.

I think there's the expectation in the photography world that guys hire me because they expect to see photos that they've never seen before. They expect something new and different. So, wing walking is just a new venture and an opportunity to visit more air shows and photograph something different. But I don't want to do anything stupid—any more stupid than what I'm already doing—but I want to bring something new to the air show industry, like being a wing walker with a camera. A lot of this has to do with the fact that these air show pilots brought me into their family. I feel very indebted to them. So wing walking is my way of, hopefully, paying them back, or at least becoming as close to a peer to them as I think I'll ever be. It seems like a logical next step for me. I might do it for a year, maybe two years, I don't know.

PETER YELLOWLEES

PSYCHIATRIST

*P*eter Yellowlees is fifty-four. He was trained as a psychiatrist in England, practiced in Australia for twenty years, and now works at a U.S. university medical center. "Being a psychiatrist, you are continuously put in a single room with someone about whom you know nothing and who has been referred to you for a reason, and some of those reasons are rather strange. You have to spend time isolated with that person. They are not necessarily the same as somebody you'd meet in a shop. Most people don't think this is a risky job because they don't think about the one patient in twenty who is potentially risky, but most psychiatrists are well aware of the fact that any patient can come in and can be a threat."

★ ★ ★

I'm a psychiatrist. I work at a medical center. In that line of work, I see a wide range of people with a large number of different types of disorders. The most typical disorders that I see people for would be anxiety, depression, and substance and alcohol abuse. I also see a lot of patients who have physical symptoms or medical problems, say, soldiers back from a war where you have post-traumatic stress disorder. So, we often see combined physical and psychiatric problems.

When patients come to see me, typically I have some information beforehand from a referring doctor or from the patients themselves; I spend about an hour with most new patients. I will go through their background history, find out what's been happening to them, why they are here to see me, and then relate that to events in their past and to any sort of biological, psychological, and social stresses that have occurred to them. Toward the end of that time, I also do an assessment of their mental state, which is simply an objective way of defining the quality that the person has in terms of their appearance, their behavior, their concentration, their thinking, their moods, and their cognition. And then I make a diagnosis from the various findings that I have, spend some time discussing that diagnosis with the patient, and look at what are the best treatment approaches.

I was born and brought up in England, and then practiced in Australia for twenty years. For one period of about three years, I lived in the middle of Australia in a place called Broken Hill, a very isolated place that I went to because I wanted to see what life was like living in the outback. In fact, the area that I was responsible for as the only psychiatrist was actually the same landmass as California, but it only had thirty-five thousand people, including quite a significant aboriginal population. I used to literally fly three hundred miles each way to a clinic with the Royal Flying Doctor Service.

In Broken Hill, I did a bit of everything. I used to see patients in the local jail; I used to be called out at midnight if there was, for instance, somebody being very violent, or if there was some sort of shoot-out going on. Or, I'd be called out by the police to try and talk people down.

On one occasion, I had to physically manhandle a woman who was threatening to jump off the top of the tallest building in town of about eight stories. What happened was, she was asking to see a psychiatrist and she was threatening to kill herself and so, as the only psychiatrist in the town, people found me, I went to the building, and up to the top. I can remember it very vividly: She was standing very close to the edge; there was a small parapet about a foot tall; she was an eighteen- or nineteen-year-old young girl; and, she was very distressed. I just went forward, went closer to the edge, I spent probably ten or fifteen minutes talking to her, just getting her to feel more confident. I asked her what her problems were and why was she wanting to kill herself, but did she really want to kill herself if at the same time she wanted a psychiatrist to come, which is not an indication of huge motivation to jump. I got her talking and listening to what she was saying, and at the same time, I gradually got closer and closer and then when I felt confident I was close enough, I jumped on her and pulled her down on the roof. Then the police joined me. She and I continued the conversation downstairs. She was admitted to the hospital.

I remember another time the police called me out. I was actually in a dinner jacket—one of the things that happens in the outback is that you have a lot of balls, so it wasn't uncommon to be in a dinner jacket—anyway, I was called out because the police had found a man who was clearly very paranoid, very aggressive, and he had a car full of explosives and homemade guns. Yes, homemade guns—this is rough country. And he was threatening to blow up a beautiful old courthouse in town. He had been convicted of some crime previously, and didn't believe that the conviction was the right decision. He had come back with his car full of weapons and explosives, and I had to talk him away from the car, and then he was arrested.

So there are things you don't expect when you train as a psychiatrist. Most people think you are going to just go to an office or a clinic or a hospital, and work there. Throughout a lot of my career, I deliberately have taken jobs where you have a little bit less certainty.

I think I'm a risk taker in some respects, and I've always liked getting my hands dirty.

I've worked in a number of jails and prisons. In one of my jobs, the State used to use me as an expert witness for patients who were in jail—primarily murderers or rapists—to help decide, as an independent person, whether they should be allowed out of jail or should they stay in permanently. It required me to see these very dangerous people, always with an armed officer either in the room with you or immediately outside, depending on the reputation of the person you are seeing.

One patient I will never forget really frightened me. He was a young man in his late twenties, maybe early thirties, who had been put in prison after three or four very serious rapes that he had committed, including one on an eighty-year-old woman where he had broken her hip during the rape itself. He was a cold, callous creature who described—when I was talking with him trying to work out why he had been doing these things—a very long history of bestiality. He had actually been killing animals when he was a teenager. For instance, he used to kill horses and then he would have sex with the dead horses. He basically connected sex and violence and killing from a very early age, and then he started raping and severely physically harming women as he got older. He was just a frightening and terrifying man. He had been convicted, but, you see, he hadn't ever killed anybody. He had been put in prison for ten years for his last rape, and he was coming up for parole. So the question is: Was he going to be let out on parole or was he going to be kept inside for significantly longer?

My charge was to review him and to try and find out why he had been doing this, because at that stage nobody knew about all this bestiality, and then to give an opinion to the State as to whether to let him out or not. My view was very clear that he should remain incarcerated, and that he would be a potential danger to society if he was let out. He was boastful, proud of all these things that he had done, and had an almost total lack of emotion. His callousness and narcissism was something that I hadn't really met before. He was thinking of the women that he raped just as things that had gotten in his way and were better off disposed of. He didn't have any form of conscience formation.

I was sitting across a table from him. It was very uncomfortable. I mean, I've had many other patients who threatened me and who got violent, and I've been hit a few times by patients, but this man struck me as being someone who just was a much more callous person who, if I had turned away from him, wouldn't have surprised me in the least if he had tried to stab me in the back. Life meant nothing to him. There are very few people around like that who really are evil. Evil does exist. You see it very seldom, but this was an example of someone who was evil.

There are several groups of patients who are potentially likely to be threatening. There are, for instance, a number of patients who want to get drugs from you or who want to get you to sign statements that get them off work, and for whom you are gonna be saying "no," and they don't want to hear that. People get angry in that situation. Sometimes you have to show them the door. I'm really clear that I don't tolerate threats and don't tolerate people getting aggressive, but that doesn't always work.

And then there are people who are very paranoid. They project their fears and uncertainties on to you and think that you are actually threatening them. Or, they may be hallucinating and may be hearing voices in the room saying, that doctor is a bad person, that doctor is gonna harm you, that doctor is affecting your brain. They may want to attack you as a way of defense. That's a psychotic defense, but it is still an attack.

The first thing you do, before you even assess risk, is set up your environment so that it is reasonably safe. Every clinic I've ever worked in has a way of getting an emergency call out to other staff. We have a phone and way of working it very rapidly that allows us to get a message out without the patients realizing it. For instance, in the outpatient clinic that I'm working in now, I supervise a lot of residents. They know that if they are feeling in trouble, all they have to do is walk out the room, come and get me, and I'll then go back in with the resident. Or, if somebody is really aggressive, we can call the police. Most doctors have a safety process, because, occasionally, patients do get very distressed.

I've never had a couch, but I try to sit in a comfortable chair at the same eye level as a patient, usually two to three feet away. I get at the same eye height to not make any sort of power differential in our relationship, but I'm also careful to make sure I'm sitting closest to the door so that if somebody starts getting very agitated or threatening, then I can get out.

In terms of how we pick out risks, clearly, if someone is obviously intoxicated or shouting, then what I tend to do is to just basically say, "I'm not gonna see you today." I leave the room and ask them to follow me. I don't mind if they smash the room up, that's fine, but the key thing in that situation is to get out of that area and into an area where there are more people. People don't tend to attack a group, so numbers is what it's about in some respects. You get out of the room, you call the police if necessary, you ask the patient to leave, you be respectful and as reasonable as you can be, and you certainly don't try and make things worse. If something has gone wrong and somebody is getting aggressive, I tend to move into the third person in talking to people, and I'll try and dampen the conversation down a little bit, or I'll change the topic.

One of the other issues about being a psychiatrist is that we do have substantial power, because we commonly make recommendations about people's freedom. Whilst it's not uncommon to be working with patients who are potentially dangerous, it's unusual for patients to actually assault a doctor. [That being said,] a few months ago, I was sitting in the nursing area in an inpatient unit that I work in, just writing some notes, and a patient—who wasn't one of my patients—came up behind me and belted me. I saw him coming at the last minute and managed to just move my head. He hit me on the shoulder, but it was still significantly painful. He was angry. I was there, and I was smartly dressed, and he knew that I was a doctor. It was just because I was an authority figure. He whacked me and then he ran away. The staff caught him and put him on very close observation. I was a little shaken up, but I made sure that the patient was being looked after, and I just carried on working.

Risks occur when people are very inebriated or intoxicated—and that happens regularly in a medical center—people come in through the emergency department, and they've been drinking or taking drugs. And we get people who were brought into the hospital from one of the jails. They come in manacles, they have correctional officers with them. Maybe they've been brought in because they were in some sort of gunfight somewhere, and they're under arrest. We are frequently asked to see them fairly quickly—you don't really have much choice, they are in the hospital—so what you typically do is get as much information beforehand and go and see with them with two people rather than one. I'll often go with a resident or with a nurse.

Another thing that happens is that people who, for instance, are addicted to alcohol often go into DTs—delirium tremens—two or three days after they've been in the hospital, and are at that stage where they're suddenly starting to get very agitated, very upset, and can be hallucinating. So it's not uncommon for us to be called in that situation where a patient has suddenly thrown their chair around the room and torn the curtains down and are throwing a nurse out of the room. Essentially, they've gone berserk.

You do feel threatened sometimes. Again, the key in that situation is going in calmly but going in with numbers of people. I've been in many situations where I'll be going in as the lead in a group of six people—there's two or three nurses, myself, maybe a resident, and, potentially, the police. You can normally start to talk someone down if you're the talker with six people standing behind you. Then the nurses will take over, manage the patient, get them back into bed, clear up the room, sort things out, and then usually you can give them a prescription for a sedative. That will calm them down and help sort it out, and then you can continue talking to them.

Also, it is not uncommon for patients to develop obsessions with doctors, and essentially stalk them if the patients believe that the doctor gave them the wrong treatment, or is really the cause of all their problems. I've had that happen three times during my career, by three different patients. One was a paranoid woman who was very angry with me but at the same time in love with me. She felt that I had somehow caused all her problems, but she wanted to see me all the time, and she was quite threatening. I had seen her as a patient, and then I had to certify her—hold her in the hospital against her will—so she was very angry with me for putting her on hold, even though she liked me as a doctor and loved me in a sort of psychotic way. I was seeing her originally because she was depressed, but eventually she became very threatening toward me. She wanted to hurt me, she started turning up at my house, and she made it clear she knew where my kids went to school. She said I deserved to be punished for causing her problems, and then she would ring my office at work to make appointments to see me. She hadn't actually caused anybody real physical harm, but she was clearly paranoid and unpredictable. In the end, I wrote her formal letters and told her not to come near me. She eventually stopped.

While we talked a lot about risks today, most patients are nice people who are motivated and want to help themselves, and for whom you can do a lot of good. Ninety-five percent of patients are absolutely fine, and in most settings most patients are very grateful for what you do as long as you are respectful of them and try to have a good relationship.

JUSTIN MCBRIDE

BULL RIDER

*J*ustin McBride won the Professional Bull Riders' world championship in 2005 and 2007. An hour before this night's competition, he talks about his profession. "It is a fearful sport. Anybody that tells you that it's not a little bit scary, they're lying to you. I wouldn't do it if it wasn't scary. I think that's part of what makes it so exciting. It's that feeling you get from being successful when it's so hard and so dangerous. It's what keeps you coming back time and time again."

★ ★ ★

My job is a professional bull rider. It means that you ride bulls for a living. You try and stay on two-thousand-pound animals for eight seconds. It's a sport where you have to be winning to make a living. There is no contract. You can't have a bad year and still make a living.

I've been around the sport all my life. My grandfather was a bull rider, as was my dad. It wasn't something that my dad ever really tried to push me into. I don't know too many parents that would like their kid to grow up to be a bull rider. But it was something my parents had seen that I was serious about, and so they really supported it.

I knew from the time I was a little bitty kid that's what I wanted to do to make my living. I tried it as a little kid and I loved doing it. I loved how challenging it was both mentally and physically, and I just kept on doing it. I competed in other sports growing up, but this was the one that I could do the best and it really intrigued me the most. I started getting on little calves when I was about three or four years old. I got on my first big bull—he probably weighed seventeen, eighteen hundred pounds—when I was eleven. I'll tell you what, what really ruined me was when I won like ten bucks in calf riding one time and I said, "Oh man, I'll never see another poor day."

If I had a boy, I wouldn't try to push bull riding on him. It's a dangerous sport. I'm glad my parents let me do it growing up, but I wouldn't want my kid to do it. I have one older brother. He rode bulls a little bit growing up but wasn't worth a damn at it, though, he's a real good saddle bronc rider.

I usually start my day midmorning. I'll have a couple of autograph signings usually at every event, then try and work lunch in somewhere. I usually get to the event probably an hour to an hour and a half prior to the event and hang out with my buddies, tell lies with them, stretch out, and then wait till it's my turn.

We have a protective vest. I got my first one in '93 or '94. There have definitely been tons of times when it's helped. Like in 2003, I got stepped on and broke ribs and had collapsed lungs. If I hadn't had the vest, I'm sure the bull would have squished me like a bug. Then we have the chaps—they really don't serve any purpose whatsoever. They just look cool and are another place to put a sponsor.

I do wear chaps when I'm at home. They're not fancy, but it's for when you're riding in brush and stuff to protect your legs. And I wear a Cinch shirt with logos of different sponsors all over it. And then you have your spurs on your boots. The purpose of those are to try and help you get a grip with your feet, but I could throw my spurs away; I don't use them. Spurs really are overrated.

Then you have a leather glove to try and save your hand a little bit. You put rosin on your glove to help it be a little more sticky to give you a little extra grip. And, we have the bull rope itself, which is a loosely braided rope with a handle braided into it. You clean it up and put on new rosin.

Of course, you always got to have a cowboy hat on. I do, anyway. You see some guys that wear helmets now. A lot of the younger guys are wearing them because they've grown up that way. You also see some guys wearing helmets because they've had facial injuries, like my buddy Ross. He never wore a helmet and then he got smashed in New Orleans in front of the chute and broke a bunch of stuff in his face. So he now has to wear one. No, I've never considered wearing one. I'm a cowboy. I wear a cowboy hat. I pull it down tight. It never comes off.

The bull riding is the payoff. Those eight seconds is definitely my favorite part of the day. When I show up, I show up to win. I don't show up to be second or third or fourth. You know, I've lied to myself so much over the years that I actually believe it that I'm going to win each time. It doesn't always work out that way, but that's how I go into it. And I show up wanting to draw the very toughest bull. When it comes to short round time—the last fifteen riders remaining—I want to be able to pluck the bull out there that nobody else wants or that people think cannot be ridden for eight seconds. That's the one I want to get on. I mean, I get a chance to be great in sports and make a living at it. If I'm going to be that lucky to get to do that, then I'm going to give it everything I got. It's like when the football game is on the line with two minutes left, I'll guarantee you Brett Favre and Tom Brady want the football. It's the same way in bull riding. When there is a bull that people go, "I don't think he can do it, I don't think that bull can be ridden," then that's the one I want. That's your chance to shine.

In the chute, you're sitting on one of the strongest animals that there is. You're pulling your rope up so you feel it getting tight on your hand. Sometimes you can feel the bull tense up, you know, getting ready to go. They're solid muscle. Some bulls are real laid back and are kind of mushy when you're pulling your rope. You can feel it sink into them. And some bulls, like a bull named Reindeer Dippin, he's a psycho the whole time. He's wound up.

I can hear the guys in the chute that are helping me out, but as far as the crowd and the announcers, nothing. You just tune certain things out. The things that are a part of the ride are the things that you're really tuned into. Eight seconds later you get off. On a bad day, you get off before that.

I don't ever have a game plan about what the bull is going to do. It doesn't matter to me, because no matter what the bull does, you have to do the same basic things right to stay on. By keeping your chin tucked, it keeps your upper body leaning forward. If you let your chin get up, your body gets raised back and that's when you come off. And you got to keep a leg on each side. Get both legs on the same side, you're not going to stay on. It's really basic stuff. It's just being able to react by being physically and mentally prepared so when the chute gate opens, you're not thinking anymore. It goes fast. You have to have yourself prepared so that you're reacting the whole eight seconds.

Some of the bulls you definitely get up a little more for because you know it's going to be a challenge. With a psychopath bull like Reindeer Dippin, you know it's going to be a fight. But that's why I do it. It's an adrenaline rush that you get that I've never found in any other sport that I've played. In most sports you're competing against another guy. In this sport you're competing against a two-thousand-pound animal that nobody is going to tell to stop or blow a whistle or throw a flag on. Once the gate opens he does not have to abide by any kind of a rule, so it's something that that is pretty out of control that you are trying to control. Actually, you're not trying to control, you're more going with the flow. You're reacting and trying to move with the bull. Once the bull turns a certain way or does something, I react to that and have a countermove for it and try to go with him. I mean, you're never going to be as strong as one of these animals and you're definitely not going to outthink him. You pretty much got to wait, let him move, and then follow him around.

In 2007, in Mexico, I got off way too early on a really good bull named Gnash. He turned back—when I say he turned back he started spinning to the left and my upper body got too far inside of the spin and I fell off right beside him. My hand was still in the rope and his horn just come around and hit me in the hand, and it caught my left shoulder. It's a shoulder that I had trouble with over the years, and so when it knocked it out this time, it just screwed it up worse. Took two weeks off, rehabbed it like a madman, showed back up in Greensboro, North Carolina, won my eighth event for the year, and finished the season out.

I kept rehabbing through the end of that year, but I kept screwing up more stuff up in it, so when I finally got it fixed after the finals, there were several things that we had to do. There was a ligament that was tore away; had to tie it back together. There was a tendon that runs to my bicep that was tore; that was tied back together. Had some arthroscopic stuff on cartilage, and then I had some rotator cuff issues. I think that was pretty much it.

This sport is hard enough to do when you're completely healthy, but then when you have something like that, it sucks. At the time, I couldn't raise my left arm but about that high [McBride lifts his arm barely to shoulder level]. I had it taped, because if it fell back out then I'd be done for the year. You then have to compensate with the rest of your body, because you can't make moves that you could before. I had to more or less just drive my right arm around to compensate for that. Say a bull was spinning to the right, I would really have to drive the right shoulder because I couldn't pick my left one up to get it where I needed. If a bull went to the left, I was fine because I don't need to be able to pick the left shoulder up for that.

It sucks not to be riding, but it was something that I knew was coming. I was just glad that I didn't have to stop last year and I got to finish out the season. Now, all I do is shake hands and slap backs, and tell them about when I rode. It's hard to sit and watch, but at the same time, you know you can't do it. The rehab is pretty slow. I'm just getting motion back in it, but I think it'll be 100 percent. It should be better than ever. When I do come back, I'll be ready to go.

There's a great camaraderie in this sport. Everybody is competing against the other guys, but at the same time, you're not really, because your competition is whatever bull you have drawn. It's a dangerous sport, so it brings everybody pretty close. You see everybody helping each other out and really pulling for one another.

I think bull riding is pretty special, because not everybody can do it. I don't think it's nothing like being a firefighter or a nurse or anything like that. They put their life on the line to help people. We're not helping anybody. We're competing in a sport. We put our life on the line because we're stupid and too lazy to get a real job. But if you're going to do it, don't be a sissy. I can't stand that. If you're going to do it, go at it with everything you got.

I've done it my entire life, and it's not something that I'm ever going to cheapen. When I feel like I'm not approaching it with everything I got, I'll quit. Maybe a couple more years. You see some guys, in all sports, hanging on. It looks to me like they're approaching it just to be there instead of to win. I'm never going to be that guy.

Being a cowboy means everything to me. It's how I live my life and how I'll always live my life. I'm really not a bull rider. I'm a cowboy that rides bulls for a living. You know, we're seeing new young guys that are coming around now that are more just extreme sports guys and are really good athletes. It's been good to attract new fans so everybody can have someone to cheer for, so I think it definitely helps our sport. But as soon as the event is over, they got the tennis shoes and ball caps on, whereas I grew up being a cowboy, worked on a ranch all my life, and that's the way I'll continue to live my life. After bull riding is over, I'll still be a cowboy.

***Author's note:** Justin returned to competition four months later. During his comeback, he received a concussion, strained neck, and facial and oral lacerations when his head collided with a bull's head and he was thrown hard to the ground. He retired at the end of that season, at age twenty-nine.*

KASSIM OSGOOD

Football Player

A two-time Pro Bowl selection for his outstanding play on special teams, Kassim Osgood wears number 81 for the NFL's Jacksonville Jaguars. After a late-afternoon practice, he plunged into a tub of ice water to soothe his muscles, then showered. We talked a little later while he ate dinner under a tent outside the team's chow hall. "They call it 'the suicide squad' because you know you're gonna have to go and hit somebody that's bigger than you. You're on the field knowing you're doing that, and you're still going down there as fast as you can with the thoughts of doing it. That's probably the insanity part. Our coach always says it's all pride, like either you're gonna want to do it and you get it done or you're gonna be scared and they're gonna run all over you."

★ ★ ★

I was the youngest of four boys, so I was always like the little one getting picked on by older brothers. They were always hitting me. I was getting frustrated, and I always had aggression in me. I found that the best way of letting out that aggression was the impact and contact on the football field. You get a rush of adrenaline after making good contact with somebody.

I started in football when I was twelve. I was a running back at first. As I got into high school, I had a growth spurt and they moved me to wide receiver and free safety. It's fun being a receiver because you can get the catch and you get to score a touchdown, and all the fans go crazy, but I always had an appreciation for defense, because you go out and just hit somebody. It's just that inner feeling, you know, when your body goes numb for a second. It's kind of like a rush of all your emotions at once; just being let loose in a physical way. It's kind of hard to compare to something else.

I was undrafted out of San Diego State. As an undrafted free agent, you're coming from the bottom to try and make the squad. The fastest way to make the squad is on special teams. I was hoping that I'd get drafted, but once the seventh round was wrapping up, I was getting calls from different teams: Baltimore, Philadelphia, New England, Jets, Raiders, Chargers. The Chargers offered the most for a signing bonus.

I had a chip on my shoulder for not being drafted, so any way I can get on the field, I am gonna do it. From the minute they put me on special teams, I was trying tee off on everybody. I was gonna hit everybody and knock somebody out, just letting the aggression come through in the course of play. I was just showing that I was hungry to make the team, and wherever they needed to put me to contribute I was ready to do it. I always play mad; a controlled mad, though. I don't like getting hit, so if I get hit or I get held or grabbed or something, then it kind of ticks you off a little bit.

Off the field, I am a quiet and silly guy. On the field, I'm bit of a loudmouth, at times. It's fun to get into a little jawing with the other guys. It sort of makes the game a little more interesting. Most of it's like comical relief. Like in the middle of a game, you're just trying to break the monotony. More often than not, you know the guys that you're going against on the other side of the ball, so you have a friendly bantering back and forth.

You're trying to do your job within the parameters of the game. In the National Football League, there really are not guys out to hurt you, but you're playing hard, you're playing fast, and sometimes you get the better of somebody. Generally, they won't talk back to you, or if they say something like, "Wow, he's a serious guy," I just hit them harder. They expect to be hit harder. You may be friends, but we still got to do our job, you're still trying to win.

The speed of the game is different in the pros. I always heard from other guys that the speed is a lot faster and you have to be a little more detailed. It's not as easy as college is. There is a smaller window of opportunity for each play. Everybody is a lot better.

For punts, you're going against two guys, and it's like a test of your strength. On a kickoff, it's like you're going against three really big guys to get to one guy behind them, so it's sort of like a test of your insanity. The craziest guys and the most insane are always on the kickoffs, definitely. They're either the quiet, crazy ones, or the loud, rambunctious ones. Both punts and kickoffs are so exciting.

Gunners are the outside guys on a punt. The gunner spot is one of the hardest positions on the field, because you're always going against two guys. If you're good, you're going against maybe three at times. I have been held, been gang-tackled, eyes gouged, hit in the back. They will hold you, tackle you, trip you, step on your toes, grab your face mask, push you out of bounds, hold you out of bounds. They're trying to put a pretty good lick on you, but their main objective is to keep you away from the punt returner. It's gonna happen every play, so you got to fight through everything.

Through studying films and studying their techniques, I find whoever is the weakest link—who I can beat off the line faster, who's rocking on the heels, what they're gonna do. I'm in the heat of the moment, just trying to move and make something on the fly. I just react to it. They could get a hit on you, and it further frustrates you, because when you get knocked down and you're trying to get up, they will hit you again and knock you back down. I get up and I'm that much angrier. So it goes back to that older-brother-picking -on-you-again thing: You get frustrated even more and you get very aggressive.

As soon as the ball is snapped, you just react to whatever they're giving you. Sometimes I don't even know what I'm doing. I just run straight at 'em and try to nail 'em because they're coming for you. You get past them and get to the punt returner. It's always like that dog nipping at your heels; like the mailman running from the dog—got to get the mail in the slot and get out of there.

If you get a solid hit on a returner, very rarely do you feel any kind of pain. It's more like there's that rush of endorphins and you're excited. It feels great. After I get them on the ground, I'll talk a little trash like, "You're not gonna score on my watch," or something kind of funny like that. Then you get up and do some silly dance, and half the time you don't even know what you're doing. The body is just moving because you have so much adrenaline pumping.

There are teams that'll try to put their best guys on me. Because of some of the stuff I do, other players are like, "This guy's crazy. Man, there's something wrong with you." They can tell there's something wrong with you in your head. They're like, "Why is he running down there and flying into people?" You're hitting people and running into people when you're supposed to be going around them.

The suicide squad is on the field for kickoffs. I'm at the three-spot on the right side. They count from one, which is the one close to the sidelines, and it goes two, three, four, five, on each side of the kicker. You got to run as fast as you can before those big guys in the wedge start coming back at you. It's the whole force-equals-mass-acceleration thing, so I have to get bigger acceleration to counteract their mass. There's some big guys in the wedge, so I try to go fast enough to get down there before they can start coming at me. I'm six foot five, 220 pounds, and these guys are like six foot five and 300 pounds, or something like that. They can move and they're strong.

I try to avoid the big guys and run to the kickoff returner, but sometimes you're not able to, so you have to split 'em and go through 'em. That's the times where you just got to load up and hit 'em. Those are the hits that you actually feel, because it jolts your whole body. I mean, that's like seven hundred pounds hitting you. I've been hit by two guys and come to the sidelines and coughed up blood, because the impact was so intense.

What you're trying to do is you're trying to contain the ball carrier from getting outside of you, so I'm trying to get kind of an angle from a wide position to the wedge so that you can kind of split through one of those gaps. If you hit straight on, they can just bounce you out, and then you open up a wide lane. Coming at an angle is easier to penetrate it. I do it so that the second line of defense can come through and make the hit. Nobody likes doing that, but you try to do the most you can. You just hope that the other guys come through and they hit the returner so that way you're not wasting motion.

Right before the ball is kicked, you hear the crowd. It's loud. You hear music. You can hear everybody chanting. We'll look at each other on the kickoff and we all know we're fighting to get that big hit. The minute the ball is kicked, everything blanks out, like you mute a TV. You hear nothing. You can't even hear yourself breathing. You're running down the field and you're making a move and the next thing is either you're getting hit or you're hitting somebody. And then you get that pop of the pads, and you're on the ground. The sounds of the crowd start to come back in, and if they're making "woooo" sounds, you know you got a big hit, you were hit hard by somebody, or somebody on the other side of the field got hit.

Referees barely call anything. More often than not, a referee is gonna ignore every penalty another player performs against you, because it happens so much. They can't really stop the momentum of the game. I kind of caught on that they're not calling it, so every now and then I might sneak a little hit in there, or step on a toe. The special team coach told me, "They're not gonna call those things. Don't come yelling at me telling me about they're holding you on this and that. They're gonna hold you *every* time, so you got to find a way to beat it."

A pile? Yeah, often there's a whole host of things going on, from pinching, pulling hair out, giving little jabs in the stomach, or someone might grind their face mask into your chin. Everything's happening. Me? I never really dish out a lot in a pile. I'm more one of the guys that wants to get out of it before something happens to me.

Anxiety? It depends on the situation. Like if it's a tight game and they call a play where the ball is supposed to go to you, then as a receiver you might get a little anxious. But as the game goes on and you're getting in the zone, finding a rhythm, then the anxiety is a lot less. On special teams, though, you expect that you're gonna be a little more amped up out there. Special teams has always been about reaction and emotion.

When you start going down and looking around to see who is coming around to hit you as opposed to just going through to the target, a lot of times people are like paranoid. They're looking around to see who is gonna hit them, so they're reacting a little slower to the play, as opposed to the guys that are just flying down with reckless abandon and just throwing their body out there. For the most part [even if I were a starting receiver,] I'd still try to finagle to get on the kickoff and a punt, because that contact is a lot different. Being a receiver you have the ball, so you're receiving punishment even though you're trying to lay into somebody and dish a little back to them, whereas on a kickoff or a punt you're going down and you have no ball to worry about, you're just going to nail somebody.

Yeah, I love the danger part of it. You slow down, you're gonna get hurt. So the faster you move, the more fluid all the hits are. Your body's reaction is a lot better when you're moving faster as opposed to being slower. Something bad always happens when you slow down, like somebody can roll up on your leg or something. It keeps you focused.

No, I've never been knocked out, but I see stars every now and then. Once, I tore my pectoral tendon in my arm diving for the returner. It was a kickoff. I split the wedge and dove for the returner. He hit my left arm and it went back at the one angle where your arm is not supposed to go back. I felt a pop. There was no initial pain in it, but the minute I went to the sideline, I told the doctor something's wrong in the arm. They did a little test where I tried to push and use some strength, but there was no strength there. I was out for the rest of the season.

Photo Courtesy of: **RINGLING BROTHERS**

VICENTA PAGES

Tiger Trainer

*V*icenta Pages is twenty-three years old. It is a Saturday morning in the
Cajundome in Lafayette, Louisiana, three hours before a Ringling Brothers
show. She talks about working with tigers as she sits a few feet from the center
arena. "It's always what I wanted. My parents wanted me to stay in school,
stay home, and have a normal life. But I wanted to be in the circus. It's what
I grew up watching. It's what I love. That's where my heart is."

★ ★ ★

I'm a tiger trainer and an aerialist.

You know, people have the idea that tiger training is not a woman's
job. They generally see it as a man's job. I've had people say, "Women

can't do that, because it's a man's job." When I hear that, I just have to say, "I'll show you how women can do it." I just want to show them that women can do it just as good as a man.

I'm a fifth-generation circus performer. I was born into it. There were always cubs in my house. It wasn't out of the ordinary for them to be in our beds, or come into the car to go drop us off at school. It was just normal for us.

My parents own their own circus, Circus Pages. You have to learn to be multitalented, because it's all family. I've done a variety of things since I was little: I've worked horses and ponies, camels, dogs, elephants, pigs, llamas, and a variety of aerial acts. I've done chiffons. I've done trapeze. I've done hand-balancing and contortions, and I've worked in a juggling act. I've pretty much done almost everything.

The opportunity came around to join Ringling Brothers when I turned twenty. It was pretty much a decision that I made. My dad said, "If you want to go, you can go. If not, we are happy to keep you home." I think deep down he knew my decision was I wanted to be in Ringling Brothers. It was my dream since I was a little girl, because it's the best, and you are at the top of your career.

The first city that I worked with Ringling Brothers was Cleveland, Ohio, in 2006. It was nerve-racking. The original storyline didn't involve the tiger act. When I came to the show, the show was already put together. It was a hard transition because my tigers had never seen anything outside of my show. They had never been around other elephants or other horses, so it was a big transition for them. And, on that particular show, there was a TV screen that sat in the back by the portal, and for my tigers to see their reflection on the TV screen was a big deal for them. They were like in a daze. They just stared. They had never seen anything like it.

I work with six tigers: two boys and four girls. It's basically like working with people. They all have their own individual personalities and their own way of doing things. It's my job to always keep everything in control, know how they are feeling, know what they are thinking before they think it, and know how they are gonna react to a new environment, new light, new music. The boys are Torres and Mohan, and the girls are Kia, Fiona, Spirit, and Makela. They range from four years to eight years old. I acquired them when they were about thirteen months old.

I started with my dad when I was fourteen, so I always had my dad to point this out or point that out. He's been working lions and tigers for years, so everything I learned, I learned along the way. When I first went to work, I didn't know what to look for. It took every bit of four or five years under my dad, in the same arena, for me to learn everything I needed to know before I started to work with tigers on my own.

Not every tiger is the same. They all have their own distinguished looks. Like I said, they are like people. To the naked eye, they are all gonna look the same, but to me, I know their differences. I work with them so closely every day. I am the one that cleans, feeds, waters, works, and exercises them, and I am one who has a relationship inside and outside the ring, so they are like my kids.

Once they see me walk out in my costume, they know it's time to work. They hear the music and they get in the mind-set that it's time. For the most part, they're all concentrated on me. If they're not concentrated on me, then I am not doing my job. When the act is over, they're relaxed. The music is off and they're out of that environment.

When the show starts and the lights come on, I'm already in the arena. The ring is thirty-two feet in diameter. At the beginning of the routine, they sit on their seats. I'm in there and the cats are in there. On a good day, the routine is roughly six minutes. On a bad day, it's seven or eight. Sometimes it takes longer for one to do something. I then have to take the time and make them do it properly.

They jump over hurdles; they lie down; they roll over; they sit up; they hop forward on their hind legs. Only Spirit walks backward. They sit on a mirror ball and it rotates around. The routine is a series of maneuvers that would come to them very easily and naturally.

Depending on what part of the act, they are right beside me and they rub up against my legs. I get close to their face. I hug them. If they didn't enjoy it, they wouldn't do it. When you acquire a tiger and bring them into this environment, of course, they're nervous and scared. They are just not made for the circus. Some adjust quicker than others. Some will be used to seeing elephants and camels and horses within a day, and then other ones won't adjust to it. It depends on the individual animals. Some learn quicker than others. Some will be ready in a month, and some will take six months to a year; it just really depends on the animal.

I can see it in the morning if somebody is not feeling well, or if they are in a bad mood, or something is bothering them. It depends really on how they act when they come into the ring. If I see that it's gonna affect their performance, then I just won't even make them do anything; they just have to sit there and do nothing. I'll adjust around them.

I have to know what they are thinking before they're thinking it. I always have to be one step ahead of them. There have been many occasions where I think they are thinking one thing, but they are thinking another: I think they are gonna go left and they go right, so I am focusing on all my maneuvers thinking that they are gonna go left. They kind of throw me for a loop. Like I said, I've had to learn how to read them.

On an off day, if I am sick or if I am tired, they know it. My eldest is then more affectionate to me. He will be like, okay, Mom, just stand there, don't worry about a thing. The other ones kind of work the act on their own, and I am just kind of there.

You are gonna have your wake-up calls. The tigers remind you that they are wild animals. They are not pets. For them, when they touch you it's not hard, but *it is* hard. You don't realize the kind of power they have in their paws. They are strong.

Afraid? No, just besides the fact that there are six of them and one of me, and outweigh me by a big margin. They all weigh between four and five hundred pounds. And there's twelve eyes on me, and

I just have two eyes on them. I always have to go in with a positive attitude and always be relaxed and calm because they pick up on my scent and my moods. They know what I am feeling.

My job is to direct them to what they need to do. They go off of my voice commands and my body language. If I say, "Up" they need to be up, or they know if I move this way they need to move that way. If I'm in a good mood and I'm uppity, then they feel the same way. They are jumping around and are in a good mood, and they move quicker and do things faster. The act seems to go a lot smoother.

When people watch my act, they see that I work with the tigers so closely and they see that the tigers don't hurt me. It's my job to keep everything in control and to make sure that nothing happens, but people misconstrue the situation. People see that my act runs so smoothly that they think that they are just like house pets. They are not. They're wild animals. They can hurt you.

Being in the show is the fun part, but the real part of the act is outside: the feeding and the cleaning and the watering. I am constantly with them. That's where all your time is spent, and that's where you learn to bond. In the morning, it's roughly about an hour and a half to two hours of cleaning, and then it's spot cleaning throughout the day. They each have an hour of exercise time, and they go out in groups for more exercise time.

They eat raw chicken and beef once a day. It depends on what part of the year it is; if it's in the winter, they'll eat in the morning. But if it's in the summer, like now, they won't eat in the morning because it's too hot; they have to wait till later on in the day.

When I started with Ringling Brothers, I had two people that were my "co-dads": two Ringling Brothers employees that knew my dad and have known me since I was a little thing. They did everything for me. They would make sure that my arena was set up properly. They would set my seats and got the tools that I need for the act. During rehearsal time, they were telling me, you need to look for this and you need to check that; basically preparing me for when I had to do. I never had to worry about anything else. I was a spoiled brat.

Now, I'm more on my own and am more responsible for taking care of my own things and checking up on my arena, making sure my seats are where they need to be and make sure they are in the right position, and make sure that the transfer cages are lined up properly and make sure all the locks are on. Leaving the other show and coming to this show has been a learning experience. If I would have stayed on with my dad's show, I would have continued to be spoiled and have everything done for me.

Yes, I also have an aerial act. Once I come out of the ring after the tiger act, I have four assistants that go in and help. It's kind of a little skit with our clowns talking to the audience. It gives me a second to take off my jacket, which comes down to my ankles, and I have my aerial costume under it. I get my mike and my shoes, rosin, and alcohol for my hands. I have about twenty seconds. Once they're done with their skit, I'm already climbing up for the aerial act. I think in this transition people can see that the performers in the circus are multitalented and there's a lot of multitasking involved in our jobs. The audience knows it's me. The lights never go out. I'm always in the spotlight.

There are a lot of risks in the aerial act. There is no net. But to me, it's another day at work. I work the Roman rings twenty-four feet in the air for roughly three or four minutes. It's basically like the rings you see in the Olympics but very different from what they do in the Olympics. It's a lot of more acrobatic movements as far as putting your feet to your head and a lot of swinging maneuvers, and things that make it more of a circus. I'm never aware of my audience when I'm up there. I'm just focused on every trick that I do. It's a routine of ten or twelve different tricks. I don't hear any music. I don't hear any applause. As soon as I start climbing up to my rings, I don't hear anything because I'm directly focused on what I am doing. If I focus on other things around me, then you are losing concentration. Once

I'm done and I'm on the floor again, that's when I start hearing music and people. It's a rush.

I was home ten days last year. We did 400 shows. This year we're gonna be doing about 350 shows in fifty-eight different cities. Every day is different. You meet new people. You see different places. For me, that's great, because I have a very small attention span and I get bored really quickly. So it's good that I move every week and see new things. If I stay in one place too long, I'd go crazy.

I'm very grateful to be working in Ringling Brothers. I work on The Greatest Show on Earth, and it can't get much better than this.

JOE DEAN THOMPSON

OIL WELL FIREFIGHTER

*F*orty-nine-year-old Joe Dean Thompson works for Wild Well Control, the world's leader in fighting oil well fires and blowouts. We talked at the company's headquarters in Houston, Texas.

★ ★ ★

I handle oil well fires and blowouts, everything from wells that are milliseconds away from potentially blowing out to full-blown surface loss of control.

There was a neighbor who lived next door to my parents and she happened to work for this oil and gas drilling company. She had heard that I was interested in getting in the gas business and said to let her know if I have problems getting on somewhere. Well, about three or four days after I turned eighteen, the company sent me an airplane ticket, and I left with a knapsack and a few bucks in my pocket. I was going to Dallas, then Seattle, and then Yakutat, which is an island in the Aleutian chain. From there, I flew about 125 miles offshore on a brand-spanking-new semisubmersible floating drill and rig.

I was supposed to be a roustabout. Well, we get off the airplane, and somebody was there to greet me. I had no idea what I was doing there. An older guy and I were sitting there, and I started asking questions like, are the roughnecks the ones that throw the chain? He started laughing. Basically, roughnecks are three men of a five-man drilling crew: there's three roughnecks, one derrickhand, one driller. They are the guys who actually work the rig floor, drill the well, and manipulate the pipe in the hole. The roustabouts help them on the offshore drilling rig as outside workers helping the crane operators, doing cleanup, moving things around, warehousing stuff, that type of thing.

I worked in the drilling part of the business for about a year or so, and then a friend of mine said, hey, you need to come over to Louisiana with me. I've got something that's right up your alley. I said, what in the heck are you talking about? Well, he started telling about snubbing, and I said, I think you're right. I had a little bit of background of how wells were drilled, so I took the job in snubbing.

The Wild Well Control founder's son got a job at the place where I was working and we got to be good friends. His dad's company was growing, and I said, what does it take to get on over at your dad's company? He got me an interview, and his dad hired me. I was twenty-three. I've been here ever since.

Two weeks after I came to work here, I went on a job up to Canada. It was winter and the weather was starting to become blustery and snowy. The temperature there was anywhere between zero degrees Fahrenheit to about twenty above. We were about eighty miles from Edmonton, in rugged country. We flew in on helicopters. It was kind of like a muskeg, down in a valley. It turns out the formation that these gas wells were drilled into was hydrogen sulfide, which is a poison gas with a very high concentration. The top of the flame was five hundred feet or so. It was coming out of a big pipe and was flowing faster than the speed of sound. It was very dangerous.

When I got there, it was all on fire, and most of the drilling rig had been pulled away. My job was to help the two guys that were in the lead, which was Joe Bowden, the company founder, and Byron Lee. I'm backing up Joe, and another guy named Irvin was backing up Byron. At the point that we got involved, the well was blowing out and we were trying to move the rig, but it was pinned to the well. We needed to try to drop the pipe in the well bore, shut the blowout preventers, and then we'd be able to skid the rig back out of the way. Because it's necessary to make sure everything's all lined up properly and the pipe is coming down smooth like it's supposed to, you have to get close to it. Byron was checking one of the snub lines, and he tripped, fell to his knees, and kind of got jarred around, but he gave the high sign to the people that could see him. He got up and walked back toward the crane, through the gas cloud. No one knows for sure, but he must have gotten a break in his face mask when he tripped or fell, and got some of the hydrogen sulfide. He didn't realize that he was in trouble. It wouldn't have mattered anyway, because, at that concentration, one breath of hydrogen sulfide and you are pretty much done.

I went to see the well, everything looked fine, and walked back the way I came because I didn't see anybody else, and as I was walking out of the cloud looking around I see Joe. He motioned me to follow him, so I did. He was quite a distance ahead of me when I realize that he was back at the trailer that has thirty-minute self-contained air packs, kind of like what firemen wear. As I'm walking in, I see him rummaging around looking for air and he threw his hands up, and I said, what's wrong, but I really wasn't alarmed at that time, because I didn't really know what was going on. Then, immediately, he grabbed the front of his face mask and ripped it off. He was about a hundred yards or so away from the well, but with the way that the gas was swirling around, it still was kind of close.

I assume what happened was he ran out of air. We've got, you know, layers of clothes on—insulated coveralls, Nomex underwear, gloves, firemen's bunker boots, a harness that holds the air pack system, and we're wearing rain suits on top of that. We're walking around like the Michelin Man. Joe had all this stuff on and he comes out from underneath this mask, which is like, oh that's not good, then he throws his hands up in the air again and just kind of pirouettes and fell on the ground. I started sucking air. He's just laying there. I picked up my pace, got to him, reached down, and grabbed hold of that harness. Well, everything is slick with oil like a bunch of sardines, and I pick him up and try to walk with him across this road and then up a hill to get him out of the environment.

I was kind of shuffling and didn't have any strength, and about that time I ran out of air pressure. I was inhaling so hard that the plastic around the seal on my mask smashed into my nose. Moving him was like an elephant stepping on my chest, that's the only way I could describe it. At some point, my survival instinct kicked in and I let go of him and walked across the road and then started up the hill. Three steps after I got there it felt like the elephant stepped off my chest and I was breathing again. I turned around and looked at him lying there, and I felt like I had abandoned him. It was like there was no way that could have happened. I took a few more breaths and then went back and I tried to pick him up and put him on my shoulders. It was like a couple of jellyfish trying to hold on to each other, slippery and sliding. At one point, I got him up and almost had him, but he squirted out of my arms and he fell on his head, and he had this big ol' scratch over his eyebrow. I dropped the boss on his head.

I get him by his feet—I got his one foot through the crook of my elbow and I pulled my arm tight to my body and I just back up and drag him. He's as limp as a dishrag. While I was dragging him, his boot came off and I landed on my ass.

As I was trying to get him across the road, I had to leave that environment three different times to get air. Finally, I got him across the road. Because of all the noise, I couldn't hear him, but I could tell he was breathing. I was cussing him out, telling him he better not die on me. I was doing some serious talking, but he wasn't listening. He was out cold. I looked around and found this guy that was wandering out like a dodo and wasn't doing anybody any good. He was disoriented. I got his attention and said, "Hey, get over here and help me." So we moved Joe up that hill and we put him on the back of a truck to a medical helicopter that had landed. We got him on a gurney and we're putting oxygen on him, and he became conscious.

It turns out that Irvin, who had gone in to try and find Byron, did find him. Byron had already taken his mask off, but he was gone. Irvin, who had been raised up in northeast Texas paper mills, was very familiar with hydrogen sulfide gas. The assumption was that Irvin must have thought he was in clean air, because he took his mask off and tried to put it on Byron. That's a classic "do not do" in rescue. He would have probably done anything for Byron. Didn't work out. Both of them were down.

They took Irvin to the hospital, but he never recovered. Byron was dead there. Joe did make it, like I said.

To finish that story, we had all the fires put out and we went back a couple days later to set the blowout preventers back down, but the seal ring had been damaged by the hydrogen sulfide, so we had to take it off and move everything back out of the way. We were preparing everything to go back in, but when there's fire in these muskegs in northern Alberta—which are basically frozen swamps—they have a tendency to burn underground for miles and then all of a sudden pop up and create a forest fire. Well, we're all but ready to start moving everything back in place and cap it, and then the swamp fire popped up. It looked like it knew right where it was going. There was probably a half-mile trail of fire that headed straight to the well, and poof! It lit the well back on fire.

So, we need to put the well fire out again, which is not a problem, it's fun. You get to play with dynamite and all that good stuff. In fact, we used fifty-five-gallon drums stuffed full of five-pound stick dynamite, and a lot of primer cord. The purpose is to starve the fire of oxygen and put the fire out.

When things get to the point where an oil or gas company has to have a well control company like ours, then things have deteriorated within the well to the extent that somebody says they need somebody that fools with this stuff more than they do. What you find is the longer an event goes on, the more things get worse and continue to deteriorate. So, we always come from the standpoint of whatever we do, we want it to have the highest rate of success that we could possibly get out of a particular option, then apply that, and get it done.

Probably the greatest risk in this business is when there's something we don't see or we don't recognize that potentially could change the circumstances. We then might be operating in a way that some small thing shifts or changes the dynamic of the environment that we're working in. That's what could possibly put us in peril. The first time that it ever happened to me was way out north of Odessa, Texas, where there's nothing but scrubs and rocks around, no one to see, no one who cared. It was just gonna be shale and gas blowing out, and it wouldn't be blowing out for that length of time, so weren't gonna impact anybody. This well was blowing out, and it was loud. We'd already figured out half a dozen different ways to put it out, but all those options were pretty lousy. Those are the things that we really hate.

I said, through sign language to one of the guys, go get the thirty-six—that's a pipe wrench—and he went to go get the pipe wrench and they got everything sealed off. It was dead quiet. Then, just as we were walking up to the well, there's a roar. Gas was going a couple of hundred feet up in the air with big huge chunks of shale rock just filling the sky up, and it's loud. That gets your adrenaline moving. Then when it shuts off, it's got to be like a cop after a shootout: All of a sudden, it's all over with.

When you've done this long enough, you realize that you take as much as Mother Nature is willing to give you, instead of being omnipowerful. When you get your hat handed to you, you go, maybe I'm not all that smart, because this well is kicking my tail with everything I try to do. There's no sense of grandeur in that. If anybody that has been doing this any length of time suggests that they are more powerful than Mother Nature, run away from them, because there's liable to be a disaster waiting to happen. This work is very humbling at times. You don't want to die, so what's the point of making a bunch of money if you can't live long enough to enjoy it?

WALTER DIAZ

HIGH-RISE WINDOW WASHER

*W*alter Diaz began work this morning at six to finish in time to talk about his job washing windows on the outside of some of Chicago's tallest buildings. After our conversation, he hurried to a local hospital to be with his ailing father.

"You always have to be afraid. I'm still scared, but I don't panic. I know how to respond to it. You got to respect that height. You can die twenty, forty feet down. See, when you lose respect and when you're not afraid of something, it's not good. That's when accidents happen. Never lose your fear, and then you can do things better and safer. That's when you become the best. Falling down, there's only once; that's it. You ain't coming back."

★ ★ ★

Walter Diaz

I'm a professional high-rise window washer. I'm thirty-seven.

I was just looking for a job to make quick cash, and I saw these guys in the air. I applied for a summer window washer job. I did some ground stuff, and it was easy. Three weeks later, they're like, "Do you care for a high-rise?" I'm like, "What do you mean?" So they explained it to me. I said, "No way." So then they are like, "Try it and see if you like it."

I never knew I was gonna go up high. I did it and loved it. I never came down. It's intense once you get involved with the guys and different buildings in Chicago. Here I am, same company, seventeen years. Name it, we do it: residential, office buildings, hospitals, hotels, everything in Chicago, and also to Indiana, but we try to stay local for safety reasons. Something happens, we respond quickly.

It's the height and the freedom. Feels free up there. When you're up high, it's only you and nothing else. Yeah. I still love it.

You have two ropes: a main rope and a safety rope. Your main rope is the one that you use daily; you rappel down on it. Your safety rope is the one that's attached to your harness. The harness is your second chance. If something goes wrong with the main rope, the other one will catch you.

You got to drink a lot of water. No pop; water. If you drink pop, your mouth will become so dry you'll be dizzy. We tie a little bottle with ice next to us, and keep sipping.

We rappel on what they call the "bosun's chair." You are sitting on that thing. They also call them "genie chairs." We call them a genie chair. It's a little board, one by two feet attached to a D-ring on your belt, and then you attach that to a cylinder. You wrap the rope around that; that creates friction. That's how you rappel down, either fast or slow. You also have some D-rings to attach all your tools—your squeegee, the brush, the water bucket. We attach the brush to a bungee cord. Once, it broke. My brush went down twenty floors. Down there, we close our working area so nobody can go in. It went right there into my drop zone, which is good. Nobody got hurt.

Soap and water, that's it—Joy soap; that's the best, and it smells good. If it's forty floors plus, we take two buckets. If it's like thirty floors, one bucket. We don't use any heavy chemicals up high, because if you use acids, that might damage your ropes, and then the next day you need new ropes; those are expensive.

Difficult to get off? Stains due to aluminum screens. There's also lime stains. Chicago's rain contains acid and it reacts with the metal and with the stone, and it creates stains on the glass. Sometimes they don't clean it for one year or two years. You have to use different chemicals. It takes three times longer than just a straight wash. With the stains, hey, we got to charge more money. People pay for it, they understand.

A swing stage? That's mainly for construction or bigger buildings. A swing stage, it can be from five feet wide up to forty feet wide. I hate those things. It's a lot more work, and you don't move too fast. You only go up and down in one speed. You work that thing up to the roof, then move it along the rooftop, and go down doing the same thing. Personally, I don't like it. I like speed. The genie chair, you can speed down whenever you want. It's better to rappel down from the twenty-sixth floor down to the ground, nonstop. That's my thing. I just love it. It feels like a motorcycle. Why you like to go fast? Nobody knows. People just like it.

I'm the foreman. I got twenty guys. I train them; I go in the field with them. Sometimes people freak about dangerous jobs. Like a week ago, my partner, he froze on me. So I went out and got him, hooked him up to me, tell him everything is fine: "You ain't going nowhere. I got you." He felt better that I got him. Next day, he was over next to me. He's okay. It's normal. My window cleaners, they're all different. The way they work, the way they move when they swing, or when they're cleaning—they're all different. Even their fear is different.

I make sure all the guys are in the right spot. For example, we are doing the building at 77 Walker. It's my favorite right now. The roof is a backward V. There is a real danger, because nobody touched the glass up there, ever. The building is like sixteen years old. I got my best guys up there. I work with them in the difficult areas. That's why I'm dirty a little bit now. And we also have our crew over at CBS News—22 West Washington—and there's also the Hotel Intercontinental.

They're all different. There's not a single building like another. Some are more aggressive than others because of the different levels, the height, the wind. Wind is an issue for us, big-time. You got to be careful because nature is very powerful. One wall can be so calm that week, and then the other week it is different. The wind, it beats you badly. The wind will lift you up like a little toy; I don't know how, but it does. It happened to me, but when you get experience, you can come down quickly. That's why I love chair work. On the swing stage—because the hoist is so slow—if you're up twenty floors, you ain't coming down quickly, no way. But in a chair, twenty floors, you like come down in twenty seconds. If it's only a little wind, you're screaming, "Whoaaaa!" going down. Oh, it's fun.

Now, if it's a seventy-miles-per-hour wind, we're not up there. Depending on the height, I work in twenty-to twenty-five-miles-an-hour winds. If it's only ten floors, twelve floors, no big deal. Hit me, I'm there. But if you're up forty floors, you might get hurt, because the wind will come so high it will swing you like thirty to forty feet one way. I don't put myself in the extremes. I check the weather daily, twice a day, three times a day. It can change in thirty seconds. You got to be on the lookout.

Once, I was on a building and a storm was coming. Nobody tells you anything, because nobody saw it coming. We were going up so slow that it felt like a thirty- to forty-mile-an-hour wind, almost lifting the swing stage; that thing was moving so bad. You're like, let's see what happens. You can't jump out; you can't go nowhere; you're just waiting, holding to the swing stage. That was wild. Thank God nothing happened. I think that's why I hate swing stages.

When it rains or is a real windy day, you got to go somewhere else, or move all your equipment from one building to another. You got to do something. We do a lot of inside cleaning then. I hate inside work. I'm not free. Everybody is watching you; you have to be neat. Outside, it's only you and the window.

When it's extreme, like fifteen below zero, we'll stop. I've worked till twenty below zero before. When it's cold, we put methanol in the water so it won't freeze. If it's windy, it gets colder. You feel miserable like, what am I doing? But if there's no wind, you're fine. You wear a snowsuit, special boots, your hat, and gloves.

The highest building on the chair for me was probably Chase Tower—875 feet. That's equal to about eighty-some floors. It was fun. I was in a chair, yeah. Well, back in the days, there were no height limits. Now there are limits: 300 to 400 feet in a chair. Because of the height, once you come down 550 feet, your ropes become so light, if you let go, you will hit the ground in two seconds. So you have to be careful. The lower you go, the faster you go down, even with the rope attached to the cylinder.

Physically, it's just like any other job, like a garbageman, because one house is easier than others. A friend of mine is a garbageman. He hates some days, because he says they are more difficult than the others. The same thing for us. It varies per building. It can go from being filthy and dirty to difficult areas to reach. You got to scrub that thing. You put muscles on the glass and then you become real tired, spend more time washing and scrubbing, but that's the nature of it. If they clean it often, it's easy. You can throw water at it, squeegee it off, and it comes right clean. Then we will make a lot of money.

It takes a little time to learn to squeegee a window where you don't make mistakes. It takes like up to three years to learn. Once you hit the three years, you are a journeyman; then you start making a lot of money because you're fast and you don't make mistakes.

Some roofs are not flat. Sometimes they got levels and sharp edges and angles. Then you got to protect your ropes when there is sharp angle. We use rope protectors. We snap those things on every area that we think is going to give friction and put us in danger.

A major risk would be to not do everything the right way. Sometimes laziness or alcohol or drugs take you to another level; that's when you make mistakes. You got to be focused all the time. I've seen it in other companies. That's why I check all my guys daily, because if I smell liquor, he's not working that day. They might lose the job. There are no games. I'm not stupid. Thank God we have very good guys.

Another risk would be not checking equipment the right way. We check our equipment every single day. The equipment can be damaged anytime, like a sharp edge, or some other guy will come and cut your rope—maybe not on purpose. There's bad people out there. I don't see it, but hey, it's in your mind, you know. If I see someone else working on the same roof that you're working on, we will stop the operation, because he might untie the rope by mistake, because he's going to work in the area not knowing that you are hanging on it. So we stop. Either they leave, or we leave.

We break windows sometimes because back in the days, they used a different type of glass on high-rises. Sometimes they are so thin. We use a suction cup on every window to control our balance to not move sideways or away from the building. That's your handle; that's your wheel. Sometimes you push it too hard and the window goes in. It happens. We try to recover all the glass and tape the window quickly so nobody will get hurt.

Up high, there's birds—bats, hawks—that throw their stuff on the windows. Once it's dry, it's hard as stone. You got to scrape that off. They might be on a corner of the windows, and sometimes you don't see them. They're screaming at you. A hawk once took my hat because I got too close to her nest. I never knew there was a nest there. I'm supposed to clean the drain in that area, but around the corner there was a nest that I never saw. So when I went there, it felt like a big baseball hitting my head. I'm like, whoa, what happened? When I look up, there was a hawk with my hat. Yeah, it took my hat. She flew away and came back again, without my hat. She thought she took my head. So what I did was, I rappelled down and called it a day. It's the law; got to respect things like the hawks. They are endangered. Someone did whatever they had to do and took care of the hawk, and we came back the next day.

There are all kinds of people. Back in the days, it was fun because nobody would care. It wasn't a big deal to see naked people, for example. I had a situation four years ago where they were loving each other. I was with my guys. When they saw us, they didn't stop. They waved and kept going. They liked it. We [washed] it quickly and moved down quickly. And there was a couple, too, like five years ago, I think they were arguing about something. When they saw us, they gave like a polite wave, were closing the blind, and they kept arguing.

Sometimes people stop to see someone hanging outside. If the window is tinted, sometimes you can't see from the outside to the inside, but most of the time you can see them. They will watch you. Sometimes people get mad at me, because they can hear me, but I can't hear them. Because they're working or sleeping, they don't want to be bothered. So we told my guys, "If you want to sing, sing in your mind. Don't bother people." And, sometimes if they see us, they don't care. Sometimes they are like, "Can you clear it better?" I like it, yeah; that means they care for our job.

But these days, people are more sensitive, and they're different. They're trying to get freebies left and right, from freebies to lawsuits. So what we do is we send notices to people. They put notes on the elevators, because you have to. Not everybody likes it; sometimes they hate it, because they get scared.

I make a living. I'm raising a family, and it's good professional work. When it's nice and calm, you can do a lot of work. My guys work ten to twelve hours to take advantage of that good day. Most of my guys are all married, with kids. My wife thinks I'm crazy. She wants to me to quit every day. She's afraid I'm not going to come back. I tell her what kind of training we have, what kind of equipment we have, and she feels better. It's exciting knowing that a lot of people don't do it. You feel macho, man. You feel good, tough, strong. That's a good thing.

MIKE BALDWIN

AUTO REPOSSESSOR

*M*ike Baldwin owns an auto repossession company. He has been in this line of work for thirty-eight years. "Repossessing cars is an emotional burnout after a time. I think you see enough hardship in people's lives. I mean, if you're picking up twenty to thirty cars a week—that's what a good repossessor does—twelve to fourteen of those you will have contact with people; six or seven of them are pretty tough stories. You do that for four or five years and it will wear you down a little bit. It's a tough business. There is danger that is always lurking. 'We're representing the lender. We got bad news: I'm here to pick up your car.'"

★ ★ ★

Mike Baldwin

People want to hear what goes on. Are you allowed to carry guns? Have you ever been shot at? Have you ever shot at anybody? Things like that. It's questions I often get. I just straight-up tell people I'm in the automobile repossession business. It always gets a reaction.

People have a preconceived notion of repossessors: stereotypical kind of tough guys, that sort of thing. I quickly try to debunk the myth of bad guys. I've always been very professional, and I've been involved with the trade associations to help more professionalize the perception of the repossessor. There are, of course, always a few bad apples in any profession.

I point out that my guys are pretty smart fellows. I don't hire them for size. I hire them for their thinking ability and compassion. In interviewing them, and in my training, I really cover anger issues and how they should deal with it. One of the classics is, there's a guy putting his finger in your chest, making a point. What do you do? Don't take it personal; the guy is losing his car; he's unhinged; back away. If it gets out of control, leave the car; it's just a car.

I had a very strict upbringing. My father was hard-nosed, and while I was under his roof, he had a pretty good thumb on my brother and I. That probably had a little bit to do with when I got away from home: I spread my wings. I tried a lot of different things: worked in construction, in concrete, made pizza, bucked hay—the hardest job ever I did in my life—and then ended up in the repossession business, which turned out to be the most interesting and exciting job I've had. I think I broke my family's heart when I told them I was gonna try and start a repossession business. I think they had higher hopes for me.

My expectation was that it would be sort of a rolling adventure. You're thinking on your feet, you're always trying to find people—that's always been the fun part and a challenge. You're not dealing with hardened people. They want to do it on their terms whether or not they're making the payments. They just don't want to lose that car until they decide they're gonna give it up.

I worked for a repossession company for some time, and the fellow was a nice guy, but he had a drinking problem. He used me to go buy him a Mickey at the liquor store—that's what he used to call it. I was his only repossession employee. He would sit in the back office and drink out of his bag. I thought that's not really a good thing to be doing. Eventually I thought, maybe I could do a little better.

When he hired me, he said, "Don't break any locks, don't go into any garages; anything else is pretty well legal." He gave me an assignment. My brother-in-law and I found the car and I then thought, what do we do now? The car was on someone's property and it was just before dark. We repossessed it by getting into it and pushing it down the street, just like car thieves—I mean, repossession does appear in some sense to be theft. When we got done, I could barely stand, my knees were shaking so bad.

Then, I started my own business. I was twenty-four years old at the time, sort of wet behind the ears. I had to get out and pound on the doors of the lenders till I started getting a little bit of work. I went up to banks asking for their repossession work.

We quickly became adept at getting cars. This was back before they had locked steering and security alarms on cars. In those days, our tools were coat hangers; you know, the old hanger trick down the door to unlock it. And we hot-wired just about everything. We got very good at that. It sounds crude, but that was what it was. Later, we had a unique little tow bar; we called them "snatch bars." They had chain binders on each side and were quick to hook up and get out of there.

We progressed to where we became very good at picking locks. There was a time where there was a competition with my repossession employees to see if they could pick the lock before I could; it was a way to keep everybody sharp. We'd have a car that came in the night before and that we didn't have any keys to. Three or four of us would go out in the morning, and you would have thirty seconds or a minute to pick the lock. I was the last guy. If they couldn't get it done, then more times than not I could get it picked quicker than anybody else. You have to have a feel for tumblers and a soft touch to make lock picking work.

But locks got more sophisticated. You can hot-wire a car all day long, but if that steering was locked, you're not going anywhere. We could defeat most of the cars except General Motors. General Motors, early on, developed a lock system that was almost unpickable.

Eventually, you had to have a tow truck. The tow truck became a tool of the repossessor, and was a lot more practical. We generally had pickup trucks that had been converted to a tow truck—beefed up with springs, a shorter wheelbase, big motors in them. They weren't your standard-issue tow trucks; they were called "repossession tow trucks." We didn't have light bars and signs and all that, because you don't want to advertise when you go into a neighborhood.

When we got into the nineties, we were into more conventional tow trucks, to handle more weight. With the old-style tow trucks, you get under there with a J-hook that had those rubber or material slings that went under the front, but they did a lot of damage to fog lights, grilles, and all that. So the wheel-lift tow truck was developed for repossessors. That's what we employ today. We've got five wheel-lift tow trucks in this company. Now it's all about picking the car up by the tires; nothing to do anymore with metal or plastic or the frame. We'll back under your car and our truck will quickly grab the tires and lift it off the ground. As long as it's a two-wheel-drive car, you can just go. If it's a four-wheel drive you got to defeat, you got to get the whole car off the ground.

Typically, your average repossession probably occurs forty-five to ninety days delinquent, but there are occasions where there may be some history on the loan and where there have been problems or phone threats where the customer was not very nice to collectors. Lenders watch them a little closer, because they think there is a real problem there. Technically, you're delinquent a minute after the end of your due date. If your payment is due on the tenth and if you haven't paid by 12:01 AM on the eleventh, that's a technical delinquency. But in practicality, it all depends on the lender and the kind of credit risk you are. If you have a bank loan at Bank of America or someplace like that, and you have really good credit, they're gonna know this is an unusual event in your life and you're probably gonna communicate with them, so they're not gonna be trigger happy. However, if you have "B" or "C" credit (people that are less creditworthy and are paying higher interest to get the loan), they're gonna be watched more carefully, because the lender feels like they're more at risk.

Lenders give basic information on the delinquent loan: They give you the vehicle information, the loan information, the best addresses they have for the customer's home, and, if they have it, work information. They legally assign it to you as a repossession. Then you go out and effect a repossession the best way you can.

Up till about the mid-eighties, we did a lot of surveillance work. If the car was in the garage (you couldn't legally go in the garage), you tried to figure out where they worked. We would set up surveillance at five thirty or six in the morning, down the street watching the house. If the car is gonna come out of the garage, we would try and follow it to work, which we did a lot of times but is tough to do: You're in traffic during the traffic hour, you get too close to the car you're following and they're gonna see you, or if you hang back too far you're gonna get a red light; when you get the red light, and if you have invested a lot of time and effort into it, you're tempted to run that red light, because if you don't get through that light you're gonna lose them and then you wasted that entire morning.

Nowadays, it just doesn't work out as much. With our world today, neighborhood awareness is way up. Go and try to park at five in the morning in a neighborhood and sit there; see how long it takes for a police cruiser to come by and check you out. You find people that are protective of their neighbors. But it cuts both ways. In some neighborhoods, the guy that gets repossessed might be the guy that nobody on the block cares for—he has got an attitude or his dog poops on their yard, or something like that. We've found many times the neighbors are very helpful in telling us his patterns and when he will be around. Or, they are vigilantes by nature and they stick their nose in everybody's business.

There's only a certain amount of people that leave their cars in their driveway at night when they're two months delinquent on their payments. Most people have an inkling that's probably not a good thing to do if you want to be sure the car will be there in the morning. You're only gonna pick some of those up. The rest of them you're gonna have to get them at work, or you're gonna have to find some other way to get them, which is going to make you have contact with those people and they're gonna know what's going on.

If the car is in the garage and the garage door is closed and locked, you knock on the door and ask politely for the car. You try and talk the people into giving it up. We're very good at that. You might not get it the first trip, but will on the second or third trip. They don't have any way out. Eventually, there is a real good chance they will open it up, clean it out, and give it to you.

If the car is sitting in the garage with the garage door open, it's a bird of a different feather, especially if the car is kind of halfway out of the garage. We can actually back up to it, put our tow truck onto it, and as long as we can do it carefully, we can bring it out, because the garage was not closed and locked; it's like a carport at that point. We can enter the property as long as it's not locked and secured.

If it's a short driveway with a chain-link fence and it's locked, we can't go on the property. If it's an apartment house with a carport, it's fair game. If it's at work and it's not a security parking lot, it's fair game. Sitting on the street is fine, sitting on your lawn is fine, and most workplaces are okay.

When they come out and our truck is hooked up to their car and one end of the car is in the air, they pretty much give up. It's kind of a visual thing. They may be unhappy, but they get cooperative, and they give the keys up a lot of time. Then, after things have calmed down, we can finish the recovery by putting the dollies under the other end of the vehicle and get it all the way up off the ground.

You got to have good people skills, and not be talking down to people. We tell them we're representing the lender. They can see the tow truck out front, so they know before you say a word why you're there. Then, you'll get response and you'll build your dialogue based on the response you get, whether it's angry or it's reasonable. If it's angry, you try and calm them down. You don't want to scream through the door; that's not a good option. You can leave a note, or you can get them on the phone to humanize it a little bit: "Let's back up and start over, maybe I approached you wrong." You have no cards except your ability to talk to them. Talk about credit, about life, about what the future is gonna be: "I've got to write a report on this repossession and I would like to write one that says you cooperated. Lenders are gonna look at what I write, for a long time. You'll get out of this eventually and you're gonna be wanting to buy furniture and another car down the line." You know, that kind of thing.

I suppose if you're dealing with better credit people, they're probably more rational. Every now and then you get into a neighborhood where there's drugs and things like that, and those aren't such rational-thinking people. Our guys are instructed that if they feel threatened, to back away from a situation. I don't want you to get hurt. I don't want the equipment to get damaged. Nobody wants to get somebody put in jail. We let them blow off a little bit, and then calm them down. It's only a car; we will figure something else out. We've been through it a million times. We understand the gamut of emotions. We've got real thick skin.

Our philosophy is to keep your head up at all times, and understand the neighborhood you're in. Don't turn your back on anything while you're doing a repossession. I've never had anybody killed. I've never had anybody get cut with a knife. I've had guns go off and aimed at our trucks or the repossessed car. Everybody in my company that works in the field understands I feel it could happen to you at anytime. Somebody could pull a gun. Like you could run into somebody just wiped out on drugs and he has lost his bearings and they have a weapon. You got to keep that in mind and be able to dodge that ball quickly and intelligently but, hopefully, it never happens.

The repossessor's bane is when you know the people are coming to your place because the lender says the debtor is gonna redeem their car from you. They have to be hat in hand with the lender and talk nice to get their car back. But we have no control over them when they get here, and boy, if the license plate was twisted or there's any damage or maybe a scratch or something, it's like their car was totaled. Psychologically, you're the person they can let go on. They got no risk with us, so we've taken a lot of heat on releasing cars.

We bring in about twenty or more cars a night, every night, seven days a week. We release twenty a day. It's just a constant inflow and outflow of cars. The cars are secure here. I've got eighteen cameras. I've got cameras on everything. No, no dogs; I've used them over the years, but they're really problematic with people trying to kill them and feeding them poison. I had a guy discharge a fire extinguisher through the fence in my dog's face one time.

If we have their car here, they have to make an appointment to come and get their personal property back. They have come to the outside of the building where we have a chain-link fence with a pass-through door in it so we can hand them their property. I remember one incident where I'm passing a fellow his property and he looks at me and he says, "You know what a drive-by shooting is, don't you, because you're gonna experience one real quick." He was serious. I said, "Would you look up and smile for the camera that just recorded that?"

And then I had another guy we repossessed, a doctor—I hate repossessing doctors and lawyers because they think they're smarter than everybody else in the world, and they think you're the scum of the earth, and they hate the fact that they had to deal with you, so they're gonna let you know in about three seconds how terrible this is. Well, I'm doing a pass-through of this doctor's property—we can see each other quite well—and he drops some of his property that I'm handing him. He bends over to get it, and a Glock automatic falls out and bounces on the pavement. If he had started shooting, and if he was any good, he would have got me. We had a few tense moments, because he was really rattled and angry, but my nature wouldn't let me leave it alone. I said, "You know, I just put you on camera dropping that Glock. Do you have a permit to carry that?" He put it away, turned, and walked away. Obviously, he didn't have a permit, and I had him on camera with a concealed weapon.

One time, I repossessed Sonny Barger's car. Do you know who he is? A high-end Hells Angel. I repossessed his car for a lender, and I did it based on the lender promising me anonymity. I said I'll try and repossess it, but the deal is I want to be totally anonymous on this. They agreed to it.

The lender had good information, so we knew where Sonny's car was. I was still young and beating on my chest a little bit, and that's probably why the lender came to me. The repossession, other than being scary, wasn't technically very difficult.

I went into the Hells Angels' encampment. You saw a few motor-cycles on the street and you saw signs of activities going on. It was dark, dangerous, and in an area I didn't want to spend much time. I pulled that car out of there. It was a something like a Chevelle; it wasn't anything special.

After a repossession, you have to make a law enforcement report to avoid a theft report. I did that, but I said I was the employee of the lender, which I was in a third-party sense, because I worked for them. So when Sonny called—"Where's my car?"—he's gonna hear the lender has it. Two days later, the lender calls me and said, "He's on his way to your office, and he's really pissed off." And I said, "How did he know where my office is?" The lender said, "One of our people in here screwed up and gave it up. We thought we should warn you."

About that time I hear this car come skidding into my parking lot. My office had a glass door that you opened up to reach the public counter, and I was at my desk and I could see the front door very well. Well, he came in threatening and snarling, wanted to get his stuff out of his car and he wanted to get his car. He was gonna do it right now, or somebody was gonna get frigging hurt if it didn't happen instantly. So I slid my desk drawer open where my .38 with a two-inch barrel was sitting. I watched him for a little bit. The people in the front office couldn't handle him at all. At this point, I saw him pull a knife out; it had about a six-inch blade on it. He started to jump up on the counter, and that's the time I put the gun in my hand. He came up on the counter, I leveled the gun at him, and I said, "If you come off the counter on this side, you're dead when you hit the ground. If you get off the counter and get out the door, you'll be safe." I'm shaking. He looked at me and said, "You and I aren't done," and he left. We moved the car about twenty minutes later to where he would never see it, and we made a police report. It was way more dangerous than it was worth. The lender didn't protect me like we agreed. I wish I had never gotten involved in that one. It didn't go anywhere, but his threat was a threat. For about a year and a half, I was very careful where I went. I figured maybe they might try to off me.

I feel crummy from time to time when you have a single mom with kids, or you lost your job, or you have health problems, or you are recently divorced, and then you have to take their car. You're never happy about a situation like that. You have compassion and are empathetic, but if it came from one of my core clients—let's say it came from Bank of America—I can't tell Bank of America, I'll take most of your work, but these I can't do. I'm out of business, end of the story. So you have to take it all.

I still love coming to work. It's very stimulating because it's still an adventure and a challenge. You get paid for finding people, whether they're hiding a $40,000 car or a $100,000 car. For the most part, I think I'm held in good stead with most of the people I've dealt with. We do it professionally, honestly, and morally. I work very hard to make sure we don't tread on the people I take cars from.

Photo Courtesy of: T. LEBARON

FRANK WEISSER

BLUE ANGELS PILOT

*F*rank Weisser joined the Blue Angels in 2007. The thirty-year-old Navy lieutenant has a distinguished flying career, including thirty-four combat missions over Iraq. Today's air show begins in a few hours. He is standing near his squadron's F/A-18s: "When you're in formation, streaking through the skies eighteen inches from another airplane, doing flips and rolls, and you're doing five hundred miles an hour and under heavy Gs, one-hundredth of an inch of movement in the stick would lead you to hit that airplane. That could potentially cause a four-airplane fireball. We do it safely every single day because of how focused everyone is, and because of the training and safety practices we have in place. None of these guys are scared when they are in their airplane, because they know they can do it. However, you have to know *that the guy flying that Number 1 jet knows what he is doing and he's not going to fly that whole formation into the ground. He is going to hit his numbers and he is going to do right every single time, because when you're flying, you're only looking at very specific parts of that airplane to make sure you're in the right exact spot."*

★ ★ ★

I'm a Blue Angels pilot. My job basically is to put on an air show for millions of Americans all over the country to showcase the professionalism in the military. The Blue Angels are a small squadron in the navy that represents everyone else out there in the navy and the Marine Corps who is serving our country. We have seven F/A-18 pilots. I fly the Number 6 jet, one of the two solo pilots.

I think everyone who serves wants to serve, and part of your heart wants to be deployed overseas. There is a time in every navy pilot's career path where they can't be overseas, where we rotate to shore duty, typically as flight instructors or test pilots. That's the time in your career when you can get to go to the Blue Angels. There are a lot of guys who want to do it, because you get to fly a lot, and it's exciting flying. You're low, you're fast, you're under heavy Gs the whole time, and you get to see the country. So for me, it was kind of an obvious choice. I don't know any navy pilots who don't want to be Blue Angels. I don't mean that to sound arrogant, I just think it's an exciting job.

The pilots that we hire don't do it only because the flying is exciting. If that is their first goal, that can't be the right goal. The first goal has to be to represent the navy and the Marine Corps in the best fashion you absolutely can, to proudly represent the guys and gals that are overseas. The fact that there's really exciting flying that goes along with it is a real added bonus for us. I don't think there's another squadron in the navy where I would fly more than I fly here: five times a day, sometimes six. And it's not just flying from one place to another. It's high Gs, flying upside down, undergoing rapid pressurization changes as the airplane goes from the surface to fifteen thousand feet in seconds, which is usually the highest we go in our air shows. It's action-packed, fun flying. It's a unique experience to your body and feels like a really aggressive workout. It's like going to the gym for an hour and just giving everything that you have. When you get out, you'll be wiped out.

Additionally, you're speeding up and slowing down. You can feel the rapid acceleration and deceleration. The biggest kind of physical limiting factor is the acceleration force of gravity, that everybody calls "G-forces." We undergo G-forces in the "Z plane," which means it's through your head and down through your stomach, rather than the "X-Y plane" like a NASCAR driver who takes Gs sideways. We take it directly through our head, which means if you're under too many Gs and you're not doing the right things to combat them, you can lose the blood to your head and you can experience either worse vision, that is, a graying effect, or total lights-out.

We go through a lot of training in a centrifuge just so that we are aware of our own limitations. Because of our training, I'm not going to let it happen to me; that's not an issue. You're aware of what you experienced in training, what leads up to it, know how close you can take yourself to that point, and then you also know to recognize it should it happen.

We have a saying that "you got to be ready to go when you strap the jet on," which means we'll envision ourselves literally strapping the jet on our back, like you're going to put a backpack on. When I put my right arm through my right shoulder strap and my left arm through my left shoulder strap, at that point I've strapped the jet on, and I have to have a 100 percent focus. It's a sixteen-point harness, so you're going to end up clicking in sixteen different spots. The straps obviously are tight, because they have to keep us in the jet when we're upside down or experiencing rapid negative or positive Gs. You've got thirty-two thousand pounds of thrust in your back, which is enough to rocket you accelerating upward.

You get in a zone in that you have to have total concentration. Everyone, you know, has problems in their life. You might have been having a bad morning, but you have to be focused when you climb up that ladder to the plane. That's our last chance to kind of check it before you put that jet on your back. There is so little room for error, especially with the Blue Angels, when you're flying so low and so fast. Even half a second of your attention taken for something like the fact that our child is sick or that you just got yelled out by your boss is enough for you to ultimately have a close call, or worse. Being with our family and friends is what we do in our life outside that airplane and is obviously important to us, but you have to realize that if you don't leave behind whatever's going on, your life is at risk. You have to do it.

Every day, the Blue Angels are striving for excellence, in every maneuver, in every single thing we do—even in every handshake with every kid that we meet. Every one of these performers put their lives on the line every day, and they do it because they love flying and they love what goes on, and they love letting people dream about being in the air. Everyone here watching imagines they are up there as pilots.

One of the things that's different for me than probably the rest of the guys you see, and probably a lot of guys in uniform that are aviators, is that I never wanted to fly. I never saw an air show till I was in flight school, but I knew I always wanted to serve. I knew that at age twelve. I was in sixth grade when the first Gulf War started. I was so proud of the men and women serving then. I said I have to do that. I felt the call to go serve my country. I decided that the Naval Academy has the most options when you leave: It offers flying, Navy Seals, submarines, being on ships, the Marine Corps. I went to the Naval Academy with no expectation of flying. I just wanted to serve. And then they told me, "You're going to fly." That was awesome. I fell in love with it on the very first flight as we rolled into a steep turn and you could feel the airplane and the wind. It was a phenomenal experience for me.

There's no military service in my family. My dad was a doctor in nuclear physics, worked for Bell Labs. My mom was a programmer for NASA. Like I said, the impetus for my career was, no kidding, the first Gulf War. I never really wavered from it. It just felt right to me, and I'm glad I did it. At this point in my life, I don't love being gone from my family all the time. I don't love that stuff, but my wife is as passionate about service to her country as I am. As much as I would like to be home more, I'm prepared to be away, because there is such a passion to serve. I would be ashamed of myself if I left the service.

I think, though, there is a point for everyone in their military service where it becomes to some degree a little bit less about serving your country and more about serving the guys and gals who work with you. I know that's true for the guys on the ground that I've talked to when they are looking at the unfortunate end of a rifle on a daily basis. There's some sort of a transformation that happens where they are serving for their brothers in arms. I mean, I'm doing it for these other guys that I fly with and I'm doing it for the other one hundred people on the team and I'm doing it for the other 330,000 guys in the navy, because they are doing it. I'm not going to shirk my duties or let up on the march if they are pulling their weight, too.

I deployed in 2005 on the USS *Theodore Roosevelt*. The aircraft carrier is a phenomenal place. It's a home for six months, twelve months. It's a self-sufficient unit and it needs to resupply minimally. Its natural weapon is not the missiles that are shot; it's not the .50 caliber guns on the deck; it's not torpedoes. Its weapon is the air wing, the one hundred airplanes it takes with it. Those airplanes and its pilots are the weapon system on that carrier, so that when something like Afghanistan opens up, or Iraq, we're already there, and we can be on the scene, no kidding, in fifteen minutes. We are always ready. The Navy has done that basically since 1776. The other services don't have a steady deployment schedule like the Navy always has had. War or not, we're always going to be gone. There is always going to be a presence overseas, because that's what we do, and being deployed on an aircraft carrier, well, obviously, you're going to be away from wife and children. If you have to be gone, it's a really neat way to be gone.

One of the real challenges for Navy pilots is you always have to come back and land on the aircraft carrier. Usually the most challenging part of our flight is landing on the boat at night. There was a study that was done years ago where they took heart rate monitors and had them on guys who were being shot at by surface-to-air missiles and were having to defend from having the airplane blown up, yet their heart rate was higher when they're landing on the carrier at night than it was when they were trying to dodge a missile. I honestly believe landing on a boat at night is the most difficult thing in all of aviation. You literally have single to double digits in feet to hook and catch, and stop in a couple of hundred feet. And, your airplane has to be within less than five feet vertical distance to be in the right spot. We're going to try to come across the back of the boat at the exact same height every time. If you're ten feet high or low with the airplane, that could be the difference of life or death. It's actually a little bit like what we do in the Blue Angels because of how exacting the air show business is; it's almost like you're going on the aircraft carrier.

We talk about being on brain stem power the first time you land on an aircraft carrier, because your body and muscles have to know what they're doing without you being able to think about it. When you see that aircraft carrier for the very first time and you have to land on it, whether it's nerves or just apprehension or whatever the case might be, it is really hard to think clearly. Your muscles are going to do what your body knows to do to that airplane even if you're not thinking about making the right corrections. After that, once you have done it a couple of times, you get the nervousness out of your system. Then it's fine. We spend a lot of time practicing carrier approaches over and over and over again so that we can do it and go out there safely.

There are so many people involved in making a safe arrest—meaning a landing on the boat—from the pilot who is flying the aircraft to the landing signals officers who stand on the back of the boat with radios and lights who talk the guys in by giving small, last-minute corrections needed to land safely. And there are the guys who are checking the gear and arresting cables to make sure they are set, and the guys who are rigging weight. There are different weight settings for every plane. Let's say my airplane and I weigh thirty-five thousand pounds and they set it for twenty thousand, then that wire is going to split. Or, if they set it for forty thousand pounds and my airplane only weighs twenty-five thousand, then it's going to rip the back end of my airplane off because it's not going to play out at the right amount, and sometimes that happens. None of us are perfect. There have been issues where someone doesn't set that weight just right, the airplane lands, and you slow down a little bit to grab that three-inch wire, but the weight is not set right, and so the wire snaps. Now, the airplane is too slow to go flying again but too fast to stop under its own brakes. There is that line snapback they talk about where that thing flings back and could cut off legs of people on the boat. It'll rip through bodies, and it'll rip through other airplanes. It's all very dangerous.

As someone who didn't know the Blue Angels before I flew, I expected them to be—I hesitate to use the word—"cowboys" who want to fly fast and aggressively, but I was really pleasantly surprised that they are a group of serious, professional men and women who really want to do their job well and safely. I was just so impressed by how serious everybody was about their job, and how exacting and how hard they work. When our air show ends this afternoon, we'll meet kids for fifteen to twenty minutes, take pictures, do some recruiting, and then we'll sit in a room for two hours and watch the tape of our show in slow motion over and over again, sometimes two or three times. The mistakes that we'll find, and work to fix, are things you never see at normal speed, and you certainly would never see if you didn't have a camera zoomed in on tiny amounts of movement. You want to see everyone just rock solid right next to each other. There always will be a certain amount of movement, but by being focused and being mentally and physically on top of your game, you can minimize it. We will work on that for hours, not because it might enhance the show for the crowd but because we are serious about what we do. If we take it serious, then our show gets better, and we won't take what we're doing for granted.

Before our shows, we talk about the wind and any corrections we need to make for showmanship and for safety. When the wind gets up to about fifteen to twenty knots, we start talking about safety issues. When you're flying really close, you feel the wind and feel each other getting pushed around together. You don't want to make the wrong correction, because someone else might make the proper correction for the wind, and that's obviously a conflict there. If the wind is twenty-five knots or more, then we will take a look on whether we should go flying.

Our longest show is forty-five minutes, which means the weather is perfect and we're going to use the surface up to fifteen thousand feet, so we might have up to twenty-five maneuvers. We do two separate things where we'll split into two groups, and pilots Numbers 1 through 4 fly together in a tight diamond formation, and pilots Numbers 5 and 6 fly as solos. They do opposing maneuvers where one will come from the left, one will come for the right, and they will cross right at the center point. They might cross right center up, they might cross ninety degrees off, like on a knife-edge. They might cross together upside down, they might be both spinning when they cross, and they'll do some things together. Then, at the very end, we have three, four, five maneuvers, depending on the weather, where we'll have all six planes together. It keeps the air show a little more exciting and action packed.

You know when you're doing well. In aviation, just like in sports, you can tell when everything is running smoothly and clicking just right. The thing is, we talk all the time in aviation about compartmentalization, where you go up there and, say, you have a maneuver that made the hair on the back of your neck stand up. Well that's fine, because you've got twenty-two more maneuvers to go. You put that one maneuver behind you and get back in, for the next one could be the best one in the whole air show. If you didn't do something just like you want to do, you can improve the rest of the flight. We do that because everyone is working so hard to do it right.

Here is a quick aside: The single best person I've ever met was my college roommate who eventually became a navy pilot. His name is Ben Becker and, sadly, he died in an airplane crash with his family a couple of years ago. He was just the most phenomenal guy I've ever met. He joined the navy and went to the Naval Academy because he saw a Blue Angels air show as a little kid. So in my mind, if I can inspire one little guy or gal to do what we do—and from that person to somebody else—well, mission accomplished for me.

R. E. "SONNY" DUNLAP

SPECIAL RESPONSE TEAM AGENT

R. E. "Sonny" Dunlap weighs 165 pounds and is six feet tall. We talked twice: The first time was at my house; the second time was by cell phone as he drove to an airport with his gear and Poncho, his trained canine, for a flight to join other agents for a special operation. "My heroes are the beat cop that's out there doing his or her job, the military, ministers, and my fellow agents. A lot of times they just call themselves 'POAs'—plain ol' agents. That's humility."

★ ★ ★

I'm a federal agent assigned to a special operations team with the Bureau of Alcohol, Tobacco, Firearms and Explosives. I'm on a SRT:

a special response team. I'm forty-five years old, and I've been doing this for ten years. You have to be with the bureau a number of years before you can be put in as an SRT member. You go through the academy, and then you make it. To make the grade, you have to be committed to this lifestyle because it takes you away from your loved ones.

I started out as a teacher, and coached football, basketball, track, and tennis. I taught in public schools for six years, and also raised beef cattle in Texas. I always had a bit of an interest in law enforcement, particularly in people like firemen, paramedics, and beat cops who were involved in any type of emergency system and whose task was to make sure we all sleep safely. When I was a young man, I would look at a photograph where you see a critical incident happen and, usually, you see the masses running away from it. But when you look into such a photograph, you'll see maybe one individual, or two, who are running toward the incident exhibiting a warrior's spirit.

I have specialized training as a special agent. It's comprehensive and it brings in all the different venues that we put together as an ATF agent. You could very well be working arsons, explosives, gun trafficking, alcohol and tobacco tax diversion. All special agents are trained in tactical maneuvers and can handle doing search warrants or arrest warrants. Agents have to know that they can mentally and physically meet that challenge to be the hands-on guys that are actually going to be laying hands on whoever poses a threat. We come with so much resolve that 9.9 times out of 10 an individual will surrender. Because of the sheer nature of an SRT operation, we can subdue a person even when they make statements like, "I'll go out shooting."

I currently have an assignment on one of five SRT teams as a tactical canine handler. There currently are a total of six canine handlers among the five teams. The dogs we use are German Shepherds or Belgian Malinois. It's the choice of the handler which dog they are going to use. I have a German Shepherd named Poncho, a phenomenal dog, extremely loyal. I've had him for two and a half years. Poncho's mission is to help us search for an individual, help us track an individual should they flee, and apprehend them if the situation merits that. Poncho brings the dimension of that individual not knowing what the dog will do, whereas the suspect knows that I am not going to use any kind of unmerited force, no matter what words are said to me. Words can escalate things, especially if there is a group—it's just the way it is in human nature—and when it escalates, then things can get out of control. The dogs have the ability, just in who they are, to show up and make people be better citizens.

Our SRT teams are strategically placed throughout the United States to respond to situations in different regions. An operation can vary from eleven to twenty members per team. A federal agent's credentials tell you that you are to execute search warrants, or make arrests for violations against the United States. What is so unique and comforting for me is that we all know one another on the team, and we all train exactly the same.

We're clothed in BDUs—battle dress uniforms—they're green, they have "POLICE" on the back. On the front, we have a cloth ATF badge, and then we have the American flag on our sleeves, and also the special operations team emblem. Then you have your belt that can be used for emergency rapelling, if you need to; you have a heavy-type tactical boot to keep your wheels safe; you have Kevlar body armor with the trauma plate in the front and back to protect the vitals; you have Nomex gloves that are flame retardant so your hands are covered; and you have a Kevlar helmet and goggles. You have also your Eagle headset. Communication is paramount, because you have to have concise communication instantaneously for team tactical unit leaders to be able to relay and make decisions. We also have, for example, an ASP—the expandable baton—and we have a Taser system, which is one of our less lethal weapons. We then go into our secondary weapons, which are our .40 caliber SIG 226 sidearm and our primary weapon, a M4 carbine rifle.

One other thing you have is training for defensive tactics, such as for close quarters countermeasures, which is hand-to-hand contact.

Our operators are trained on subduing people if it's deemed that you need physical defensive tactics to restrain a person, because some day you may have to engage a person physically.

When I first came on, there was an SRT operation, and in that operation a suspect justifiably had lethal force used on him. As a law enforcement agent, you're always reacting, and in any type of conversation you have with anyone in this occupation, reaction is slower than action. So you're already behind the eight ball. When individuals are approached and lethal force is used on them, agents muster up the courage to react and make the situation safe for society. That is why I will always respect the men and women that are in this line of work.

I rely on training and the people I work with, and I believe that every operator has some type of belief. For example, each operator has their own Pelican—it's the hard suitcase–type deal that we carry our gear in—and in that will be all kinds of different things: It may be a charm, or it may be a photograph of your children or your family. You can look in a man's helmet, and inside, he will have taped there a picture of his family or something that is important to him. I have a photo of my daughter in my helmet, and I also taped one on the inside of my Pelican so when I open it up to start putting my gear on before I go into an operation, she is the first and last thing I see. So, there is training and then there is the sense of belief.

What we do prior to an operation is that the intel on the place is worked up, and we will do an operational plan. Then we will have a briefing on the breakdown of the individuals, what we need to look at, and how to facilitate this arrest warrant or search warrant without there being any injuries or deaths. Right before the initiation of the operation, we're pretty well in tune with what we need to do. Now, that is never 100 percent, because even when you have a schematic of a building, once you walk into the building it may not be anything like that, or you may have a person that is deemed to be very violent but they, that day, decide, okay, I give up, and become very passive. Or, you may have [a person] identified as maybe not much of a threat who then becomes a person who decides to shoot at you. All these different variables are going on, but you still have this feeling of comfort because you are as prepared as you can be prepared.

There are always threats, because, as an SRT operator, when you go into a situation the first thing is that you try to render the area safe. We have criteria that we look at when it comes to a situation, which is, number one, keep things safe for a hostage, should there be one. The second [concern] is safety for the general public. Those are the two things, besides our partners, that we put our life and limb first for. Then there is the suspect. What keeps us different from the criminal are the laws we enforce and our professionalism in keeping society safe. Sometimes we have to go into a situation knowing that we may have to kill. There is a distinction in killing and murdering, and to have a sovereign and safe society to live in, sometimes lethal force may be administered.

What we do isn't a game. There is human life on both ends, whether it's the person committing the crime, or the people that have sworn to render that situation safe so that it can be adjudicated. It was explained to me one time that it's kind of like being a professional athlete, except it's not a game. You are paid to travel, you are expected to stay in condition, you are expected to work out, you are paid to perform, and you are mandated to perform, but the end result can be something that can stay with you the rest of your life and it can trouble your soul. When we go into like a home that has a meth lab or you go into where they're selling drugs, or there are explosives that are used to inflict harm, and you see children exposed to this, and you have to arrest their parents, you see their eyes and their little hearts. You do the job, and you get it done, but I've realized that you just don't separate it, you carry a little bit of them with you. I guess, being a father and a person, hopefully, of compassion, you hope that in the goodness of society they have a chance and that they will live as a functioning person that adjusts.

The adrenaline spikes in this job are a big thing, because you can guarantee that it's gonna happen. I think a person would be a bit foolish to not have an understanding of the potential of it, because, like I said, it's absolutely not a game. Going into a situation, you have the adrenaline spikes to begin with, and then as soon as shots happen, that's when your ears really become perked. But through training and experience you tend to start leveling off a little bit, and you are assessing quicker. But no matter how trained you are, when you hear rounds go, it checks you up a notch. Even though you are going to facilitate an arrest, you are going after a person who is breaking federal law. Being an SRT member, you have resolved to get the job done. You are the last line of defense for society. If you don't get it done, the person escapes, and more can happen down the road.

This particular operation is pretty typical: You have a prior felon with semiautomatic firearms at a methamphetamine lab. What we do is we're given a federal search warrant and/or a federal arrest warrant, and then we implement the will of the Justice Department. The individual came out and began shooting at the team. This is out in a very rural area with a lot of outbuildings, a lot of cars with the hoods up and the trunks up, just a lot of junk.

The individual came out with his buddies and they began shooting. I think what had happened was the individuals had come out and seen that it wasn't going to go their way. I was assigned to the react team covering off the threats, that is, the team that covers our forward observers, or snipers—the term "forward observer" is the common term used now, but that person is indeed trained as a sniper. I was also trained as a forward observer, but here, I was looking for any kind of potential lethal threat. So anyway, we came in to help, because some of the individuals had run into the woods. Obviously, with meth labs, they knew that they're breaking federal laws, and as prior felons with firearms, it is breaking federal law anyway. They engaged the team. The team, with resolve, ended that. Two people were shot. One was shot by one of the other criminals in the mayhem that was going on. Everyone was apprehended.

These people that we're asked to serve our resolve on are people that are committing the crime knowingly and defiantly, and on that day you're gonna have one of two people: You're gonna have the one who puts up a fight, or the one that says, "Okay, I give up." It's not that they want to give up, it's like a reaction: "They caught me."

I was in either fifty-two or fifty-four operations last year. To an operator, it's the job we love, but it's really just what we do. There may not be a whole lot of excitement always, but about half of the ops have had some type of incident that requires an adjustment. Now, that being said, there is always the comfort level of an operational plan. What's so beautiful about being able to do our operational plans is that the field agents doing the work that goes into the SRT operational plans spend copious amounts of hours making sure that we make it as safe as possible and still carry out a federal magistrate's issuance of a search warrant or an arrest warrant. In every operation, we hope for good things to happen, but we plan for the worst. We never go into it with a laissez-faire kind of attitude, mainly because anything can happen, and it does a lot of times. There's kind of a running joke that we always know that "Mr. Murphy is in our stack." What that is saying to the layperson is that Murphy's Law is out there, and as much as I believe in fate and the grace of God to continue to do a taxing job, I also believe in Murphy's Law. It just happens, so you have got to be able to prepare on the fly and make adjustments.

Another operation that I'll relate to you is an incident that happened in Colorado. This operation was deemed a home-invasion operation: two individuals who conspired to hit another known drug supplier and take their guns, their dope, and their money, which to a lot of people would think, let them fight amongst themselves. But the scary part of that is when that happens, the people that will do that have no regard for the personal safety for the civilian that's out there, and a lot of times if things start going bad, they will shoot at random.

In law enforcement, you have to have an acquired target before you deploy lethal force, and that target has to be someone that's a threat. Gang members, as drive-by shootings obviously show, will shoot at will, so we have to always keep that in thought wherever this situation goes down. In the background of an operational plan, the agents are always given a heads-up if a person has had any type of specialized training—military, martial arts, or being a member of a gang—because if they're armed, they have their pecking order and their people genuinely are good fighters.

So, we get a call that there's a warning order going out; that warning order will tell us where we're supposed to be and the briefing time, usually the following day. I was at the SRT office in Los Angeles. Through the warning order, we know if it will be a rural or an urban operation. Most operators have two sets of kits with our gear ready to go, a rural kit and an urban kit. I check my kits, make sure I'm good to go. I have my dog squared away, ready to go. I start making my flight arrangements, then I deployed.

I made it to Colorado, squared myself away in a hotel, received a briefing that evening, and had a night's rest before the early morning operation. We had, I believe, sixteen operators. The number of bad guys is sometimes an unknown, because it can vary, but in this operation he—the main gang player—showed up with only one other gang member.

Our team split into two formations so we could address both individuals. When I say "split," it's a controlled division. You are told to stay with a group but I, as a canine operator, can float a bit, because things can change—a person can fight or run, or if the forward observers say he may be armed, then I can flow into that group and help. It's a very, very quick adjustment with a whole lot of variables that have to be assessed, and then you just have to make a decision on which way to go. Here, we have the team deployed out in two different areas, one to address an individual in one spot and the other team to address the other in another spot. It's never a luxury when you're going after armed individuals, but for us as operators it's a luxury knowing that our forward observers are giving us real-time information so that we can rapidly deploy. It can be a bit overwhelming for the bad guys, so nine times out of ten they will surrender, but the one that doesn't surrender still has fighting on his mind or he tries to escape.

I had to quickly assess the two suspects as to who would be the most likely to pose a problem, and if it merits me deploying Poncho, then I would do that. When I'm with a canine, I don't have my M4 carbine. I have him on one hand, and when I do have my pistol out it's in the other hand. When we deployed, there was one individual on our left, a forty-five-year-old; the other is a twenty-six-year-old. I addressed the forty-five-year-old, who we anticipated to be probably the most violent of the two. About twenty-five yards from him, we came from concealment—I can't tell you where; I wish you could, because it would click a lot and you'd think, wow, that's really ingenious, but I can't do that. So anyway, we're coming from cover. I address him first, and the other operators who I'm with kind of break off. We're in our uniforms so we're obviously the police. We're giving him commands like, "If you have a weapon, drop the weapon. Do it now. Follow our commands." The individual to my left starts crow-hopping like he is maybe going to run, or put up a fight. He did neither one of those; we subdued him, handcuffed, and then secured him.

However, as I told you before, it's a bad feeling to be behind the eight ball—reaction does not equate to action; action has already got you. When I turn to address the second individual, I heard escalation in the voice of the operator who I was standing next to: "Drop the gun! Do it now!" That's an indicator to me that things are going downhill. So as I'm assessing on deploying my dog, that individual draws a weapon from his waistband and starts casting it in our direction. At that time, another operator addressed him with lethal force. What happened is that the operator shot three times in rapid fire, but as his weapon was coming up, the suspect—only through the grace of God—was not hit because he had started falling to the ground just as the operator deployed his rounds. In the wall behind this individual, there were three perfectly grouped rounds, exactly where they needed to be to stop the threat. Due to the fact I'm deploying the dog and also probably gonna be hands-on with the individual, I have my weapon holstered, for I'm relying on the professionalism of the operators next to me to get things done. But because of the threat level of this happening, I'm reaching for my weapon. This individual who drew his weapon still is not completely compliant, so I addressed him verbally, telling him to follow our commands: "Do it now, or I will release the dog!" At that point, he became extremely compliant as most people do when they understand the magnitude of things. We continued our advancement and cuffed him.

These individuals violated federal statutes, because one was a drug user, both of them had prior felony charges, and they're bringing firearms, which they cannot be in possession of in a situation in furtherance to commit another federal violation. Also, we found out that these two individuals confessed to being involved in a couple of bank robberies in that area.

The job is a lifestyle; it requires an enormous amount of travel with an enormous amount of gear, which can be taxing on your body. Part of the job is flying commercially, getting from point A to point B. The glamour of travel, for me, went out the window the first week. You have so much gear and you're responsible for it, which can affect you professionally and monetarily, but you deal with it. Also with the travel, you miss family things. You miss graduations, you miss singing Christmas carols, a lot of things. I feel a bit of guilt rides with us.

All the men and women I work with in ATF are brave people, but even with that, there's adrenaline spikes in every operation we do. When a weapon is deployed in your direction, or shots are fired in your direction, obviously it takes the ultimate adrenaline spike. The beauty of the way that the ATF and other law enforcement agencies work is that you brief out an ops plan, you rehearse it, you execute it, and then you debrief it immediately after to find out what you could have done different. As I said, Mr. Murphy is always in our stack, so there's gonna be issues at the debriefing. Then you can make your adjustments for something that happened in that situation to make it better next time. And then, later that night is when you really have a kind of adrenaline dump.

The element of danger, whether it happens or not, is there and sometimes it happens. What happens from the initiation of an operation through completion is you do the job, and when it's done, you go back with your buddies. If that buddy just happened to keep you alive that day, you slap him on the back, you thank them, and then you tell them, "Hey, I'll buy you something to drink," a soda pop or maybe something stiffer a little bit later on when things are taken care of. To be in any special operation, be it federal or local, you are kind of a silent professional. You don't really talk about a lot of things about the job, which is really good, because, to me, it keeps humility. Wherever there is humility, there is always professionalism.

Faith is paramount, because my daughter is the most important thing to me. The way I adapt with the possibility of not getting to see her again is through the faith that I'm relying on my superiors for training, I'm relying on my team leader for operation development, and I'm relying on my teammates 100 percent; they have helped me stay alive, and they know I will do 100 percent for them. Faith in God is important in my walk through this occupation. If you have a belief in a supreme being, that's when a lot of calls are made to the family, "Hey, you might hear about it on television, but all is good, nobody is hurt, we caught the bad guys."

JOHN KABAKOFF

CAB DRIVER

*J*ohn Kabakoff drives a cab in Chicago. I am waiting at the curb for him. He stops, then drives us to a café where we can talk. "I've never had a person pull a knife or a gun on me in the cab," he tells me. "I've been robbed a couple of times by people with guns, but not in the cab. The last was six or seven years ago by some guy outside my building. I don't know if he followed me home from where I parked the cab, but he was behind me when I was going into the side door of my building, and he had a gun. I was tired and wasn't very cautious. He surprised me."

John Kabakoff

Later, Kabakoff continues describing his job as he drives me around town. "Most people are strangers, but almost all the time people are very honorable. I try to use good judgment."

★ ★ ★

I never get lonely on the job. I value my solitude. When I'm driving, half the time I'm alone and half the time I'm with other people. That's a nice mix. There are times when I like the quiet and there are times I have moods. They're not as extreme as they have been at certain times in my life, but I have moods sometimes. Sometimes I don't want any conversation.

I'm a cab driver. Most people have this concept in their mind about what a cab driver is. What does a cab driver do? How does he earn his living? Everyone has an impression. To some extent, it depends on your experience. It could be positive, it could be negative. It could depend on the person's station in life and where the person is as far as valuing you as a cab driver.

I'm sixty-nine, and have been doing it a little over ten years. My last regular job was working for the State of Illinois. I was a caseworker, dealing with welfare situations like issuance of medical cards, food stamps. A lot of it was over the phone, but most of it was routine paperwork and thousands and thousands of pages of rules and regulations. It's not pleasant memories, not because of the recipients, it was the bureaucracy. I knew I couldn't stay where I was; it was too painful.

I was outside a 7-Eleven one night having a cup of coffee, trying to figure out what I was gonna do next. Along comes an old friend, parks his cab to go inside to get some coffee, and we struck up a conversation. I asked him how he liked his work and so on and so forth. A light went on inside me: I realized that what he was doing was something that I should be doing, for the freedom, and because I've always loved to drive and meet different people. You can drive wherever you want, you can take a break if you want, you can have lunch if you want, and you can go home early as long as you put in your time to make the money you need.

Although drivers often refer to themselves as working, say, for Flash or Yellow, we really are all independent contractors. I'm not affiliated. I don't have a dispatching radio. I get my passengers from the street. They wave me down. Sometimes I work the hotel lines and the doorman will whistle for me.

I work approximately fifty hours a week, which might seem like a lot for a guy my age, but I enjoy my work. I like working in the afternoon and the evenings best, because people are more relaxed, the traffic isn't much, and the tips tend to be larger. Most days, I start at two or three in the afternoon, and I work until anywhere from eleven until maybe two in the morning. I cut it down to maybe five or six hours on Sundays.

When you're talking about risky occupations, most people would think the risk involved in driving a cab would probably be about passengers who might be dangerous, but there are other risks, most of which are other drivers. Drivers who are the riskiest ones are the phone talkers. Between 20 and 30 percent of the drivers in Chicago are on their phones, and they can't possibly be paying attention to their driving. They're kind of like people under the influence of alcohol; their driving amounts to the same thing. While they're having a phone conversation, they're totally into that and are not paying much attention to what's going on around them, like other cars or traffic lights.

A few times people have run into the side of my car at the rear end, maybe because they're drunk or under the influence of drugs, or because they're on their phone or they're looking back. I've got to be careful all the time. It's important to remember to always to drive defensively, and also not to become angry. You don't want to ever be angry. I work on not being angry. I mean, I'm a human, so I have gotten angry, but I try to get over it as quickly as I can. There are things like when someone is on their horn behind me and I'm going the speed limit. I'll give you another example: I'm at an intersection where I've got a red light and I want to make a right turn, and there's a sign there at the intersection that says, "No turn on red," and there's an individual behind me on his horn, he wants me to turn right. Now, I might slip into anger; however, I don't want to hold any anger. I want to get over that anger quickly. Once I recognize and acknowledge my emotion, then it kind of evaporates, it's gone. I certainly don't hang on to that anger, because it can easily turn into resentment. You don't want that to happen, because it's not fun being a resentful person.

I don't take all fares, but I don't drive along thinking about what kind of person I want in my cab or what kind of person I don't want in my cab; it's an automatic subconscious situation, it's built in. Say if somebody is waving a bottle of beer and wobbling around on the curb wanting me to pick him up, he's obviously drunk; maybe he's got a beer in one hand and a phone in the other and screaming and hollering on his telephone where you can hear him two blocks away. I'm not gonna pick that person up; it's trouble. You don't want him creating disruption in your life, you know. I want civility and someone who's friendly, nice, polite; someone who's pleasant and not screaming and hollering behind me.

I go out there and do what I do best, which is driving the cab, being nice to people, getting them from here to there smoothly, safely, and expeditiously. I'll play some nice music for them. I tend to play classical music, but if they want classic rock or country, or whatever, I'll be happy to. I often ask them if they have a favorite radio station or type of music they like to listen to. Most of the time, they're happy with what I have on.

Sometimes there's something about a passenger that I sense where I feel that person wants silence, so I don't say a word. Other times people are very inquisitive, they want to talk or they want a story, or what's the funniest thing that ever happened, or what's the most dangerous thing that's happened. Sometimes people want me to tell them my experience, how did it come about I'm driving a cab. Often, the passenger really isn't trying to pry into the driver's personal life.

I think they're just trying to make conversation, or maybe they are just generally curious about other people. And some people just like to have someone to listen to their heartaches or troubles; maybe they want advice, or they just need to vent.

Sometimes you get difficult people. I had a couple who seemed to be nice people when they got in the car, but after we started off, it was apparent that they had had some drinks. The woman had maybe a couple more than the man, and she kept mentioning that I was going the wrong way. She kept telling her boyfriend, "He's going the wrong way; he's taking us for a ride," and I was reassuring them that I was going the right way. She kept bringing it up. After the fourth time she brought it up, I noticed there was a service station up ahead, and I pulled in there and stopped the car. I just walked around and opened the door and said, "This is the end of the ride. Sir, you're a gentleman and you're polite, but your lady friend here, she's been nothing but disrespectful toward me all the way, implying that I was trying to cheat you. I don't want to deal with her anymore. You're gonna have to get another cab." He said, "I understand." He paid me what I had on the meter, gave me a nice tip, and then they got out.

When I'm in the cab, I don't have any fear. If I were feeling fear, I think it would be time to hang it up, you know. I use common sense and good judgment. If someone wants to go somewhere, it's only proper to take them wherever they want to go. Now, you might not feel comfortable going there, but none of those places really bother me. I might not hang out there, but if someone waves me down and if they seem to be okay when I see them—if they don't look scary or there's nothing about them that's apparently wrong—I take them anywhere they want to go.

Sometimes, though, a passenger might be suffering from delusions, might be totally wrecked on alcohol, or maybe he doesn't even know his own name, or he can't verbalize where he's going. Perhaps you didn't really realize how drunk he was, but once he's in the cab, maybe he's slouched down or he can't verbalize where he wants to go. So, I keep trying to get at it in different ways: Do you have a key from your hotel? Do you have anything? Sometimes nothing I say penetrates, and the person is nonresponsive. He just wants to go, and maybe he'll be screaming, "Go, go!" but you don't know where he wants to go and he's not capable of verbalizing. So you step on it and you go, because you realize the setting isn't the best setting to deal with this individual. You need to go somewhere where there are a lot of lights and where there's a police officer. It could be a 7-Eleven, or it could be in front of a tavern in the Rush Street area where you always have police officers. Then you pull next to a squad car, see an officer there, and you let the officer know that you got an individual that is unable to express himself. The police will always help you out. Oftentimes the police officer will say, "How much is on the meter?" Then they say to the individual, "He's got seven dollars on the meter," or whatever. "Pay the driver, please," and then the person is usually responsive when he sees the officer. It kind of sobers him up just enough to realize what's going on. Then usually the police officer will say, "We will get you another cab," just to facilitate it, and I'm on my way again.

A couple of times people have gotten sick in the cab. One time, a young man got a little sick in the back. He was talking to me about some emotional problems that he was having. He had had a couple of drinks, but he wasn't stinking drunk or anything. It was mostly because it was an emotional problem that caused him to throw up. I pulled in a gas station. Fortunately, I had a bucket in the back. I had some rubber gloves and all the cleaning things, so the two of us cleaned up the mess together.

Another time, I picked up a guy late one night. He got in the car and then right away he's screaming at me, "Follow that car!" But there was no car to follow. He kept carrying on and making crazy talk, and hollering at me to follow the car. I got somebody who's really out of it here, so I figured the only way to get rid of this guy is for me to, again, go where I knew there were police. I slid into that place, put the car in park, opened the door, motioned to the police to come over, and I said, "I got a guy here that needs to get out of the car, because he's screaming at me to follow imaginary cars." They helped me get him out. I didn't want any money from the guy, I just wanted him out of the car. I don't know what they did with him.

Sometimes there may be a couple in the back and they're having an argument; it's happened a number of times. What I do oftentimes is, I'll pull over and stop before I say anything. That will catch their attention. Or maybe I won't do that—it depends on what the circumstances are; I'll turn around and look at them and I'll say, "Look, this cab ride may be a little bit unusual for you, but I'm gonna share something with you: In this cab you got to behave yourself. You got to be kind to each other. You got to be loving toward each other. None of this anger and fighting going on, because I don't put up with this. If you want to be mean to each other, you're gonna have to get out of the cab." It always shakes them up and takes them out of their temporary insanity. I don't tolerate people fighting in the cab. I won't put up with that.

I remember another night, I was working in the Lakeview area. There are taverns and clubs there that don't all close at the same time; some of them can stay open longer if they pay more money for their license. I was waiting out front, and a man came out. He looked like your average Joe College. He looked clean and presentable. He got in the back, and I could tell he was just a little drunk. He said, "Take me down to Frank's." It's another drinking place, maybe a half a mile away. I said, "Yes sir." So we're on our way, and before the main intersection up ahead I turn left at a side street (because I couldn't make a left turn up where the main intersection was even though that street was the street on which his place was). I turned where I could and zigzagged to get to where I needed to go. He says, "You took the wrong road, you suck." I started to let him know that you couldn't turn there (maybe he was new in the neighborhood or maybe he was too drunk to remember, but it was apparent when he opened his mouth that he was in no mood to listen to what I had to say). So I didn't say anything after that. The more he spoke, the more he got himself worked up, and he became very loud and aggressive.

He swore, and said he was gonna hurt me. I thought the best thing for me to do is just keep my mouth shut, because no matter what I said he's gonna grab on to it and make something out of it, and maybe it will be just what he needs to hurt me.

I continued driving to where he wanted to go—to Frank's—and he's still carrying on about what he's going to do to me. When there was a pause, I politely let him know that we were at his destination. He didn't totally acknowledge the fact that I got him there; that would have been too much for him to do. He puts some money on the seat next to me and I gave him his change, then he got out of the cab and was still carrying on. Five or ten seconds later the door opens. It's the same guy, and he said, "I gave you a twenty." The money was still on the seat, and I said, "You see, that's what you gave me, it's a ten." Then he started muttering like I'm trying to cheat him from the money.

You know, I try to work with a peaceful heart and operate with a fearless attitude. The important thing to remember, when you think about things like dangerous situations or dangerous people, is that we tend to draw to ourselves the very things that we fear the most. If you have an attitude of fear, you will be a magnet for those very same things that you're afraid of. That same principle applies not just to driving a cab but to people in general, whatever their occupations are. If you expect people to be nasty, rude, or dangerous, they probably will be. But if you look at other people as decent people and maybe they're having a bad day, if you are kind to them, then maybe everything will work out.

Sometimes, though, it doesn't work out exactly their way and they will give you a hard time or be dangerous, then you have to just deal with them and do the best things under the circumstance. You certainly don't want to take them to a dark alley somewhere. If you got someone who you sense might be very dangerous, the best thing to do, like I said, is go somewhere where there's a lot of light and where there are other people, and then help the person to exit the cab gracefully. Whatever you do, don't raise your voice. Don't become retaliatory or abrasive, none of that. Just keep an even, calm tone even if the person is acting out in a bizarre way.

Oh, another thing: People might pound on the car when they want to get in. Maybe you're going down the street where all the bars are. You know the guy is drunk, it's apparent he's not behaving, and you know he's trouble. You don't want him in the car. So he's pounding on your car. You try not to stop if you can avoid it. You just pray that he doesn't break a window or anything. It's annoying. How would he feel if I were to do that to his car? What gives him the right to do that to me? He's certainly not gonna get in trouble, so he's got nothing to worry about, because he'll just walk away. People aren't gonna run after him, and probably there's no police around.

If someone sat directly behind me in the car, I might suggest that they move over a little bit to the right on the passenger side; I would prefer that they sit there. No, I'm not afraid if they're sitting behind me. There's a basic trust that you need to have toward others. If you're distrustful or paranoid or scared about having someone behind you—not knowing that in the next second they could get you in a stranglehold or do this or that to you—it's best that you not drive a cab. It's not the right occupation for you if you have that kind of fear. If the person is right behind me—because of the headrest—then I can't really see the person's face. I like to be able to see a person's face when I'm speaking. It's not that I'm staring at the person or looking deeply into a person's eyes or anything like that, it's just that it's my nature when I'm speaking with someone to occasionally glance at the person's face. I don't really think in terms of protecting myself, because if that person behind me is perceptive at all, he can see me looking in the mirror and knows exactly where my eyes are. I might glance at them but I try not to make it an issue. And, when you're driving, it's best to keep your eyes ahead to look for pedestrians or traffic lights. It is good, though, to be aware of the type of individual that you got, because you really don't know.

JERRY HURLEY

Timber Cutter

*J*erry Hurley's house is at the end of a secluded dirt road and is surrounded
by some of the world's tallest trees. We chat awhile with his wife and watch
a video that shows him cutting a massive tree. He begins talking about
his profession. "Probably three times every year you get the crap scared out
of you."

★ ★ ★

I cut timber.

I don't have a crew anymore. My son, Blaine, works with me. I
geared back to just me and him. We cut trees, that's all we do. No,

we're not loggers. We're timber cutters. A logger is the one that gets the timber to the landing and sends it to the mill. I'm a timber cutter. There's a certain amount of pride in the woods for timber cutters. We're respected. I don't know really why, but I think people like timber cutters because they know what we got to do.

I bid specialty jobs, trash, or whatever. Trash? We call it trash. It's a mixture of oak and alder. I'm cutting a lot of tanoak right now. They're twelve to twenty-five inches on the diameter of the stump. It's mainly ground reclamation where the oak has taken over. Oak is like a weed, and when they clear-cut years ago, the oak got a start, and it really took over. It's all on a timber company's property. We cut it and they sell it.

I started working in the woods when I was eighteen, when I went to work for Weyerhaeuser setting chokers (a choker is what you wrap around a log to get the log from the woods to the landing, where they load it on trucks). While I was setting chokers, I was watching timber fellers, and I thought that's something I always wanted to do, so that's what I did.

I was still pretty green when I started cutting timber. I tore up more equipment than you can believe. I broke a lot of saws; it was an expensive learning. By the time I was probably twenty-two, I felt I was good enough to kind of do it. It's only a tree, but it takes a long time to get confidence. It doesn't come easy. My confidence level now is very high, but it's only because I have been there, done it, and know what to expect.

After Weyerhaeuser, I went to falling timber for gyppos here and there—a gyppo is an independent logger. Falling? It doesn't matter: I say "fall." I think the correct term is "fell." The falling is getting the tree on the ground, and then "bucking" is cutting it into log lengths so they can haul it to town on trucks. So, you fall trees, buck them into logs, and haul them to the sawmill. Anyway, gyppos were like logging contractors that, at that time, would contract with Weyerhaeuser or Crown Zellerbach. A job would end with one gyppo, then you'd go work for another gyppo. Pretty quick, they all know you and they kind of like pass you around, keep you working that way. Did that till I was thirty-three, then I logged a little bit on my own for a time, that didn't seem to work out too well, and I ended up being a mechanic, but I could make much more money on a saw. So I got rid of the equipment, and I went to contract cutting, and then I ended up going to Roseburg, Oregon, to cut for Roseburg Lumber and stayed there for about seven years.

I learned to jack timber at Roseburg. Jack timber? You jack timber away from rivers, streams, property lines to save the trees. There, it was on steep ground and they wanted the Douglas fir saved because it was at a premium price, so they wanted to utilize everything that they could get. You jack timber because you couldn't possibly wedge it. Wedge? Well, you wedge a tree when you put an undercut in; that gives the tree room to move forward. You then put the backcut in and put a wedge in. Okay? When you jack it, it's like it's got an extreme lean to where you cannot possibly wedge it where it needs to be, so you put a jack notch in and then you put these jacks in there and you jack it to wherever you need it to go.

In this work, you're humbled almost daily. They're big trees, they intimidate you. You walk up to something and you go, I got to cut this down? I'm not even sure where it leans. What you do is you stand right at the base of the tree on the upper side right between your feet, and you look straight up, you follow that invisible line right up the middle of the tree. That will give you a good definition of where it kind of leans. The tree will lean one way or the other out of that invisible line. Then you got your limb weight, and the tree will predominantly pull to that side. Trees, in a patch of timber, believe it or not, only grow limbs on the upper part on one side, usually the sun side. The backside is usually clear. Also, wherever the top leans, that's where the tree leans. That's the best tell: that top. If you can't see the top, you got to go with limb weight. But, if you look at a tree from the lower side, it will lie every time and could lean everywhere. You got to get on the upper side and see where the limbs curve. That's how you pick the lean.

Falling is the funnest. The idea of a good falling job is to get the tree where you can cut it safely, then buck it safely. Bucking is not fun. Bucking can be really dangerous. Some guys will fall a tree right down the hill and go, "I can't buck that." Well, of course you can't, you didn't work long enough falling it and you didn't put it where you could buck it. You should have put it here, or there on the side of the hill instead of down the hill. You want it where you can stand in a safe spot, and if it rolls away from you, nothing's gonna chop you. But a lot of guys are lazy and they all lean down the hill, so they do the easy thing. Now you buck it and the boss is gonna be mad at you because he's gonna have to hook the tree with a choker and hold tension on it while somebody bucks it. That's when things can fly up and whack you. It just makes sense to always stay above everything you've done. A good falling job is when it's all bucked and taken care of correctly. It's like playing with gigantic pick-up sticks: You don't want to just move anything, you want it to be on purpose.

It's a tense job. Every day is tense. I think your biggest worry is something falling on you while you're cutting. In 2002, I was cutting just a regular redwood tree right here in Smith River, and this other tree that I hadn't even touched broke off halfway up and slipped out of nowhere when I felled this one tree, and it hit me right on the top of the head and broke my neck. Got a compression fracture of the vertebrae that controls your breathing and your heart. Well, the tree probably broke the winter before, from wind or snow. They break off sometimes. About thirty feet was broke off, probably three inches in diameter. When I fell that one tree, the other tree just kind of fell straight down on me. I didn't see it. It knocked me right down the ground. I got up, I went, "Boy, my whole shoulder is stiff. I'm hurt." My arms were tingling and was all numb. I could feel my hands, but I could tell that they ain't right. It was six months before I could pick up a saw again.

No, we don't yell, "timber!" If there's somebody around me, we say, "across the hill; up the hill; down the hill," depending on where you're falling the tree. We say exactly where you're going with the tree so if somebody is coming to talk to you, you give a holler right when you're ready to fall it but before you put the backcut in. If nobody answers back, then you go ahead.

Another time, I cut my left hand almost off. That would be in the days before they had chain brakes. Chain brakes are on the saw. If you fall on your saw, the chain brake will go on, or if you overrev your saw, it will go on; if the saw kicks back, the chain brake will throw the brake and stop the chain instantaneously. If I had had a chain brake, I wouldn't have even got a ding.

Well, I was in Grays River in Washington, three hours from the hospital. I bucked a log and I stuck the saw dog in a fir tree (the dogs are the pointy things on both sides in the front on your saw) and I stepped up on the log that I had just bucked, and it fell down just enough that I lost my balance and fell forward. My hand went right down on the chain and wham, it cut all the way up my forefinger and thumb. I felt like I had been shot. Oh, it really hurt.

I went to the doctor, and he said, "I don't know if I can save it. We're gonna put it together and see what happens." Then he said, "We can cut it off later if it doesn't work." The doctor worked on it hard and I went to therapy. In six months, I was back to sawing. I've still got a hand.

I got back to work for about eight months, and then up at Mt. Rainier a guy felled a tree on me and broke my left leg. I was up the hill from him. It was a tall Douglas fir. In wedging the tree over, he first felled a little short tree into it to give it a push. Well, the little tree pushed the Douglas fir forward, but not enough to make it go, and when the Doug came back, it broke off and come right up where I was bucking on a log. It hit me and shattered my lower left leg. That was the closest to dying as I think as I've ever been. I wasn't very happy. I had just got healed up from my hand injury and back to work, starting to get things going again, and then that happened. The doctor looks at the X-rays and says, "That's the straightest breaks I have ever seen, just like they were cut with a knife." The doctors didn't have to operate on it, because the breaks were so straight.

I think it was like five different breaks. It didn't break the knee joint or the ankle joint, but it just broke all the bones in between, so they were able to put traction on it and it healed on its own.

A lot of times I've seen young cutters get out there and they go, "Oh, I can do that, I can do this," and then they can't do it. That's one thing about this trade, there's no bluff. I've had guys come out and they would be woodcutters. I would take them out and after just a little while I'd say, "You aren't gonna make it here, let's just get you out of here right now." He'd say, "Are you firing me?" I said, "No, I'm saving your life." They said they were timber cutters, but they were woodcutters: somebody that goes out like on the weekend and cuts some wood. They haven't got the credentials to be here. I'll be packing them out before the day is over, and I don't want to do that.

The first thing in timber cutting is safety: Get your ass out of there, that's primo. The timber is second. Take care of the man's timber, but not at the cost of your life. Leave it if you have to. There's nothing out here so bad we can't just leave it. If it's too nasty, you just have to walk away from it, or you get help. Don't let your pride get you killed like, oh, I think I can handle it. Well maybe you can, maybe you can't. When you start cutting trees, everything moves, and you're dealing with so much weight. That's the biggest deal. What's gonna hurt you is something falling.

Black bears are a problem here. The moms and their cubs are the worst. We stay away from those as best as we can. Most times, bears are scared of you, but they will chase you, and they really haul. Once you move into a job, bears usually will leave in the day and come back at night. We know there's bears because of the signs: tracks and poop. As long as you keep working, you're all right. Make a lot of noise, and they stay away from you. I'd hate to sneak up on one. I don't go down there in early morning without making a lot of noise. Bears can hear pretty good. I like it, though, when they eat bees' nests, and then we don't get stung. Over at Mt. Shasta, you get the crap stung out of you, because there are no bears.

Cougars make me nervous. There's a lot of cougars around this country. I had a job three miles from here up on a hill. I took my wife up to babysit me while my son was laid off with a broken ankle. We have two-way radios, so I go and cut and then I check in with her from time to time. If I get hurt, she can call for help. Anyways, two little cougars, they weren't much bigger than a good-sized dog, they stayed around there the whole time I cut a patch. They would kind of stay up on the hill and watch me. They never really bothered me, but they made me nervous. Fortunately they were young, but I didn't want to tangle with their mom.

Yeah, it's a profession. It takes a level head and concentration. Some people think that it's macho; it's not macho. You got to be focused from morning to night. You got to pay attention to what you do. You can't go out there hungover or have trouble at home, things that would get in the way. Don't go out there angry. If you're angry at work, then you shouldn't work. I know one guy, one time, he was angry with his wife. He come out to work and is slamming things around, and then he got hung up in a log. He pulled the saw out and he still had the trigger pulled back and it cut right across his leg. Well, there you go. You shouldn't work when you're angry.

Every man I work with out here is a professional. They don't want to damage the streams, they love to fish, they love to hunt, they don't want to damage the habitat for the creatures. I mean, this is where we live, this is where we play. In a way, it's a world order. I know some people are just butchers. You can find those guys in the bars who probably got fired off of these jobs because of the stuff they've done, but most of these guys out here have good moral values as far as the forest. When we do something, we do it right. I feel good here, because we're reclaiming this soil. Not in my lifetime, but the next generation will come through here and go, God, that's beautiful. We got lots of spruce here, and then you got a lot of redwood mixed in with that, and a lot of Doug fir. I would say within fifty years you will drive through here and it will be gorgeous, because we're getting rid of the oak and the weeds and getting this crap off the ground. Man, I'll tell you what, there's places out here you couldn't find the ground if you had to, it's so full of old logging debris. We're getting rid of it.

The largest tree I've cut, I think, was twenty-one feet in diameter, a three-hundred-foot-tall redwood tree. I think it was about 1,100 years old. I can still cut a lot of timber, but I've got to use the noodle more than I used to. Before, I could just go hard and not really pay that much attention. Now I got to think more so I don't hurt myself. I got arthritis in both knees. I wear a brace on my back that is preventative to keep the pain toned down. I got a few years to go. I'm still in good shape. I'm sixty, but I've still got good lung capacity.

GRIFF WITTE

JOURNALIST

*T*he *twenty-nine-year-old Jerusalem bureau chief for the* Washington Post *sits on a couch in his office talking about his new job in Israel, and his previous work in Afghanistan and Pakistan. The day before, Griff Witte interviewed smugglers who were transporting goods in underground tunnels from Egypt to Gaza.*

"As a human being, you don't want to be there, you don't want to see these things, you don't want to hear these things. It makes you sick, it makes you depressed. You see things that are so awful that you wish that no one ever has to see things like this, but as a journalist, you would much rather be there than be a thousand miles away, because it's not often that you get to witness the moments when the world changes direction and empires fall and new *empires rise. We are in the business of covering these turning points of history. I hate violence, I hate blood, I hate death, but I am intrigued by conflict and why human beings can't seem to get along. It's a strange fascination: You wish you didn't have violence, but on the other hand you know that you are out there representing millions of people who want to know what's going on, and they're relying on you to tell them accurately what has happened. Someone has to be there to cover it."*

★ ★ ★

I'm the Jerusalem bureau chief for the *Washington Post*. I'm a newspaper reporter. I cover Israel and the Palestinian territories. I write about anything that is happening here, which is often involving violent things that have happened the day before, but I also cover politics and do features writing about offbeat things.

I was raised in Nyack, New York. From the age of probably seven, I can remember waking up to the sound of the newspaper hitting the front walkway and running down the stairs to open it up and read it. Usually, I wanted to check the Mets' scores, but occasionally I'd glance at the front page. It was amazing to me the way in which the entire world could be processed and analyzed and packaged together in those little sheets of paper that was delivered to my front doorstep every morning. There were datelines from Jerusalem, datelines from Moscow, datelines from Afghanistan; these are places on the earth that I could only dream about, but there they were in my morning paper in Nyack.

My dad is a freelance cartoonist, but he works for just about every magazine you can think of. My mom is a psychologist. I think that in many ways a journalist is a good combination of those two professions, because as a cartoonist you're observing the world and you're rendering it in your own way, and a psychologist, obviously, has to understand what is driving people and what makes them tick, and has to be able to listen. As a journalist, you want to be able to listen, be able to understand people's perspectives, and then render what they tell you in a way that means something to a wider audience.

Right out of college, I went to work for the *Miami Herald*. I was at the *Herald* for just a little under a year, and then I had this crazy idea that I would go back to school, and actually went to Columbia University for just a few days. I had moved to Manhattan on September 7, 2001. Four days later, the planes hit the Trade Center and before I knew it, I was heading downtown to cover it for the *Herald*, even though I was not working there anymore. I recognized that the *Herald* didn't have any reporters in Manhattan at the time, and I guess my instincts kicked in. So within a couple of hours of the attacks, I was at Ground Zero reporting on it.

I remember that I paused for a little bit. I think there was about an hour or so where I didn't go down there and just watched it on television like the rest of the world did. And then I realized that there were stories to be told, and there would be some value to me witnessing it firsthand, not just with mediation of television. I took the subway half the way, but then you couldn't go much farther after a certain point, so I walked the last twenty or thirty blocks. It was very strange, because everyone else was headed north, moving away obviously from the Trade Center. I remember very acutely thinking what's wrong with me that I am going toward these towers that have fallen rather than away from them.

I wondered why I was still taking notes. Well, I said to myself that we need witnesses, too. We need people who are recording. This is history that is unfolding right here, and we need people to keep their eyes open to see what's happening, and tell the stories of the people who died, tell the stories of the people who lived, tell the stories of the rescuers.

After that day, that was basically the end of graduate school for me. It lasted four days. Strangely enough, I got a call just about a week or two after that from Steve Coll, the managing editor of the *Washington Post*, and he was doing a book about the antecedents to September 11. He wanted to tell the story of how September 11 happened—going about twenty-five years back to the Soviet invasion of Afghanistan—and he needed someone to work with him on that. He needed someone who came cheap and was not gainfully employed at the time. A week later, I was down in Washington talking with him about the book, and a week after that he offered me the job.

I worked on the book for about a year and a half, and it was an amazing experience. I got to travel to Afghanistan very soon after the Taliban fell in the fall of 2001. I'd been out of the country maybe two or three times in my life before then, and all of a sudden I was in Afghanistan doing a lot of interviews. It was such an opportunity that I couldn't turn it down. I mean, it was such a critical subject at that time. It was the question that the entire world was asking: How did this happen? I had a chance to contribute to the answer, so it was very alluring to reconstruct a narrative of the anti-Taliban forces in Afghanistan who had been pleading, begging, getting down on their knees, telling Washington, "We need to do something here, the Taliban are destroying this country and Al-Qaeda has moved in." These were people whose stories had been completely ignored by the media and had been completely ignored by policy makers in Washington, and when I got to Afghanistan, they were all incredibly eager to tell their stories.

I was nervous and definitely apprehensive about it. I had never done anything like it before. The U.S. had just defeated the Taliban, but it was well-known that there were remnants of the Taliban that were running around all over the place. It was unclear where people's loyalties stood, and I was very concerned about my own safety going into it.

I was working out of the *Washington Post* house that had just sort of been set up in Kabul, but everything was done on the fly. The communications were poor. You have to have your antennae up all the time. There was one moment where my driver insisted on telling me exactly how much money he could get by turning me over to the Taliban. I think it was a couple of million, or so. I'd never considered myself that valuable and important a reporter, but he felt pretty confident that he had a gold mine in the backseat of his car.

For my security, whenever I travel in Afghanistan or Pakistan, I completely avoid having anything that calls attention to myself. I never travel with weapons, and I also don't travel in nice cars and don't wear nice clothes. I travel in beat-up old taxis without tinted windows, because I don't want anyone to think that I'm anyone they should care about. I want to be as low-key and discreet as I possibly can. As an American in Afghanistan and Pakistan, you are automatically a target for people who are very anti-American. Here in Jerusalem, in situations that are potentially dangerous, I do want to stand out more as an American, simply because Americans aren't combatants here. Because of the conflict that is going on between Jews and Palestinians, I want to establish that I am part of neither camp, that I am completely apart from it. So here, for instance, we do have an armored car that we will use if the situation becomes dicey.

In general, journalists are on their own. They want to be independent and don't want to be associated with the military. They don't want to be seen as a target. In essence, they want to blend in as much as possible. I don't exactly blend, as you can imagine. I have blond hair, six feet tall, and I'm fair skinned, but you want to do everything you can to, you know, make sure that people just don't give you a second look, or at the very least they are confused about who you are.

By and large I have to say that in Pakistan and Afghanistan, people were just incredibly welcoming and went out of their way to help me in amazing ways. Some, though, were reflexively anti-American, who don't like the fact that you're there in their country, and on a handful of occasions, people really made it clear that they didn't want me there and you realize this is potentially pretty dangerous. You wish you could disappear and be anywhere but where you are at that moment, but the mission I was on was something that was exactly what I wanted to be doing: going to a corner of the globe that most Americans will never visit, a corner of the globe that's hugely important to the lives of Americans, and trying to convey a little bit of what that place is like to anyone else who cares to read back home.

I covered the siege at the Red Mosque last summer, where a group of radical students and religious leaders took over a mosque in the heart of Islamabad. There was a big confrontation and live gun-fire between the Pakistani armed forces and the radical students and the mosque leaders. They were shooting at one another. Thousands of people came out into the streets to support the students and the mosque leaders, and I found myself right in the middle of that mob while they were chanting anti-American slogans. It was a very, very angry crowd. They were angry at the government. They were really angry at the military. They were angry at the U.S.

I was in this mob the entire day, interviewing people, and seeing whatever I could see of the gun battle that was raging next to me. Everything seemed fine from a security perspective, or so I thought, and then the battle died down just around dusk. Everyone started to go home, people stopped shooting, and everything seemed to have completely calmed. I think I let my guard down to a certain extent, and I went walking right in front of the mosque where the fire had been going back and forth just minutes ago. Someone jumped out and shoved me in the back and started screaming, "CIA! CIA!" He was clearly trying to get things started again, trying to use me as a prop for getting the crowd energized again. He started to incite others in the crowd to attack me. He was shoving me and hitting me, and trying to get his friends to join in. I realized at that point that I was completely surrounded by this mob, and there was absolutely no way out. I was completely at their mercy.

I tried to look into the eyes of the people closest to me, and even though I didn't speak or know their language, I pleaded with them. I said, "Please, I'm a journalist. I'm not here to hurt anyone." I doubt if they understood what I was saying. I pointed to my notebook. I pointed to my pen, "I'm a reporter. I'm a writer." To the credit of one guy next to me, he basically told the guy who had been pushing me to leave me alone, and he told everyone else in the crowd to leave me alone, as well. Then he escorted me out. Afterward, he said, "I am so sorry that that happened. You are a guest in this country. You are guest of mine. They shouldn't be treating you like this." I was afraid. I mean, it was apparent I didn't have control over the situation. I was completely at the mercy of the people around me and they could decide to rip me limb from limb, or they could decide to save me.

I always think of this incident whenever people talk about the "angry Islamic world, or the angry radical Muslims." This guy saved me, and he didn't have to. He could just as easily given in to the mentality of the mob. It would have been quite a coup if they had managed to string an American up from the nearest tree. But his sense of hospitality, his sense of just being a good host, overwhelmed that anger.

I stupidly felt more confident after that, and I think the lesson probably should have been that I should be more careful but, instead, the lesson that I took from it was that no matter how angry people are, when it comes to human beings standing next to them, most people are gonna want to help that person, rather than hurt that person.

I worked on the book until the summer of 2003. Then I became a reporter at the *Post*, first in Alexandria, Virginia, which was a far cry from Afghanistan. I wanted to go back to Afghanistan, because I loved it there and I loved being out on my own. I love foreign correspondence because of the sense of escape and the sense of discovery that goes along with it and the chance every day to stumble upon something completely new.

After Virginia, I did a short stint in Afghanistan during the winter of 2005, the coldest winter in my life. It's very cold in Kabul, for one thing, and there was no heat. I was shivering so badly that I couldn't sleep. I never thought that I didn't want to be doing it, but I remember being more miserable than I ever been in my life. I had pneumonia and it was like negative ten degrees outside. I remember being in my bed, just incredibly sick out of my mind and really, really cold. I thought, "Gosh, isn't this wonderful. I'm in Afghanistan, and who else gets that opportunity as a correspondent for the *Post*?" I'm sure a lot of people think that's crazy.

It had been relatively quiet in Afghanistan throughout '02, '03, and '04—not that things weren't happening—but the level of violence had gone down quite a bit. In the fall of '05, the Taliban came back with a vengeance and started to really flex their muscles again. At first, they were quite inept. They kept sending out suicide bombers who would manage to blow themselves up in the bathroom on their way to carrying out their mission. By 2007, they had executed a massive campaign of suicide bombings that killed hundreds and hundreds of people and they'd obviously gotten a lot better at their trade.

You find yourself thinking like a suicide bomber, which is a scary thing to do. What that means is you think, if I were a suicide bomber, would I want to attack right here? You think constantly about, is anyone around me potentially going to hurt me? And then you also think about, are the people around me people who a suicide bomber would want to attack? This became very important in Pakistan last year, because I was constantly in crowds. It was a year of major political upheaval. There were all sorts of rallies and demonstrations, and there were constantly people gathering in hundreds, thousands, tens of thousands, hundreds of thousands, and I was always in the middle of those crowds. You have to be alert at all times to who is around you. I actually didn't feel that often like I was being targeted, but I mostly felt like the people I was covering were being targeted.

I would often travel with colleagues, because there's some safety in numbers. If something does happen, you want someone to be there to get help. I grew a beard when I first went to Afghanistan thinking not that I would fool anyone, but that I might confuse people—that maybe for a minute or two, people would wonder who I was and not immediately jump to the conclusion that I was a Westerner.

As the Islamabad bureau chief for the *Post*, I was supposed to also cover Afghanistan, but there was so much turmoil in Pakistan

I ended up spending almost all of my time in Pakistan. For example, I covered Benazir Bhutto's return to the country after her eight years in exile. I flew from London with her group of her supporters to Dubai where we picked her up, and then we landed together in Karachi. Hundreds of thousands of people were there to greet her. She was on a truck that was going through the streets in a big procession, and I was on the truck next to her truck, watching her as she waved to the crowd, and as people welcomed her back. I had never seen so many people in one place in my life.

At around 7:00 PM, I decided that I needed to file my story. The battery on my cell phone had run out, so I couldn't just call it in. I went back to the hotel room and was completely exhausted. Whatever energy I had left, I just poured into the story, wrote it all up, and sent it to Washington. No sooner had I sent it in, the television in the hotel lobby flashed that there had been a suicide attack on Benazir's convoy. I immediately jumped back in the car and away we sped toward the scene. We got there within a few minutes of the attack. There were 140 people killed. There were parts of people everywhere. The truck that Benazir was in was still on fire.

I spent a couple of hours at the scene and then went back to my hotel, and completely scrapped the old story. I had a lot of energy at that point as I wrote the story the second time around, but I remember just sobbing because of the horror of what I had seen. I earlier had been interviewing some of the people who were now killed.

Two months later, I was standing outside the operating room at the hospital when Benazir died. That was December 27, 2007, and strangely enough, I had just found that I was going to be leaving Pakistan and coming here to Jerusalem. I'd come to Jerusalem for a few days to check it out, to work on some of the logistics of my move, and then flew back on an overnight flight from Amman to Bahrain to Islamabad on the morning of December 27. I went to my house, took about an hour's nap, woke up, and heard news that there had been a shooting.

I got in the car and started to drive over with my driver to see what had happened. While we're in the car, we got word that there had been an explosion at Benazir Bhutto's rally. I immediately called her spokeswoman and, amazingly enough, she picked up the phone—this was probably about the minute of the bomb going off—I remember hearing people screaming. Clearly something major had happened. We started to go to the scene of the bombing, but the traffic grounded to a halt. It just so happened that where we were stuck in traffic was right next to the hospital, so I went to the hospital expecting to do a story about another attack on Benazir's rally. Word started to spread that she was hurt very badly, and then a crowd started to form around the hospital. It started with dozens, then it became hundreds, and then it became thousands. The crowd grew more and more anxious, more and more angry, and eventually the doctor came out and said, "She is dead." I've never seen such grief. People started hitting themselves in the heads, started to pound on the hospital, they broke all the glass, all the doors, all the windows, and they eventually tried to get into her operating room. I didn't know what direction the crowd was going or how out of control it was going to get. I was stuck in the crowd.

I was pretty focused on making sure that I stayed safe, but also making sure that I observed everything. I was caught in a space where I couldn't get my hands free to write, so I just had to focus on seeing and hearing and smelling everything that I could. I felt how wrenching this was for everyone there, but it's a strange thing with journalism: You have to be able to remove yourself a little bit and remember that you're not a participant—you're trying to be a witness.

I moved here in February. Israel is more livable, and I still get to cover the things that drive me. This is a place that challenges me in a way that Pakistan didn't, perhaps because in Pakistan and Afghanistan you have a conflict where one side has clearly embraced this sort of nihilistic culture of death, of killing. Al-Qaeda and the Taliban are truly extreme in their views, and in terms of how our readers interpret it, it's a one-sided conflict. It's clear who's right and who's wrong.

Here, it's murky, very ambiguous. Opinions are so sharply drawn, and people disagree so vehemently over who's right and who's wrong. That puts an extra burden on the reporter to get it right.

I spend a good amount of time in Gaza. I was there yesterday covering smugglers. A lot of what comes into Gaza, comes in through smuggling. So I decided I would go see if I could find smugglers. I went down to Rafah, which is the southernmost town in Gaza, right on the Egyptian–Israeli border. I drove myself down, but then you can't take a car into Gaza, so you have to walk. They have a very elaborate security center there. You hear rockets going off and you know that the buzzing overhead is a probably a Predator drone. I feel generally safe, but there is combat going on in Gaza just about every day. And there are also a few people who would like to kidnap a Westerner, so that's always a concern.

There are all these white plastic tents that look like greenhouses right along the border. In each one, there are four or five guys digging a hole and crawling to Egypt. Amazingly enough you catch them on their cigarette break and talk to them. I mean, they don't seem to have anything better to do, so why not talk?

I learned that just about everything travels through those holes. They are amazingly sophisticated. They dig them about fifty meters deep and are about a kilometer long. They are reinforced on all sides, have intercoms hooked up, lighting, and little rooms off to the sides to store things in. That being said, it's also incredibly dangerous work. These guys know, at any time, the tunnel can collapse. A lot of them have suffocated.

I don't enjoy taking risks. There is no thrill of risk itself, so in that kind of situation, you can go in the tunnel but what have you learned by going in? I mean, you can learn maybe a little bit more about what it's like, but there is the chance that the tunnel will collapse or that the Egyptians will throw a smoke bomb in while you're there.

One of the things I really love about reporting in this part of the world is that people rarely make you feel as though you're unwelcome, or you shouldn't be there. You could be in Washington, D.C., and call some highfalutin guy on the phone who will slam the phone down and make you feel like a jerk for calling him. You feel embarrassed that you picked up the phone in the first place. Here, you wander into a smuggler's tent, and there's no "Get out of here." It's, "Sit down. Please have a cup of tea. We'll talk."

I will be here about three years. I think that's a good amount of time to get to know a place but not so long that either you get completely embittered or you get so completely used to everything that it stops being novel. It still feels new for me, everything still feels fresh. I feel like I'm where I want to be right now. This is part of the world that we, as Americans, have to understand better, and people in the Middle East have to understand America better, if things are gonna work out.

Photo Courtesy of: **T. LEBARON**

JODIE WILLIAMS

RESCUE SWIMMER

*T*wenty-two U.S. Coast Guard rescue swimmers are stationed in Kodiak, Alaska. Jodie Williams is twenty-six years old. She is the only female rescue swimmer on duty there.

"Size obviously does come into it. I can't say that I would be just as good handling someone that's two-hundred-plus pounds as the guy next to me, but I know that I can do it. I can handle myself. I know my techniques and what works for me."

★ ★ ★

I'd say the first real case that I actually got in the water was a night cave rescue. It was like two in the morning; something like that. It was just a pleasure craft. It had a cabin in it and it was good sized. Some storm was coming through and they got pushed into a rock; got a big ol' hole in the boat and the boat beached on its side on rocks. They were sleeping, and their boat had pulled off the anchor. They were drifting and didn't know it. The dad got blown off into a cave. His two sons were still on the boat.

Because it was dark, all I could see were little whitecaps on the water. I had butterflies beyond butterflies. This is real, and they are going to put me in the water all by myself. I think any swimmer that says they're not even a little afraid when they go into the water at nighttime is blind. You're the most alone and you can't see. It was scary.

They lowered me down. The instructions were to go to the boat and assess the situation. We knew that one person was missing, but I had to talk to the other two on the boat first. The helicopter couldn't hover right next to the boat, because there was a cliff and a down-draft. So they put me down by a hook in the water, and I swam maybe around seventy-five meters to the boat.

One son had a broken leg. He had fallen off the boat, and then climbed back in. The other one couldn't swim. They told me, "My dad is over there, my dad is over there!" They were older, and their dad was probably in his sixties. I said okay. So I walked along the rocks to where they're pointing. They're pointing into this cave, and I am like, oh, God, please don't be in the cave, because I don't want to go there. I'm thinking to myself (like we're always told), because of the currents, don't blindly swim into caves. Sure enough, I shine my flashlight in and I can see reflective tape on his vest. I'm yelling at him and he's not answering me, so now I'm thinking he's dead. Without even thinking—and this was my biggest mistake on this case, because something could have gone wrong—I just jumped and swam in. I didn't call the helo crew to let them know what I was doing. I was so tunnel-visioned.

As soon as I got to him, he answered me. He just said, "I'm really cold." He was okay. He had some cuts on his face, but he was fine. So I swam him out of the cave, no current or anything. It was pretty calm. Pulled him back on the rocks. He was a big guy and didn't have the strength to get up on the rocks. There would be a wave that would kind of push him up, and then he would drag back down on the rock. I'm pulling him by his back and I'm like, "Oh, come on," and he is like, "I can't." I said, "You're gonna have to or you're not going to go anywhere." So he muscled up some strength to hold on when a wave came, and then I was able to pull him up. The helo couldn't hover there, so I was going to have to swim him out. The waves were like crashing over and over, and the guy was terrified of the water. Every time a wave would come, he'd get down on his hands and knees, because he is terrified of getting pushed back in. Right as I was getting ready to take him into the water, the helo said that they were out of gas and they left us.

So we hung out on the boat. Another helo was en route, and came and picked us up. They were able to hover right there. The basket came down and I helped him into the basket and then he went up. The old man was ecstatic and glad to be alive. He was like, "You're such a good person." Then the guy with the broken leg and then the other son got into the basket. The brothers were kind of quiet. We dropped them off at the hospital, and then we went back to the base. It was a good case.

Rescue swimming really is the smallest part of our job, but it is what we train for the most. We do the majority of our work here in the shop, working on survival gear, working out, and doing all the stuff to prepare. I don't go flying every day. I don't go jumping in the water every day. But you have to train every day for it to be somewhat second nature so you can think outside the box for what comes up, because every case I've had has been different. I've had to think differently about how to do something, but I always revert to what I've been taught, which is what we go over and over and over.

I'm from Colorado. Out of high school, I was looking for money for school. I'm sure that's probably a good reason a majority of people join the military. A friend of mine—his dad was retired Coast Guard—he talked to me like, "You should really think about the Coast Guard." I didn't even know what the Coast Guard was. I thought coast guards were lifeguards.

I played sports in high school. Oh, gosh, every sport. I played softball, volleyball, basketball, track, you name it. I'm not coordinated, though, so I wasn't good at any of them. Never swam. I always thought I knew how to swim. You know, you go to the pool in the summer and play around.

I've always wanted to teach, but I don't know if I was ready to go to college. I actually wasn't thinking college right away. I knew that I didn't have the money for it. My sister was joining the Marine Corps, so I started thinking about the military, and then different branches. The Coast Guard came up, and I decided that's what I'll do. I'll get out after my four years, have money, finish college, and then teach. I've been in almost nine years. No end in sight for me.

It's so different than what you think going into the service is. It's so funny to me about people in high school that are set, you know, "I am going to do this when I grow up. I am going to do that." And they go to college, and change their majors four times. It's the same way joining the military. You go in thinking you're going to do this, and get out. I don't know how many rescue swimmers have told me, "I joined the Coast Guard to be a rescue swimmer," but then their path takes them somewhere else. It's just because you're young; you don't know what you want. I didn't know what I was going to be doing.

I actually was a dental tech in the Coast Guard before I ever even thought about being a swimmer. I was stationed in Puerto Rico. I had never even seen the rescue swimmer rate. [A "rate" is a Coast Guard enlisted person's pay grade.] I didn't know anything about it, and I sure as heck didn't think it would be anything that I would be doing. I met the swimmer guys while cleaning their teeth, and I would see them in the gym. I kind of got to know 'em and started doing running races with a couple of 'em. One guy said, "Have you ever thought about going to rescue swimmer school?" I said, "Oh, no. I don't even think I know how to swim."

As a dental tech, you are required to do two years, and then you automatically become a nurse, or you can put your name on a list to do something else. So it was coming time for me to make my decision about what I wanted to do. The dentist I worked for said I should really try rescue swimming, just to see if I can do it.

If you don't know a rescue swimmer, you put them on this huge pedestal. They jump out of helicopters and they rescue people in crazy conditions. They seem like they're so far away from you. So I never even gave it a thought. But then when I got to meet 'em and know 'em and run with 'em and stuff, it really didn't seem like it was something that was out of my reach. Once I kind of realized it was somewhat in my reach, then I started thinking about it more and more, and then I was like, yeah, I'll try it. I didn't have that deep passion that they say that you have to have, because I didn't know anything about the job.

When I finally decided I wanted to be a rescue swimmer, I put my name on the list. I went to the pool at ten o'clock that night just to see if I could swim. We had an outdoor pool, and you could buy a key to go in. I was so embarrassed. I didn't want anybody to see me. I didn't know how to put my head in the water or anything. I couldn't swim even a length of the pool. Yeah, a twenty-five-meter pool. I made it halfway, if that. It was awful.

I went to work the next day, and I was telling the dentist I worked for, "What was I thinking?" And I'm crying, like this is so dumb. He was like, "It will work out." And just a stroke of luck—I would not be a rescue swimmer if this had not happened—there was a captain that was temporarily filling in at our clinic. He was friends with the dentist I worked for, and he just so happened to be an Olympic swimmer for Canada. My doctor talked to him, and told him my story. He offered to take me to the pool twice a day, for two weeks, and teach me how to swim. He taught me how to put my head in the water, and everything.

For two weeks, he taught me how to swim, and then I had the rest of my time as a dental tech to train. So I went to the pool every night, went to the gym; spent a lot of time working on my pull-ups and chin-ups. Pull-ups were a big challenge just because girls don't normally do those. It was really hard. I could not do one pull-up when I started, and then, over time, I could do ten pull-ups and ten chin-ups. I was, though, still kind of shy and embarrassed about telling people that I'm going to go to rescue swimmer school. Doubts? Oh yes, I felt like that all the time. I called my mom once—this was when I started the airman program. You do four months as an airman before you go to swimmer's school. It's kind of a screening process; they weed out the people that they know won't make it. So I started my airman program, and I remember my first day at the pool, they just killed me. I thought I was going to drown the whole time. I called my mom, and I was crying, and I said, "I can't do this." She is like, "Don't you quit. If you're not meant to do it, they will tell you can't do it." So I struggled through it, and they never told me to go home. With repetition, and training with the rescue swimmers over and over, you become conditioned, and it wasn't so difficult anymore.

The training center was in Elizabeth City, North Carolina. It was roughly four months long. Oh, gosh, the first month of it is probably the most anxiety I've ever had—not being able to eat before you go work out, and then feeling like you're going to be sick, and being dehydrated all the time, and a lack of sleep—just all the stuff that comes with a program like that. It's all high intensity. And then you get into a rhythm.

There were six of us when we started. Two people didn't make it. I had the fear that it's a male-dominated job. You always had the fear that they're not going to give you the time of day, and you're not going to get your chance to prove yourself; kind of you get shot down before you even get started kind of thing.

The guys in my class were great. They have what's called "squad base." It's kind of a bonding thing. They sleep together there, they eat, tell their stories, they do everything together. I slept in a separate room, but I was always in their room. I never let myself get separated, because I know how that is. Maybe I just got lucky, but I didn't have any problems, and I didn't have any deferential treatment.

When I got to the school, the very first guy I met was muscled and tall, and I looked at him and thought, "What the hell am I doing?" A couple of the guys in the swimming class were real big guys, and I'm thinking to myself, "Oh, Jodie, what did you do?" The biggest guy in the class lasted maybe four days, and the one guy that I kind of picked to be the guy that goes home first—real skinny, wiry, goofy, an awkward kid—he was the strongest person in our class, by far. So it just goes to show that a good majority of it's in your head. One guy that didn't make it could have set push-up and pull-up records. He was good at all the physical stuff, but he just didn't have the water confidence in his head.

One of the instructors said that I was the underdog, the one that people pull for because I have the heart. I imagine that that's what they saw: somebody that wants it so bad and really gives it their all. If you don't really want it, you can't make it through. But there are guys that slip through the cracks. They just have it physically and can do it, but their hearts are not there. I called my mom the second I got out of the pool. I told her I made it. She was ecstatic. I felt like a million dollars, because that's when like you start thinking, I can't believe I did this! There are two other female swimmers in all of the Coast Guard, and now I am one of them. I became the third. The Coast Guard hadn't had a female graduate for, I think, five years or something like that. And I'm like, "I can't believe how close I was to not going and not finishing."

There's still a lot of old-school thought in the rate. You know, everybody has these preconceived notions about these girls: "They're giggly. Oh, can you pick these up for me," that kind of thing. There's a lot of people you're not going to change and who are not going to like girls in the rate. That's just the way it is. I truly believe that if you pull your weight, you're going to get respect. I was lucky because I didn't have anybody talking bad about me or down at me. You want people to know you are a hard worker and that you can keep up even when the guy next to you wouldn't do something. I volunteered a lot. I went on flights a lot and I always PTed with them. PT? Physical training. So I always did everything with them because I didn't want people to think I have it easier, you know.

My first unit was in Los Angeles. I was there for roughly a little over three years. I flew a lot there just because there's so much boat traffic and so many people in the water. It's just a different type of flying than here in Alaska. In L.A., we got tons of false alarms and false flare sightings. You would be flying for hours searching for something that isn't there. Here, you get a call and you know it's going to happen; you know it's real.

In L.A., we did a lot of getting people off their boat and to a hospital. We can go quicker than an ambulance, or sometimes the ambulances cannot get there. The percentage here isn't as high as it would be in L.A. In L.A., it seemed like a good majority of the rescue swimming were all medevacs and a lot of diving injuries. Here, we do get medevacs because people have heart attacks on boats that are far out, but not as many.

We get a lot more of the water-type rescues here. For example, two people ran out of gas on a pleasure craft. Oh, gosh when was it? I would say probably last August. They ran out of gas and the waves were too big that the boat tow couldn't come and get them. They were probably about an hour or two away. They were an older couple, in their seventies. They didn't have survival suits. Usually the way it goes is, if you have a big enough platform that you can hoist right to their boat, then that's what we want to do. But their boat was so small, and it's anchored. If the helo were to come down, it would kind of blow their boat around. So they put me in the water to get them—a free fall, fifteen feet into the water. It's not bad.

I swam over. The man had a life jacket, and the women didn't. It doesn't make any sense. She's a rather large woman and she couldn't swim. I asked him, "Do you have a life jacket for her?" He said, "There's none that fit her." And I said, "Would yours fit?" He also had a float coat. So he gave her his float coat, and then he put on the life jacket. I feel for anybody that doesn't have a [survival] suit on because the water is so cold here. I would say upper forties, or so.

You tell them what is going to happen. You have her get in the water first. She gets in the water and panicked instantly. She was hugging me for dear life. I said a couple of times, "Can you turn around so I can swim?" She would say, "Yeah, yeah," but then she wouldn't move. It was clear she was panicked, so I just let her hold on to me that way, and I just kind of swam away from the boat with her latched to me. She wasn't going to pull me under or anything, so I just let her hold on until she went up in the basket. She was surprisingly calm, compared to her husband.

He's going to have to get into the water and he's a little worried about it. I went back and got him. I had to help him into the water. He had really bad arthritis. He was in a lot of pain, like almost instantly. So he got in the water. He is like, "Get me out of here, get me out of here," because he's scared. I finally made it to the basket and got him in. Right as I got him in, a wave came and went over his head, and he just freaked out. He was standing up in the basket, holding the cable. I had to tell him, "I can't let you go up until you sit down." He just didn't want to sit down because he didn't want the water over his head. Then he went up in the basket, I went up, and everything was fine. We took them to the nearest island to drop them off. And you know, after everything was said and done, he gave me the biggest hug. He is like, "You are so great. Thank you," and he is holding his wife's hand.

People love Coast Guard rescue swimmers, especially here. People have so much respect for what you do. The job's definitely got the glory.

It's funny how people fall into jobs. Just kind of happens. I don't want an office job where you spend eight to ten hours seeing the same thing all day long. Looking back, I don't know how I got all turned around, like how I went from Colorado to join the Coast Guard to what I'm doing now. You would expect someone that knows how to swim. I wouldn't think in a million years I would end up here. It's the coolest job in the Coast Guard.

I will do it as long as my body will let me do it. I would imagine that sometime down the road I'm going to get too old, and then I'll be a salty chief somewhere.

JOE BAUMGARTNER

BULLFIGHTER

*J*oe Baumgartner is one of three bullfighters who travel on the Professional Bull Riders (PBR) circuit protecting bull riders, from the moment a bull charges out of the chute until the rider safely leaves the arena. At forty-one years old, he is the only bullfighter to work at all of the PBR World Finals.

He sits on a metal storage trunk at an arena, two hours before this night's competition.

★ ★ ★

I'm a PBR bullfighter. That means I travel around the country and go to PBRs, which is the professional bull riders' tour. People in this industry, they don't forget where they come from. One thing about bull riding is that people remember how they were raised and where they grew up. It's pretty good that way.

I keep cowboys safe, by any means. There is no set game plan. You never know what's going to happen. You kind of look for what's going on. There's a lot of bulls that you'll see every week. Some of the bulls are mean, and some of the riders have a history getting off bad. Those matchups are the ones that really get your motor going.

It's the life I chose, so that's what I do. I don't give a shit how bad I get beat up, but as long as all forty-five guys that get on can walk out of the arena and get on again tomorrow, that's a good day for me. I mean, that's not only for the satisfaction that you did a great job, but that's doing what you are hired for.

The one thing about the PBR—the forty-five guys that are getting on tonight—is they voted for the three guys that they want to be at all these events to protect them. The PBR has been in existence now going on its fifteenth year, and this is my fifteenth year working here. I've been to every one of the PBR World Finals—the only guy. So it's pretty cool. I think they know that I'm going to give it 110 percent every time, and if somebody gets hit, it's not because I wasn't trying.

My office is in a big arena full of dirt with a lot of big bulls running around in it—one at a time, of course. Every day is different. It's not like you're a football player, like a running back where you figure you're gonna get hit every day. There are some days here when you get hit a lot. And there are other days when you don't get hit at all, and things just seem to flow good and flow smooth. You usually can tell pretty much right off the bat how it's going to work. If the first couple of guys are getting a storm, then you know that your day could be long. Bull riding, it's just . . . I don't know the word for it. If things start one way, they tend to stay that way. If things start the hard way, they're going to be hard all the way. It would be like a basketball team when a team goes on a run and you're waiting for that time-out so you, hopefully, can break that run and your team could come back and do something.

We got to be on every day. I mean a bull rider can have a bad day and get on a bull and get only one jump. Granted he's not making any money. People seem to forget about it. But in the bullfighting business, if you make a bad mistake, people remember that stuff. I've got days where I've been off a little bit. Everybody has one. Like if somebody got thrown off a bull, and you were supposed to make a move. Say you're late making that move and you only got part of your move made, and the rider might have got hooked a little bit, it's something that you could have maybe done to prevent it from happening. Most of the time it's just kind of you grab the bull by the horns and try to distract the animal so the cowboy has a chance to get away. Sometimes you're there for five to ten seconds; sometimes you're there for a split second. Every situation is different.

In the last couple of years, I really had to work on my self-discipline because I was never a guy who liked going to the gym. With the PBR schedule, it's hard to make yourself go to the gym, because your travel schedule is pretty much all year long anymore. You're home for maybe three days a week, so it's hard to get that regimen. When you're home for only that short amount of time, you got to have your own life, but at the same time, that life is being a bullfighter for the PBR.

We finished last night's performance at about eleven, and then we got in the truck and drove up here. We had to go do an autograph deal for one of our sponsors this morning, so we did that from eleven to one. We got done, ate a little bit, and kind of just hung out in the room and relaxed a little; now we're here.

There's three of us that fight bulls during every PBR event. We're pretty tight. The three of us do well together, I think, because there's nobody out there to be a hotshot. There's nobody out there trying to steal the glory. It's just three guys working good together. We get it done. One of the guys, he brought his wife and his daughter with him this week, so he has kind of gone off on his deal, but the other two of us are hanging out.

We got to the arena about four o'clock today, two hours before tonight's performance. First, I go look at the draw. The draw is what bulls are matched up against what cowboys have drawn. It's just so you can kind of see the potential wrecks that might happen. Like I said earlier, there are some guys that just don't get off good, or maybe the bull is terrible and the rider might have the bull that is going to run them down.

Then, I just kind of go in a room, relax for a little while, and start changing. Get my garb on, and then I'll head into the sports medicine room and ride the bike for a little while and have them give me a good stretch. I then just kind of stretch a little bit on my own; just get ready to go into the arena. My stomach nerves up pretty good, so I'll not eat four to five hours before a performance. It's like part of my warm-up. Even after all these years, them nerves get to going, and I get some butterflies in my stomach. I think that's what probably keeps me going. It's part of your mental game. I don't get superexcited, like I don't go slapping my face or anything like that to try to wake up and get my thoughts cleared. I just try to stay relaxed until the first chute opens. It's kind of a rhythm that you get into when you're doing thirty-five events a year.

Afterward, we kind of get together—the three of us bullfighters and Flint the entertainer—and we do a little prayer; just thanking that we had a good night and everybody got away okay. It's nothing fancy; it's just asking to keep everybody strong to do their job as best as they can. Then, we head back to the locker room and just kind of shower, relax, and then probably head back to the hotel.

Bulls are a lot like people, you know. Some people like to go to work, and then after work they like to go have a drink at the bar, kind of party and live it up a little bit. And some bulls just like to go do their job and go home. Bulls are like that. They are also like football players. Some bulls are like the linebacker or a lineman, just big and strong and want to hurt you. Other ones are like a running back or wide receiver that uses their speed to do their job. There are certain bulls like you go, damn, this is a counterfeit sucker. The bulls I mind are the counterfeit ones, which are the ones that when a guy goes to get off and you are in a position to take that bull away, and then he swamps back right to the cowboy instead of being honest.

You want to be the invisible guy when you're a bullfighter. You want to be the guy where the bulls don't see you until it's time to see you, because some bulls will see you and they will come at you when the ride is going on. I try to get really small, just kind of hanging out on the side, invisible until you're needed. And then even when you're needed, be that invisible guy that just slips in there and jerks the bull out of it, help the guy up, and nobody notices.

The good way is for the riders to wait for us to get there, wait for us to set the bull to make sure that its focus is on us. Then the guy can get off pretty easy. There are some guys that when the whistle blows, they just pop their hand out of the rope, and whatever happens, happens. I prefer the guy that waits for you, or the guy that lands on his feet and is getting away.

One bullfighter will try to beat the bull that likes comes back around to [him], and if that works good, then pretty much all you're doing is being there to protect the bull rider. And if that guy can't get 'em—if that bull doesn't pay attention to him and he keeps coming around to try to hook [the bull rider]—then *you're* the guy. That's what happened last night. That bull hooked me in the hand, and hooked me in the side of the face, but, that's what they pay you for. I'm a little sore from last night. I took a pretty good shot. I think I broke my knuckle. This knuckle right there. I don't worry about it. I don't have to run on my hands. So as long as it's not my feet, I don't really worry about it.

We used to wear baggy shorts, but I always felt restricted, and you'd wear a really loud-colored kind of shirt, and you put makeup on your face, like clown makeup. That was kind of part of the gig; that was the way it was. You never got really treated like an athlete because of that. Now, we have kind of a uniform, which is shorts, a jersey, and no more makeup. I wear a chest protector, too. Just to cover the vitals. It's like plastic with foam in it. It fits tight around you so them bulls can't get a hold underneath it. And I wear a cowboy hat; that's my helmet. I've been in some hellacious wrecks, and it doesn't come off.

People seem to respect you more now for being the athlete that you have to be. Yet, even to this day, there's a lot of people that when you say, "I'm a bullfighter for the PBR," they look at you like you're kind of funny. They think of you as you're one of the funny guys. They have a guy that's hired to entertain the crowd and do that. He entertains people on the breaks. But then you say, "Okay, I'm *like* a rodeo clown." Then, all of a sudden, it clicks. My crowd participation is nil. I was never a funny guy. My job is to protect the cowboys. I'll tell you what: I don't hear the crowd, and I don't see it. I never look up. My focus is right there in the arena. I hear the whistle blow, or the horn toot, when the ride is completed, and that's about it.

It's just something you can't be halfway doing it, because your life is depending on it. The two guys you are working with are depending on you being good, and the guys riding depend on you being good. You know, it's a life-and-death deal here. I mean, I've seen people get killed bad. Three times in one year I saw. . . . Well, I can tell you about all three of them.

One was a bull rider that didn't have a protective vest on or anything, and he was doing what we call a "day money drag" where the guy was hanging off the side of this bull—he was a just a little cute black mule, never hurt anybody in his life—and the guy just hung on and hung on upside down, and his head was dragging on the ground. Finally he let go. He hit the ground, and when he did that the bull turned and stepped on his back and just broke him up in the middle. Well, he was still making a qualified ride, so I had to kind of stay out of the way. I can't do much about where the back feet land on 'em, but the head and horns I can keep off 'em pretty good.

Then I was in Brazil—nobody was wearing protective vests there, either—and the guy got jerked down on top of the bull's horn. He was still riding him when the bull threw his head back and the horn hit him right in the chest. Done. Right there.

And then I did lose a good friend named Brent Thurman that same year at NFR [National Finals Rodeo] in Las Vegas. It had to be like '93 or '94. He had this bull drawn. I actually helped to get the bull to the NFR that year, they were going to take him out, I go, "Man, this bull is good." So, Brent, he walked up and he goes, "Hey Joe, how am I going to ride that son of a bitch?" And I go, "Brent, this is a fucking-bucking fucker." I mean, I was all straight with him. That's one thing I never did: I never bullshitted nobody. Still, to this day, I don't. If people ask me an opinion, I'm going to tell them what I think, and if you don't like it, well. . . . And so that's what I told him and, boy, the next thing I know he kind of hung his foot in his rope and that bull jerked him down underneath him and stepped on him. Stepped on his head. It was a rotten deal, man. I lost a good friend. But at the same time, you look at it as I lost a good friend doing something he loved to do. I mean, he was a bull rider through and through, and that's a chance you live with. That was by far my worst day, when Brent died. The other two guys, you know, you kind of shake it off.

Injured? Yeah. I've broken both my ankles; broke both my legs. Two years ago, I broke my leg. A bull stepped on it. And then I got healed up from it, went back to work, and then last September, I had a bull step on my other leg and broke it. I was at home for two months. During that two months, somebody else is making my money. If you're sitting at home, you're not getting paid.

I wrenched my back the other day; pinched my sciatic nerve. We've been on ground on the East Coast that's been really bad. It's all indoors there, but the dirt has to come from somewhere, you know. So the dirt's been really sticky and wet, kind of leaves big holes in the ground when the bulls buck. That happened the second night in Massachusetts, with about five bulls left to go. So I just kind of got through the rest of that night, and then went into the sports medicine room and had them guys work on me for a couple of hours. I got there a couple of hours early the next morning and had them work on me again. The magic that they pulled on me last week was pretty phenomenal. With that, and a back brace, I was able to work.

Physically the worst time for me was I had a bull hit me dead on the knee and tore my ACL and PCL. I sat home for four months wondering what I was going to do for a living. That was probably like in '97, '98, maybe. I lived at the gym; went six days a week, twice a day. For a complete tear of your ACL, that's a seven- to eight-month deal. Hell, I was back in three weeks and five days from the day that it happened to the day I went back to work. I was a little scared, you know, because I knew I was probably only 80 percent. But I knew I had a really good partner that I had worked the NFR with three or four times, so I knew that if I was a step slow, he would cover the slack. The best thing in the world that happened was the third bull knocked me down and had me down, and it was just knocking the crap out of me on the ground, and, well, I started to get up and bent my leg and I go, "Still feels all right." Right there, bam, it was done. I saved a cowboy.

I really haven't even noticed it. To me, forty-one years old—that's an age; that's all it is. I mean, my body still feels good. I still feel as quick as I ever was. Unfortunately, for me, when I started the pay scale was low. I used to go work a rodeo for a hundred dollars a day. Now, a guy can do pretty well. I mean, you're not making what a baseball player does, but at the same time, I'm comfortable in my life. I look at it two ways: Damn, I was born a little too early, and then I think, damn, at least I'm making it good for all the younger guys coming up so they might not have to fight bulls for twenty-some-odd years. I think when I walk away from it, I'll walk away from it. If there is anything I can ever do to help I would, but I don't want to be one of those guys who just drags around.

I will tell you what, man, it's my life. There's very few people in this world that get to go to work, make a living, and love what they do every day. That's the life I got. There's not that many guys that are making a living at it. There's probably two hundred to three hundred guys that call themselves bullfighters, but the good ones get the work, and the other ones just sit at home and call themselves bullfighters.

★Author's note: *The day after the interview, Joe jumped in front of a bull named All In to protect rider Colby Yates, who was thrown to the ground. The bull's right horn hooked Joe's chin, hurtling him high into the air. Joe landed on his head, stayed on the hard dirt for several minutes, and needed help walking out of the arena. He suffered a concussion.*

RICK LEE

IRONWORKER

*R*ick Lee's son and brother also are ironworkers, and are working together with him on a new high-rise building. The construction crew was sent home this morning, because it was too windy to work. "A lot of people look at what we do and think we're just a bunch of dummies up there, that all you got to do is put a bolt in the hole. It's not that the work is overly cerebral, but there's a lot of thinking that goes on. And if you don't think, you're going to be injured. It's the same kind of idea that you see with people that climb Mt. Whitney. People will climb Mt. Whitney and think they are ready for Mt. Everest. Whitney is a hike; Everest is a climb. The difference is that if you lose your focus on Whitney, you come back down. Lose your focus on Everest, *you die. Our trade is exactly the same way. It's not brain surgery, but it's not a walk in the park, either."*

★ ★ ★

I'm an ironworker. Yesterday, you referred to it as a steelworker. That's a misconception. But, that's all right. It's something that is thought of by ironworkers as almost disrespectful, because steelworkers are people who make steel, the guys who are in the foundries. We're ironworkers. That's what, by trade, we are.

I do structural steel. That's the framework for any building, high-rise, low-rise, don't matter. We do the stuff that's covered up. From time to time we will work on projects where the architect will expose some of what we do on the building where you can see it. That's kind of gratifying. I dig that. We can always look back and say we did something. I enjoy seeing effort, that's my reward. Part of the reward is money, there is no doubt about it, but part of the reward is actually getting to see something develop from just a slab on the ground. I mean, what's the use in a slab? It's just a parking lot. We turn a parking lot into something that's useful.

My dad was a mechanic when he got out of school. He was working in a garage, and the guy who owned the garage kind of helped him along. The family was starting to grow, and I guess my dad just wasn't able to make ends meet as a mechanic. Well, his boss somehow heard that they were needing ironworkers to do the rebarring on all these small bridge decks on a highway, and he asked him if it was something he wanted to do. So he did, and he joined the union as an ironworker. It wasn't a lucrative career, but we always had everything that we needed.

I remember going with him to job sites as a kid. We thought we were part of the gang, so we would go. I enjoyed it, so I thought that would be a good thing for me. I wanted to do the same for my family, so that's what I did as soon as I got out of high school.

I graduated in June, and started in July 1980. It's been really, really good to me. I mean, I raised my family and now my brother and son are in it. My son, Kip, is connecting—the one that's putting all the iron together on top. Kip, yeah, that's his name. "Kip" is a term that engineers use for load. It's a measurement. It's called "kips." I thought that was pretty cool.

I started as a connector. The connector is the guy who actually takes the iron that is coming from the crane and puts it together. I always wanted to do it. I don't know what it is, but I like being off the ground. It's kind of crazy. It's not that I like the danger of it, but there is a certain rush from working on the edge. Maybe that was part of the intrigue.

I was connecting for probably the first seventeen years of my career, then went into running raising gangs—which is raising the iron. You have a small group that consists of two connectors and two people that are hooking the iron on. On some jobs, you have a phone man who's making contact with the crane operator and is giving him direction. At other times, the crane operator can see you, and you can signal him by the universal hand signals that we have for moving the crane in any direction you want to move it. So that's what I did. Basically you look at prints and what iron you need, and you put the iron in a sequence that it has to go together. If you have a thousand pieces, each one of them has a number on it and has to go in a specific area. You can't just come out and say, okay put that over there, put this over here.

You are continually climbing and moving. You're never just standing still. Maybe that's the sadomasochistic side of me. It's just hard, and not very many people can do it. There are a lot of people who can connect, but they're never, ever going to have that title "connector," because it's not one that you make for yourself; it's a title people give you. It's a level of respect of grown men that is earned over time. Once it's earned, then you know you made it. When you're able to pass that threshold and carry a level of work that transcends everyone around you, they place you in a special spot. There is no shortcut to the kind of respect that you have to earn. If you shortcut anywhere, the respect isn't there and people will not follow your direction. You have to pay whatever dues is necessary to earn respect. That is very difficult in our trade.

I want people to trust me, because if people don't trust your judgment about what you are doing in life-and-death situations, they're not going to perform to their potential. There were many guys that did the same for me. There are some things that will kill you dead as a hammer; I mean, right now. In my career as a connector, four guys I've worked with as a team have fallen. Three of them were killed by impact on the ground, or hit things on the way down, or were hit with iron and were swept off. I mean, it could happen. The dangers are so varied. When you relax and lose focus on what you're doing, you are exposing yourself to an injury. It's a sobering experience; not that somebody was doing something that was unsafe or doing something that they shouldn't have been doing. Sometimes they just put themselves in a bad position. There is a term that's called "the hospital side." If you get on the wrong side of something, let's say I've got a wall to my back and a piece of iron coming in: that would be the hospital side, because that's where I'm going to be trapped. So what we do as a trade is we train our people to be where there's always a route to escape or something to get behind, so you're not going to get smashed.

Let's say, for example, on a daily basis we put in 125 to 150 pieces of iron. Of those pieces, potentially probably 50 percent of them could smash you or hurt you in some way. Every single second you are on point. That's what I like about it. You're on this sharp edge of your focus, and as you as you turn your back, something's fixing to get you. You just have to be on for eight hours. It's very strenuous, but you forget it when you go home. When the belt comes off, you're done.

When you first get into it, you feel overwhelmed because everything is happening around you. You always feel like you're behind and are always reacting. You're not the one who is in control of where you want to be, or what you're doing next. You hear about athletes, they'll say, I was in the zone. You get that way in our trade—at least I do—where you don't think about anything you're doing. You don't think about being off the ground, nothing. You just think about what you're supposed to be doing and then you can run along the beams as fast as you want to go. You should be a little afraid, because if you don't, then this kind of trade will eat you up. You can't afford to fall. This trade is dangerous.

Because of the inherent dangers in what we do, there's high risk. I don't know where the ironworker lists on the most dangerous jobs, but it's got to be up there. There are some people that can handle the risks that we take, and some people can't. How you handle heights and handling a crane that's swinging beams at you can get a little hairy from time to time. Sometimes you think the guy that's trying to control a piece of iron, anywhere from a thousand pounds to ten thousand pounds, with a piece of equipment is fighting against you. Some people can't manage that.

You are at heights that will obviously kill you if you fall. You don't have to go very high. You can go twenty feet, twenty-five feet and you can die fairly easily from that. The risk of falling is probably the greatest risk that we have to manage as ironworkers, and as a company. We have the same goal of doing what we do in a way that is safe enough that we can keep doing what we do, because if we do it in such a way that we're not concerned about the people around us, we are going to kill them all off, and there's not going to be nobody left to do it. So, we manage the risk of falling by training people and by implementing safety programs that are tried and true.

There's no absolute way, but there are techniques to walking a beam. If you ever see the guys doing the high-wire walking, they step just the right way: You place your feet in a way to have the most stability on a small surface. I like to get people to get in their mind that this is something that they have to get over. You know, we'll walk down the sidewalk and never think once about falling off. I mean, how many times do you walk on the sidewalk and are afraid you are going to fall down? Very seldom. If we can walk a line that's on the sidewalk, we can walk a beam that's up in the air. What we have to overcome is our own mind. We should have some fear, but not a fear that overwhelms you. You just get used to it so that it's second nature, then you don't even think about it.

The more narrow the beam, the more focused you have to be. The beams are from four inches anywhere up to fifteen to twenty inches—it's like a highway when you get something that big. Your feet go on the bottom flange and then your knees can almost hold yourself on there with no hands. Sometimes the smaller beams are so small you can't get on that bottom flange for stability. It takes a lot of practice.

Guys will talk about their tools kind of the same way that a baseball player talks about his glove, because our life relies on our tools being good. A lot of times we'll climb a column and we'll stick a spud wrench, or a sleever bar, in a hole and we'll sit on it. A spud wrench is a wrench that has a pointed end; it's another aligning tool. A sleeper bar is a longer tool for leverage and for aligning. We also have a crescent wrench and bolt bags. The tools that we use are very minimal. There's a whole shack full of other tools, but those are the basic tools that we use to really put together. Because of the shape of what we do and the size of what we do, and because there's variables in how iron is forged, it takes a lot of work to pull and pry to line up the holes that we are going to suspend a piece of iron on.

My job is to manage the manpower, the materials, and the tools. I try to meet the production schedule by having enough material and enough manpower and enough tools to complete it. It's kind of challenging, because you have days like today where it's windy and you can't do anything. The wind is blowing probably at least in the high 30s and low 40s. We're working around the top of the building at three hundred feet, which of course there's nothing there to slow the wind down; it's going full speed up there. And with this particular crane, because of its design, it has a pretty low toleration for wind, so things can go wrong at twenty-five miles per hour. And with the brake systems that are on it, it doesn't have the power to stop in the wind. So what do you do with twenty-two guys with nothing to do? We're all going home because of the wind.

When I first got into the trade, I was working for a company whose reputation for safety is not the greatest. There are a lot of companies out there that are unscrupulous in how they use their manpower. I'm almost ashamed to say that I worked for this particular company or that particular company because of their apparent disregard for human lives, rather than what can we do to manage whatever risk that we have, so that you can go home at night and be with your family. It's a combination of a company using practices that aren't safe and tools that aren't designed to do what we were doing, just to save money. A lot of companies will cut costs on safety because it affects how much profit that they get, how big a house that they have, and how big a car they drive. I got no problem with somebody having a big car and big house, but not at the expense of me or somebody that I work with.

So, I was working for that company and I'm on this beam, and the beam rolls over. I jump off, because I think the beam is going to fall in a hole. I land on the concrete from maybe twenty-five feet, and I broke my left arm at the wrist, right arm at my elbow, fractured my skull across my eye and into the eye socket, and fractured my pelvis. I was probably in my mid-twenties. Laid up about two months. Do I hold some animosity toward 'em or anything like that? No. But I would never work for them again. Never.

There's just so many circumstances like that. Hairy stuff happens all the time. It becomes routine to us, and how we manage that internally is the difference between those who can and those who can't.

I'm still amazed at what we do. You know, you stand back and look at this building, and you go, that's just a building. But it's cool what we can accomplish with a group of guys who, a lot of times, are unrelated. At the height of our crew—maybe twenty-six, twenty-seven guys—we have the same goal in mind. It's almost like a football team. Not everybody is a quarterback and not everybody is a wide receiver and not everybody is a lineman. Everybody has a thing they have to do, and you just go do it. We have a group of guys that all want to put this building up, so you're gathered around even though in other circumstances you would never meet them. There is no way I would meet any of these people that are here if it were some other circumstance, because we don't all have the same interests or the same likes or dislikes, but because we are doing this one thing, we're all friends and associates. We may not go out and have, you know, lunch every day or go out somewhere on the weekend, but while we are here we are committed to each other, because we have the same kind of goal: that's to put this building up, make a living, and do it safely.

No, I wouldn't classify myself as a risk taker. I would classify myself as not being afraid to enjoy. A lot of people are afraid to enjoy stuff, you know what I am saying? I will accept whatever risk there is in order to enjoy life and experience things. I've never really thought of myself as an ironworker that does other things. I like things like riding motorcycles and fishing, but I would rather be considered a father and a husband, who also does ironwork for a living.

GENE HAMNER

CROP DUSTER

*A*s a young man, Gene Hamner was a smoke jumper with the U.S.
Forest Service, and flew 565 combat missions in Southeast Asia during the
Vietnam War (including receiving four Distinguished Flying Cross awards,
and twice flying into North Vietnam on search-and-rescue missions for
downed American pilots). After his combat career in Southeast Asia ended,
he flew C-141 transport planes for the Air Force and, for a short while, flew
charters for hunting and fishing trips. He then continued his flying career as
a crop duster for thirty-five years.

"I've always liked the idea that whatever I've done, it's me versus whatever,
from smoke jumping where you're with other guys against a thousand-acre
fire, or in Laos, flying solo except for a Laotian guy in your backseat talking

to the ground commanders. Where I was working, I was butting up against China. There were no American assets to get me out. You get shot, it's Air America or it's Laotian or you're gonna walk home. If you weren't picked up in a very short period of time, the bad guys got hold of you, I mean you were done. They didn't take you to the Hanoi Hilton. You died there in the jungle, and probably not a very pretty death, either. It was all you against whatever in the world is out there."

★ ★ ★

My most formative years were up in a little town in the forests and mountains of Mt. Lassen. Those were the years when I realized that an eight-to-five job of sitting behind a desk is not for me. Then, as a forestry major in college, each summer I worked for the Forest Service doing various things like fire control, marking timber one year, two years floating in the Middle Fork of the Salmon River on a rubber raft, cleaning campgrounds. Those campgrounds were in primitive areas. I'm talking about no motorized vehicles, no airplanes, nothing. You're dependent upon yourself.

The whole thing that I loved about that, and everything else I've done, is that it's me against something. It's me out there against the river. When you're on a fire and you parachute out of that airplane, get to the fire, you're up against that fire. You got the adrenaline going and you're fighting that thing, and you got the camaraderie when the fire alarm goes again and you go running into the airplane, put on your jump gear and the parachute. It isn't like somebody is dragging you out there to do it. You get on fires for a couple of days and you're just sucking in the smoke and ash and hoping like heck that everything goes your way. You're concentrating on what you're doing when you're out there doing that, and you're getting paid to do it. You're in such great physical shape that you do this for hours and days, chopping line, felling trees, or doing whatever, but when you're off, you just live life. I mean, you drink beer, you go to the bars, you go down the river. At the end of all of that, you just have that feeling of freedom and exhilaration. You know you have gone out and done it.

I had six summers with the Forest Service. The first summer I was strictly on a fire crew on a tank truck, just digging fire lines. We were on a pretty major fire that was getting out of control, and we had the tankers come in dropping fire retardant, and they brought some smoke jumpers. When I saw these guys jump, I was hooked. So, I went over to the jump base on our time off, found out what's really required. Everything I did from then on was geared for smoke jumping.

Our jump training was a two- to three-week affair, and then you made seven practice jumps at the end. The first was in a huge field— you couldn't miss it. The last jump was into timber, and you had nowhere to go but into the trees. Imagine you've been fighting fire for, say, a week, and at the end of that, now you got to go back and spend hours cutting your chute out of a tree, packing it, and walk out with hundred-pound packs on your back.

When I smoke jumped, I went to Fairbanks, Alaska. But the Vietnam War was then heating up, so I applied for pilot training in the Air Force and the Navy. Both actually came through, and I'm sitting there looking at the Navy and I'm looking at the Air Force thinking, would I rather come back at midnight in a battle-damaged airplane in a storm and look for 1,100 feet of steel floating in the South China Sea, or eleven thousand feet of concrete right from where I took off? I opted for the Air Force. I finished that summer of smoke jumping and then went to the pilot officer training school. I was twenty-three.

Well, the war was on, and the fighting part of you—I mean, that's what you're there for—wanted to work the war. I wasn't married, so you might as well go to war. I was motivated and it was just a natural progression for me. In my case, I asked to be a fighter as my first choice, and then forward air controller. I went to Southeast Asia as a forward air controller.

In '71–'72, I was in Laos with the Ravens, as a volunteer with the Royal Laotian Army. We flew mostly at night, in a modified Cessna

337. We'd fly east to the Ho Chi Minh Trail, be assigned an area, and then we would begin looking for trucks. I was flying the airplane and you kind of look over at your airspeed, look over at your altitude indicator, and if things were getting out of hand, then correct it. You'd get into a turn and you had to keep the nose moving, because the ground gunners were looking and if you give them a target they'd shoot. In the daytime, you couldn't see the tracers. You wouldn't know how close they were until you see the air burst around you. At night, you could see the tracers coming up at you, which had a tendency to make it a little more uncomfortable, because if you saw tracers were moving relative to something on the windscreen, you know they were way off. But, if they weren't moving, then those things would come straight at you and be getting bigger and bigger and bigger, and then you'd have to take evasive action. I never got hit, but one time it was close when a 37-mm line came up from a seven-round clip and the last round was probably about a foot and a half off the nose of the airplane. If there had been an eighth round, it would have been right through the center of the airplane. I could smell the cordite when it burst right above us.

There was a lot of that in combat, you know, with shrapnel going over the top and other stuff, and losing an engine one night and then, as soon as the ground gunners knew that you had lost that engine, everybody was shooting. I had my right seater throwing everything in the world out of the window trying to lighten up the plane, because I couldn't maintain altitude. As long as an airplane is responding to the controls and you have any hope of that thing flying, then stick with the airplane, and we did. Then, everything else just turned into a bucket of worms all the way down because of the altitude of the mountains around us and the distance getting back. We battled fog all the way down to the ground, and when I landed and got to the other end of the runway, it was so foggy I couldn't see. We had been at a point where we were too low to jump, and we couldn't climb.

But, anyway, you didn't want war stories. But all of this leads up to the thing that, when you get finished with all of the stuff in

Southeast Asia—six months of living and fighting the war, with rounds coming during combat—those situations are very formative.

In one of the charters that I took, I was waiting for the people to come back and a crop duster came in and landed. He was waiting for his crew and I was asking if there a big demand for crop dusting, or is it something that's going to just peter out? The guy says it's a gold mine: "It's a lot of flying, but it's a lot of money." So I went down to a crop-dusting school, and that was it.

In Laos, I was flying an O-1—a little tail dragger—or a U-17, which is a Cessna 185, and a T-28, which was guns and rockets. With the O-1 and the U-17, you're looking for little dirt strips out in the middle of a jungle. I figured what's the difference between that and crop dusting where you go out to an 1,800-foot strip, fly in there, get a load, and fly back out. From the standpoint of the flying, it was the same kind of flying. I'm looking at crop dusting as a piece of cake.

You can't even imagine what that was like. I mean, I was in hog heaven flying around with binoculars and listening to the engine. There is nothing inside of a crop duster other than looking to see what your load is, or once in a while looking at oil pressure and temperature. The airspeed on 90 percent of the airplanes that I have ever flown doesn't work at all. Once you get in the air and you set everything, then it's just a question of what's going on outside and how does that airplane feel. When you come around in a turn, is it sagging, can you feel that tail end kind of letting down and the airspeed getting slow? Maybe you're kind of getting blown away from your turning point. You know exactly what's going on, because you better. The airplane is talking to you, just like we're talking right here.

Sometimes, I fly from four thirty in the morning till two thirty or three o'clock in the afternoon, never a drink a water. You don't eat anything, you don't want anything, and then you land and you shut the airplane off, and all of a sudden, you're just drenched, you're thirstier than heck, you want to get something to eat. It's just adrenaline and concentration. You're thinking of everything else, and not your belly. Time goes by fast.

You're trying to get your wheels so they are not more than a foot above the crop, so that puts the spray booms about probably thirty inches above the crop. The chemical comes through the spray booms right on top of the crop. The speed is about 105 to 120 miles an hour. If you're gonna fly under a wire and there's a road there, you need to see if there's traffic, or maybe a standpipe coming up, or a tractor, or whatever you're looking at, and you're thinking of the next swath; you're already one swath ahead of the airplane. Most of the time, going under the wires is not a big deal. They are either high enough that it's not a factor, or if it's really low, well, I've brought back salad greens in the brakes.

Some farmers are putting in owl boxes. There's a lot of little critters, like mice and gophers, that get out in the field and they'll eat the crop—grapes, asparagus, tomatoes. Everybody now is getting more environmentally friendly to where they are using predator insects and other things. They are not using so many chemicals. So, farmers put up the boxes all along, and sometimes they tell you they have just put them in and sometimes they don't. The owl boxes are up probably about eight to ten feet, and they all want to paint them in environmentally friendly colors like green or brown. If you got stuff on your windscreen and you're looking out across a field into the sun and there's owl boxes and standpipes, I mean it's a pucker factor. These things are out there and they are big hazard, and is gonna be very detrimental to the airplane. It's difficult seeing them. I mean, you're trying to stay down on the crop, and sometimes you can't really see that owl box. If you see it, it's not a factor. It's when you've got sulfur or stuff on your window or when you're looking into the sun, or its a murky morning in the spring and you're doing a fertilizer or doing seed and you're flying out in this field and you're supposed to have a mile visibility, but a lot of times you really don't, so it makes it very difficult to see them.

One time we were flying at night and there was a field that was over east of Victoria Slough, and they had these tall transmission lines. It was eleven thirty at night. We were gonna spray a field of tomatoes on a very irregular-shaped field on a delta island. The high lines kind of came in on an angle just off to one side, but didn't go through the field. We were using flaggers who stood on the levee that goes around the island, and they would—because it was at night—wiggle a flashlight so that you'd see a little flashing light. You'd come around with your turn lights on, pick up the rows, pick up the flagger, and then you'd fly down and spray. Then the flagger would take whatever interval that we tell him to—thirteen steps or whatever—and they would mark off the next pass. We would do this in a big, circular racetrack pattern and the flagger would move right across the field.

On this field, there was a tree that marked where we started, but there was more field to go that was south of it. It was so close to these transmission towers that we couldn't come into the field, get down in it, and then be able to climb out over the towers, and then come back around, because the plane would be too heavy. Well, some fishermen had come in and had sat down on the levee on the other side, and they had a lantern.

I pulled out of the field and made my first pass, and come back around to turn away from the wires. As I was coming around, I was looking for my flagger with her flashlight, but I was seeing the fishermen's lantern. When you're making that 180-degree turn, you're looking up and down, and you're also looking for that flagger while knowing those wires were there. All of a sudden I'm feeling vertigo. It was a very black night, no moon, few lights out across the fields of farmhouses, and no definite horizon.

So I come around and I dove into the field, and I realized I was flying cross rows on that field and I wasn't lined square, and when I pulled out I wasn't picking anything up in my turn lights. I thought I was in a climbing left turn and, with vertigo, I was actually climbing straight ahead, and there were these huge transmission wires. I hit the top, outside 60,000-volt line that threw me up and over, and I hung with my landing gear in the 240,000-volt line while the 60,000-volt lines were falling into themselves. The sky was a brilliant blue.

The engine stopped, and it almost ripped the wing off. I had enough time to look at the tower way down the line, and I had another tower about ten yards away from me over on my left side. I hung there long enough that I remember thinking, how in the world am I gonna get out of this? I was hung up there upside down in the wire. The wire that I was hung in broke at the far tower—it just couldn't support the weight. The top of that tower to the river was 210 feet, above a river. I could see the water, and I thought to myself, well, this is it. I figured there is no surviving this.

I don't know exactly what happened, but the plane dropped into the water going pretty much straight in, prop first. I was wearing a helmet that had a double visor. As I was going forward, I went into the padded dash and it busted both of the visors, and I broke the hand grip off of my control stick.

The airplane was sitting upright in the water, floating, but sinking. When I was aware of what was going on, water was seeping in through the tail. I stepped out onto the wing, took my pocketknife out of my pocket, cut the laces on my boots, and threw them into the water. All I could think of was my Air Force training and how I didn't go through all this to then jump in that water and drown—because I couldn't swim with my boots and coveralls and everything else on. So I took the boots off, took my coveralls off, and put the knife into my teeth. By then, the water was waist deep. I mean, the airplane had sunk that much. I got down in the water and swam to a little land that was near. And then I watched the airplane's spray lights sinking.

Fire engines were everywhere. This ambulance came in across the levee from where I was. My boss showed up, and everybody was standing there. Somebody yelled at me, "Are you okay?" I said, "Yeah, I'm all right." I wasn't hurt at all. Later, I complained about my elbow, but it was nothing that they ever did anything to. When I took my Levi's off, the broken control stick had nicked the inside of both legs and they were bleeding just a little, but there were no broken bones and no major cuts.

A couple of months ago, I was dusting grapes with sulfur for a grower. It was six thirty in the morning. I went back for the last load and come back out. The wind had quieted, and there wasn't anything moving the sulfur. As I pulled out on the second pass, I was looking into the sun, but I had no trouble seeing the vines. I was just thinking that was a lot of sulfur there. I came back for the next pass, spraying down into the field, and everything was fine. I could see what was going on, but all of a sudden it was a wall of tule fog in the worst situation you ever flew through. I mean, one minute you have referenced everything and the next minute, in the space of a snap of a finger, there is nothing. I looked to my right to establish the grapes, and all of a sudden I heard the sound of the landing gear down into the wire in the vineyard. I remember I pulled back, but the nose pitches down into the grapes and, well, I was along for the ride. A wall of fire came up and burned my face and burned my eyes and burned off my eyelashes and eyebrows. I had my visor down, my glasses on, and I had a dust mask that I was wearing, which probably kept me from sucking flames into my lungs.

The plane ended up flipping over on its back, and I was hanging upside down. I reached down, popped my seat belt. There was fire all over to the left of me. The right wing was up in the air, the window was busted out. I was worried about the sulfur, because when sulfur burns, it puts out sulfur dioxide, which is extremely toxic. It only takes a couple of breaths of that and you're unconscious. I mean, it will knock you out. I was fully aware of the fire and the sulfur burning, and I'm thinking I don't want to breathe in deeply. At some point in the crash, my head had rocked back, which moved my helmet forward and my visor broke my nose. My nose was pouring blood out into the dust mask. That kept me from sucking in any of the sulfur dioxide. As I crawled out, I can't breathe. Now, I'm kind of concerned. I jerked my helmet off and I take the mask off. I'm thinking where the fire was and that there was the full gas tank. I just want to get out because of the gas and fire, and it might blow. I didn't want to be in the middle of that.

I skinnied out of the plane, stood up, and took a deep breath of air, and I thought to myself, I don't have any lung damage. I'm between rows of grapes in the vineyard. But things were starting to get a little fuzzy out in the distance.

I had my cell phone with me in my pocket, and I called my partner and told him the airplane was done, I just tore it up. He is going, "Holy mackerel, where are you? How are you doing?" I'm telling him my eyes were toasted, but I said, I'm fine. I walked out a half mile, heading east. I ran into a guy who drove me up to where my partner had just shown up. I jumped in his truck and went to the hospital. When I went over to the doctor and he takes a look at me and he says, "What happened to you?" Then I say, "I've been in an airplane accident." He didn't believe me and thought I was just some smart-ass son of a bitch that wouldn't tell them what in the heck went on. He said, "Well, you look pretty good having been through an airplane accident."

I don't know how to describe this to anybody who would understand it. I mean, here is a situation where you truly cheated death tearing up that airplane, being upside down, and there's fire in the plane. You're going along and you run into this unlucky situation, but on the other side of that unlucky situation, you're alive, you're fine, nobody is hurt. There is a feeling of exhilaration from that.

I go to work, get it done, I come home. It gives me good money, but I don't feel like I need to brag about it. You go to work like a bus driver does. Crop dusting is not a big deal.

But you can't give up on a flying an airplane. This is what you do. I'm not looking for any more flying stories. I don't need any more of those. I've had a good run. I try to put everything in my favor and always have, and I've always survived it all.

MATT CORRIERE

CRAB FISHERMAN

*K*odiak, Alaska. Easter Sunday. Matt Corriere invited me to have dinner with his family and several friends. After his friends left, we grabbed a couple of beers and talked late into the night about crab fishing. "It was the worst experience of my life, but it was also the best experience of my life. I wouldn't trade it for anything in the world. I think that shaped who I am today. I'm a confident adult male who is comfortable in my own skin. I've been to the edge, and then brought myself back. I know what I can do and where I can be pushed. No one can take that away from me."

★ ★ ★

There were several years where I lived on a boat. I didn't have a home other than the boat. I would have girlfriends now and then and spent time at their houses, but there was about three years where I pretty much lived on a boat. I fished halibut and went crab fishing—king crab, opilio crab, tanner crab—and then we'd start over again with halibut. You'd spend nine months a year out at sea.

King crab has always been the World Series of crab fishing. It's the most prestigious crab to catch, and the biggest. You could do good on that short season; it was only five to eight days long. We had just spent two months out there. You know, out at sea is where the bad stuff's supposed to happen: accidents, boats sinking, people dying. When you get home, you're in your backyard, your guard is down a little bit maybe, and you're not expecting anything to happen.

King crab fishing used to start on November 1, so we would leave Kodiak maybe a week and a half before that to get enough time to get out to Dutch Harbor. We'd get there, where the Coast Guard would do inspections to make sure you didn't actually have any crab on board beforehand. If you had pots on board, they'd check to make sure they were set up to regulation. Then you'd take off from there with thousands of pounds of bait on board, and thousands of pounds of groceries. Any mechanical breakdowns can cost you the season. Everything had to be in tip-top shape before you left racing out for pots of gold. It was exciting.

The last year I fished, I made $90,000. I was twenty-three years old. I spent that time on the *Massacre Bay*. It was a crab and halibut boat, and it tendered salmon in the summertime. It was ninety-eight feet. Not the prettiest boat in the world, but it was in pretty good mechanical shape.

After the king crab season, there was like a week break, and then we went tanner crab fishing, which are known as snow crab in restaurants. We did that till right up to Christmastime, then we brought the boat back to Kodiak. We spent Christmas here, and then January 1 was supposed to be the tanner crab opening, but the fishermen went on strike for twelve or fourteen days. The price of crab was too low, so they just stand down and won't go fishing until the cannery offers a price that they can all agree on. So we just kind of hung around town and then the skipper of the boat, Jock Bevis, wanted to get out of town. It was usually good for the crew to get out of town, because you're not spending any money when you're on the boat, and you're not drunk and you're not doing anything stupid and getting into trouble, so it was a forced sobriety. We actually used to look forward to leaving, because things could get too weird in town.

We left a little bit early before the season opened and went to the south end of Kodiak, about ninety air miles from town. Jock and I were the only people on the boat that was the normal crew. There were two other people, so we were a little short on the deck, but it was just supposed to be a quick opening and the fishing wasn't going to be very intense to need extra guys. Everyone was an experienced fisherman.

We took the boat to the south end of the island and into a bay called Lazy Bay. It doesn't have very good anchorage, because it's full of kelp, which is a seaweed that fouls the anchors up. This was the night of the sixteenth. It's after midnight. The wind had come up that night, we were kind of dragging anchor, and Jock decided to move the boat so that we'd get next to a village that was close by because he could pick up a football game the next day on the TV antenna on the boat.

We pulled anchor and left Lazy Bay—there is an island on the port side of the bay as you're coming out, so you got to make a wide turn to go around this island and then go inside. The rest of the crew—Bill Corbin, Tom Salisbury, and me—went downstairs and we're all sitting at the galley table reading, doing whatever, and it was only going to be like thirty minutes till we went and dropped anchor again. Unbeknownst to us, the skipper is upstairs in the wheelhouse, asleep. He had been doing drugs and alcohol all day, and I didn't know it. He fell asleep, and we drove all the way across Alitak Bay, which is probably fourteen miles across. It took thirty-five to forty minutes to get across.

It was snowing. It's the middle of the night, now maybe two o'clock in the morning. The sea conditions were probably running five feet or so. The boat is wobbling a little bit, but it wasn't anything terrible. I was reading a book, and then all of a sudden the boat just stopped, the refrigerator fell out of the bracket that it was in, and all the dishes came flying out of the cupboard.

Jock hit a reef. The boat came to a sudden lurching with a loud and very unusual sound. We all came flying off of the galley table. I didn't have any idea. It happened so fast. The stairs going up the wheelhouse are right there, so we're up in the wheelhouse within seconds after we hit. Jock had woken up and thrown the boat in reverse to try to get it off the rocks, and instead of assessing the situation, he ripped about a nine-foot hole in the bottom, up in the bow. We might have had some holes, but nothing big. The boat might have been crushed up a little bit, but if you start towing that much dead weight it is going to tear a hole in the bottom.

Crab boats are half sunk when they leave town, because they have holding tanks that are full of water to keep the crab alive, and they're constantly being pumped, so that the water is coming out of the hatch and then goes across the deck and out the scuppers. You're constantly filling it back up, because, if you didn't do that, you would end up with a free surface effect, and then all that liquid would go to one side of the boat and the boat would roll over.

The boat was empty other than water, and then we've got fuel tanks. The boat is full of fuel, so it's heavy. And it's got ninety to a hundred crab pots on deck. Each pot is a thousand pounds with gear inside it. You've got one hundred thousand pounds of weight on the deck, plus all the water in the tank and ten thousand gallons of fuel. You're sitting pretty low in the water before you even start. So one of the biggest areas of flotation has just been breached, and Jock continues to back the boat up.

There is a swell coming into the reef where we just crashed, and the boat is riding kind of funny. You can feel that the bow is not responding the way it should; it's not riding with the waves. So I went out of the wheelhouse, climbed over the pots, and looked down on to what would be the whaleback—that's where the generator was— and there was water just pouring out of the hatches and the whole deck is awash. I go back and tell him, "We're sinking. There's water across the deck and we're sinking!" He says, "No, no, no. We're fine, we're fine." You know, he's just been caught asleep, drunk, and high, and he's in denial. So he keeps backing up, and we're crashing into rocks behind us. It's not pretty. There's a nasty swell running in there. We're bouncing off more rocks. There wasn't a lot of time.

Jock wouldn't stop the boat from backing out. There was a beach in front of us and he could have just poured the coals to it and ran the thing up on the beach. The boat might have been a total loss or it might have been savable, but who cares, everyone would have gotten off the boat. But he chose not to do that, and he continued to drive the boat backward out of the reef. I don't think he really understood how much trouble we were in until the boat listed over about twenty degrees to the port side. Then, I think, he realized we were in trouble.

During this time, I had gone down into the engine room. I was the engineer, so it was my responsibility to take care of the mechanics of the boat. I reversed the pumps on the tanks for the crab, and I was trying to pump the water out to get us more flotation. I was under there when the boat lurched over and one of the engines rolled out of its cradle and went tumbling across the engine room. That's when I knew it was time to get the hell out of the engine room.

It took fourteen minutes from the time we hit the reef to the time the boat rolled over.

Bill and Tom were trying to get their survival suits on. I grabbed mine. Jock still was up in the wheelhouse. I'm not real sure what he's doing, but he did get a Mayday radio call out to the Coast Guard. We're trying to get the life raft deployed, and then we decided to just let the life raft go with the boat, because we couldn't get it out of the cradle. They're supposed to release when you go underwater—they have a hydrostatic release on them that's supposed to break them free, but it's got to go down fifteen feet before it does that. The boat just rolled and stayed upside down right there in twenty-five to thirty feet of water. I think when the boat rolled over, the chains on the pots broke, because the weight was too much, and they tumbled down and kind of supported the boat a little bit. The boat never really sunk and we weren't terribly far off the shore.

As the boat is rolling over, myself and the two other crew members are on the bottom holding on to the propellers—maybe it was just one other crew member; I really have to think about it; it's so foggy in my mind; all that was happening so fast. That's where we should have stayed. I don't know where Jock was at the time.

I'd always thought that when a boat goes down it would suck you down and you had to get off, so I jumped off into the water. Tom was with me. Jock had come to both of us at some point. He had a top-of-the-line survival suit that automatically inflated when you got in the water, but its hood was stuck between the airbag and his back, and we couldn't get him up high enough out of the water to get his hood on. The three of us were in the water. I don't know where Bill was. I think Bill had a heart attack before he really even got in the water, from just from being scared. He wasn't in the greatest shape. I never saw him again.

So we couldn't get Jock's hood out, and seawater is flooding inside his suit. He became hypothermic within five minutes. This is January; the water is probably forty degrees. It's still snowing. The air temperature is at least thirty-two degrees and the wind is blowing twenty-five to thirty miles an hour, so you have a wind chill probably down to ten degrees. It was *winter* in Alaska.

We spent some energy trying to get Jock's survival suit fixed up so it would work. We would pull on him, and we'd go under, and then he'd come up. We couldn't get the hood out. When people become hypothermic they become incoherent, and they won't listen to anything that you have to say, and he was getting to that point and becoming difficult to deal with. He then swam off on his own or he drifted off. Somehow he became separated. I think he swam off on his own.

I was still in that mind-set of a very young man who was invincible, and this was just another adventure. I remember telling the guys, "This is nothing. This is just crab fishing." I was trying to cheer them all up. At no point did I think was going to die. I was too young to even think that. As we get older, we know we're not invincible. Those guys were in their mid-forties, and they knew they weren't invincible. But to me, it was just another adventure. It was just another story to add to my repertoire of Alaskan adventures.

And then it was just Tom and I left. We were trying to swim to the beach and we could see there was a big bluff that was maybe 150 feet tall. The only thing I had grabbed from the boat was my Maglite 3D cell battery flashlight. I was using it to shine on the bluff. I used that to direct us to the beach. Tom was lying between my legs, kind of with his arms draped over so we wouldn't become separated, and we were backstroking.

I'd never been in the water with the survival suit on up to that point. I had been in the water before by accident, but I had never been in the water with a survival suit on. So we had these pieces of equipment, but no one really knew how to use them. We didn't know how to use the life raft, and none of us really knew how to use the survival suits correctly. We'd catch crab and that's all that really mattered at the time.

Tom and I are still together in the water and we're swimming to the beach. It was at this time that the clouds parted, and it wasn't snowing anymore. I could see the handle of the Big Dipper pointing in the direction I wanted to go. Using the Big Dipper, I didn't have to keep stopping and turning around to see if we were heading in the right direction. It saved quite a bit of time of having to stop every couple of minutes.

We swam for maybe an hour, and then Tom was becoming hypothermic and incoherent, and we were getting into the surf. We were pretty close to the beach. Then he just swam off on his own. He was cold and he wouldn't listen to reason. I was telling him—I don't really remember verbatim what I was saying—but I'm sure I was telling him, "We're close. The beach is right there." We could hear the surf. We just had to get through the surf and on to the beach, but he just wasn't listening and wasn't responding. I don't know the medical reason behind it, but I know what I have observed: He's not listening anymore, he's not helpful anymore, he's not paddling anymore. He's too cold and too weak and he's tired. So, as we're getting into the surf, he swims off. I yell back and forth to him for three, four minutes. We can communicate. He was responding and he wanted to find me again, but we could never get back together. He'd gotten into an offshore current and was getting pulled away, and wasn't strong enough to come back.

I was probably on the beach five minutes after he left me. Tom died from hypothermia and was picked up that night. He was picked up pretty close to where Jock was, so he got into the same current of water and they ended up in a line separated maybe by a hundred yards. Bill was found the next morning.

The surf was pulling me in, and it was just booming, and I couldn't hear anything anymore. Once I got on the other side of the surf, there's this beach—this isn't a beach like when you think of a beach—this is a beach that's got boulders on it the size of Volkswagens, and the surf is running maybe six or seven feet. You can't get your feet down in a survival suit; you can't really get yourself vertical. It's pretty difficult unless you have other people there to kind of balance each other, so I can't get my feet down, and I'm going through the surf, and I'm thinking, I've made it this far and now I am going to break my back on one of these rocks? I'm trying to get myself positioned between the big rocks so I don't get smashed when the wave throws me up on the beach, but a wave picked me and just gently put me right on the beach between two big rocks. I stood up and I couldn't believe how gently I landed. I didn't get beat up at all.

I made it to the beach, and there is no one around for a long ways. There's no cabin. There's nothing there. I had been in the water a couple of hours, maybe, in total. I'm tired. I sat down on a rock. I could see boats out in the bay kind of doing a grid pattern looking for us, and there is a C-130 flying around, and a couple of helicopters.

Well, now I was excited and happy that I was on the beach and I proceeded to cuss the ocean out: "I beat you!" It was a formidable enemy. It was trying to kill me. You know, sailors make all kinds of stories about the ocean being a jaded lover—you do one thing wrong and then it will kill you. There are hundreds of stories about stuff like that. I beat it that night, so I was pretty excited.

Then I start trying to get my bearings on where I am and what I have. I've got this flashlight, this Gumby suit and a pair of rubber boots, and a dirty old sweatshirt and a pair of sweats, so I don't have a lot. But I am alive, and I am on the beach. I sit down for a little while and I'm looking around and I see the helicopters flying around. There really isn't anything there that's of any use to me in any way that I could save myself at this point, but I am on the beach, there's people looking—eventually they're going to find me. So I sit down and just try to conserve my energy and get out of the wind a little.

I've been on the beach maybe thirty minutes and a helicopter is doing a search. They fly past me, then back up, they put the light on me for maybe twenty seconds, and they fly off. Okay, I can deal with that. They're going to look for other people. They know where I am. Twenty minutes go by. Thirty minutes go by. An hour goes by and they haven't come back, and I'm thinking, oh shit, they didn't see me! You know, you start doubting, why haven't they come back to pick me up? And the tide is coming up. The tides in these bays are quite extreme; they can be eighteen to twenty feet, so there's a lot of tide movement in a short period of time. I'm starting to climb up this bluff and I'm running out of beach and they're not coming back!

Unbeknownst to me, they're looking for people who are in worse condition than I am and who might still be in the water. They're actually picking up Jock and Tom in the water, but it takes longer to recover a dead person than it does to rescue a live person, because a dead person can't help themselves; they got to get pushed into the basket. So, it's taking a while to get them.

Then a helicopter comes back and drops a rescue swimmer named Steve Todd into the water. Rescue swimmers are a breed unto themselves, especially in Alaska, volunteering to get thrown into that water from a perfectly good helicopter. Steve swam through the surf and made it to the beach, came up to me, and asked me all the pertinent questions, you know, like "How are you feeling. Are you injured?" I said, "I'm fine." And he said, "Okay, we're gonna get back in the water, and they're going to pick us up." I said, "The fuck we are. I ain't getting back in that water!"

He had a radio and said that I wouldn't get into the water and that I was combative. So the pilot said that there was a spot down the beach maybe a hundred yards that went out into a little point. It wasn't much, but there was enough dry land there that they could get the helicopter close to the cliff, deal with the updrafts, and pick us up. It maybe ten or fifteen minutes to get down there. Then Steve told me they're gonna drop the basket, but with the updrafts from the cliff they are not going to be able to hold it very steady and for me just to jump in the basket however I could, and hold on. So they got the basket, it hit the rocks maybe ten feet away from me, and I just dove into the thing, legs sticking out, arms sticking out. They picked me and it smashed into a rock and smashed into another one going the other direction, and then they hoisted me into the helicopter. Steve started doing a medical exam on me, and he asked how many people were on the boat and what happened. Then I saw that Tom's and Jock's bodies were lying in the back of the helicopter.

The helicopter crew had spent quite a bit of time and energy fuelwise picking up the two bodies, and they were getting low on fuel. I understand the Coast Guard has spots all over Alaska where they keep barrels of fuel. They were now trying to find a spot and can't find the darn thing, and they're looking and looking. Everyone in the helicopter is starting to get a little frantic that a perfectly good helicopter is gonna fall out of the sky because they're out of fuel. With only about fifteen pounds of fuel on left on board—which is nothing—they find the spot.

And, so, I'm stuck in this stupid cocoon thing of a survival suit and I am thinking, I've made it through the ocean, have been picked up by the helicopter, and now I'm gonna crash in a helicopter, and I can't help myself. I was getting pretty panicky, because I could sense the urgency of the men in the helicopter. I felt like I had no control at that point. Now, my life is in the hands of this pilot and this crew who can't seem to find this fuel dump. Finally, they found it. There couldn't have been five minutes of fuel left on board. We fueled up and flew back to Kodiak. They took me to the hospital, ran tests, and kept me for a twenty-four-hour period to observe me.

I had a sister that lived in Kodiak at the time. My dad was out fishing and he was told that the *Massacre Bay* had sunk, and all hands were lost. They turned his boat around and came back to Kodiak to drop him off. Before he got back to town, he thought that his son was dead.

Kodiak is a small town, so it didn't take very long, I am sure, for the coffeehouse to be full of rumors and stories of what happened that night. For weeks, everywhere I went in town I'd get hugs from mothers and ladies. People would shake my hand. Everyone was supportive.

You know, I was from an underprivileged family and I had a criminal record, and really had not done anything with myself, so I wasn't really important to the community. But I had the sense that I was important as a person. This town has been good to me. It's allowed me to do things I might not have been able to do somewhere else.

I have a sense of place in my life with a good community and a good church. I have a family that loves me, and I love them. It's a good place to be.

I was upset for a while that I didn't die that night. That funeral they had for those guys was huge. It filled up the whole high school auditorium that seats about nine hundred people. It took me a long time to get over that. I was depressed afterward. I couldn't get a job. Nothing was panning out. It took about six months to get my feet back underneath me. I never went crab fishing again. That chapter from my life was done. It wasn't even an option. I could have, but it was time to do something else. I'm a general contractor now, and I am doing well.

ACKNOWLEDGMENTS

I am indebted to the men and women who graciously shared their stories with me, and now with you. They are the soul of the book. I am humbled by their trust that I would get it right. I hope I did.

There are others whose interviews are not here. Space limitations preclude their fascinating stories from being included. While your names are not listed in the table of contents, please know that what I learned from you helped me to ask better questions of those who followed.

Rich King, the U.S. federal marshal you read about, is the only person I knew before this project began. That meant I had to find everyone else. Through Google searches, cold calls, e-mail requests, and word-of-mouth luck, many good-hearted people gave advice and opened doors that made the interviews possible. Without their help, *Jobs That Could Kill You* could not have been written. Thank you to Denise Abbott, Johnny Armento, Aaisha Ali, Ann Barker, Dove Bock, Sarah Clark, Scott Emmert, Kurt Fredrickson, Jason Gibson, Patti Green, Megan Hafenstein, Christina Higgens, Jennifer Jo, Doug Kelly, Jan Kemp, Jamaal LaFrance, Norm Leong, Bill Mahler, Jeff Meyer, Matt Schlager, Phil Smith, Gina Swankie, Ken Thomas, Terry Thornton, Tom Trinen, Dace Udris, Janet Upton, and Ted Yerzyk.

My deepest appreciation to the amazing Mark Weinstein, senior editor at Skyhorse Publishing, who believed in my first book and decided to take another chance on me. Thank you, Mark, for being patient when I was several weeks late delivering the manuscript. Thanks also go to Mark's colleague, Julie Matysik, who assisted in the editing of the manuscript.

And gratitude to my agent, Bob Diforio, who found a home for this book.

Sanjay Kedambadi and his superbly talented team at Bharathi MediScribe in Bangalore, India, transcribed hours upon hours of voice recordings. Sanjay is the best!

A comfortable bed, several evenings of entertaining conversation, and directions for getting around town in Jerusalem were a special gift from hosts Nathanael and Liz.

Thank you to JC, Christine, and Jamie at the Starbucks down the street for always having a smile and a tall cup ready when I came in to write.

To my sister: You know what I mean when I say that you made my travels possible, from Alaska to Israel and every place in between. Thank you, Bev.

As always, my incredible wife kindly tolerated my frequent aimless babble about whatever point I was trying to make. Thank you, Sher, for your love, understanding, and support.

Finally, to my precious grandchildren: Abby, Caitlin, Jason, and Ryan. Your love was a close companion to me during those many long days and nights away from home. When your working days arrive, may you be passionate about what you do.

ABOUT THE AUTHOR

Tom worked for thirty years as a legislative director in the administrations of the past five California governors, negotiating legislation and testifying before committees of the state's Senate and Assembly. He is the author of *Working at the Ballpark: The Fascinating Lives of Baseball People—From Peanut Vendors and Broadcasters to Players and Managers*. He also wrote a coffee table book for Wild Well Control, based in Houston, Texas, called *Beyond the Blowout: The Risks, The Challenges, The Stories*; and a coffee table book for Superior Energy Services, based in New Orleans, Louisiana, called *The Making of Superior Energy Services: Roots, Entrepreneurial Spirit, Global Footprint*.

His life on the edge (but never for pay) includes bungee jumping, hopping freight trains, free diving in the Pacific Ocean for abalone, and driving quarter midget race cars from the age of five to fourteen years old, including once setting a world record for a one-lap time trial.

He lives in Sacramento, California.